ISBN 978-1-333-05483-0
PIBN 10457993

1 MONTH OF
FREE
READING

at
www.ForgottenBooks.com

By purchasing this book you are
eligible for one month membership to
ForgottenBooks.com, giving you
unlimited access to our entire
collection of over 700,000 titles via
our web site and mobile apps.

To claim your free month visit:
www.forgottenbooks.com/free457993

TO HER GRACE

THE

DUTCHESS OF PORTSMOUTH.

MADAM,

WERE it possible for me to let the world know, how entirely your Grace's goodness has devoted a poor man to your service: were there words enough in speech to express the mighty sense I · have of your great bounty towards me; surely I should write and talk of it for ever: but your Grace has given me so large a ·theme, and laid so very vast a foundation, that Imagination wants stock to build upon it. I am as one dumb, when I would speak of it: and, when I strive to write, I want a scale of thought sufficient to com‑ prehend the height of it. Forgive me, then, Madam, if (as a poor peasant once made a present of an apple to an Emperor) I bring this small tribute, the humble growth of my little garden, and lay it at your feet. Believe it is paid you with the utmost gratitude: be‑ lieve that, so long as I have thought to remember how very much I owe your very generous nature, I will ever have a heart that shall be grateful for it too. Your Grace, next Heaven, deserves it amply from me :

A ij

*that gave me life, but on a hard condition, till your
extended favour taught me to prize the gift, and took
the heavy burthen it was clogged with from me, I
mean hard fortune. When I had enemies, that with
malicious power kept back and shaded me from those
royal beams, whose warmth is all I have, or hope to
live by; your noble pity and compassion found me,
where I was cast backward from my blessing, down in
the rear of fortune, called me up, placed me in the
shine, and I have felt its comfort. You have in that
restored me to my native right: for a steady faith,
and loyalty to my Prince, was all the inheritance my
father left me; and, however hardly my ill fortune
deal with me, 'tis what I prize so well, that I never
pawn'd it yet, and hope I shall never part with it.
Nature and Fortune were certainly in league, when
you were born; and as the first took care to give
you beauty enough to enslave the hearts of all the
world; so the other resolv'd to do its merit justice,
that none but a monarch fit to rule the world should
e'er possess it; and in it had an empire. The young
prince you have given him, by his blooming virtues,
early declares the mighty stock he came from: and
as you have taken all the pious care of a dear mother,
and a prudent guardian, to give him a noble and ge-
nerous education; may it succeed according to his
merits and your wishes: may he grow up to be a bul-
wark to his illustrious father, and a patron to his loy-
al subjects; with wisdom and learning to assist him,*

whenever called to his councils; to defend his right against the incroachment of republicans in his senates: to cherish such men as shall be able to vindicate the royal cause; that good and fit servants to the crown may never be lost, for want of a protector. May he have courage and conduct fit to fight his battles abroad, and terrify his rebels at home: and, that all these may be yet more sure, may he never, during the spring time of his years, when those growing virtues ought with care to be cherished, in order to their ripening, may he never meet with vicious natures, or the tongues of faithless, sordid, insipid flatterers, to blast 'em. To conclude, may he be as great as the hand of Fortune (with his honour) shall be able to make him; and may your Grace, who are so good a mistress, and so noble a patroness, never meet with a less grateful servant, than,

   Madam,

    Your Grace's

     Entirely devoted Creature,

      THO. OTWAY.

THOMAS OTWAY.

LITTLE is with any certainty known of the great Author of VENICE PRESERVED.—In the licentious days of Charles II. it is believed neither the *virtues* nor the *vices* of OTWAY were sufficiently prominent to distinguish him.

His father, Mr. HUMPHREY OTWAY, was the Rector of *Wolbeding* in Sussex—THOMAS the poet was born on the 3d of March, 1651. He was first sent to *Wickeham* School, and thence removed to Christ-Church, Oxford, of which he became a Commoner in 1669.

On leaving the University, the *histrionic* frenzy possessed him—He found the bent of his mind led him to the Theatre, but he mistook the part he was to perform there: instead of exciting emotions himself upon a stage, he was to furnish others with a *cue for passion*, as long as the language he spoke should exist. He made as an

Actor but one attempt, and in that he is said to have failed.

The army and Otway had as little congenial between them—He served in Flanders, but, versatile and facile, he soon became disgusted, and at length resolved to write for the Players—How, well he succeeded, is impressed upon every heart.

Imprudence, however, is said to have left him never above want, and sometimes, it is reported, had plunged him into all its severities. We hear continually an idle reproach upon the ingratitude of an age which can suffer the indigence of Genius. But it should be confidered that, for the most part, such dilemmas are voluntary inflictions, and that he has slender claims upon the sympathy of men, whom calamity cannot make wise, and whom pride prevents from soliciting relief.

OTWAY died in 1685; but, it is hoped, the wretched fate said to have attended him is fictitious—Nothing, however, can with any certainty be advanced respecting his *end*.

Few of the Professors of Literature offer so striking an example as Otway of the sublime pre-eminence, and indiscreet abasement of GENIUS.

His productions are as follow :—

Alcibiades,
Don Carlos,
Titus and Berenice,
Cheats of Scapin,
Friendship in Fashion,

VENICE PRESERVED.

ACT I. SCENE I.

A Street in Venice. Enter PRIULI *and* JAFFIER.
Priuli.

No more! I'll hear no more! Begone and leave me.
 Jaf. Not hear me! By my suffering but you shall!
My lord, my lord! I'm not that abject wretch
You think me. Patience! where's the distance throws
Me back so far, but I may boldly speak
In right, tho' proud oppression will not hear me?
 Pri. Have you not wrong'd me?
 Jaf. Could my nature e'er
Have brook'd injustice, or the doing wrongs,
I need not now thus low have bent myself
To gain a hearing from a cruel father.
Wrong'd you!
 Pri. Yes, wrong'd me! In the nicest point,
The honour of my house, you've done me wrong.
You may remember (for I now will speak,
And urge its baseness) when you first came home
From travel, with such hopes as made you look'd on,
By all men's eyes, a youth of expectation;

Pleas'd with your growing virtue, I receiv'd you;
Courted, and sought to raise you to your merits: 20
My house, my table, nay, my fortune too,
My very self was yours; you might have us'd me
To your best service; like an open friend
I treated, trusted-you, and thought you mine:
When, in requital of my best endeavours,
You treacherously practis'd to undo me;
Seduc'd the weakness of my age's darling,
My only child, and stole her from my bosom.
Oh Belvidera!

    Jaf. 'Tis to me you owe her:
Childless you had been else, and in the grave
Your name extinct; no more Priuli heard of.
You may remember, scarce five years are past,
Since in your brigantine you sail'd to see
The Adriatick wedded by our Duke;
And I was with you: your unskilful pilot
Dash'd us upon a rock; when to your boat
You made for safety: enter'd first yourself;
Th' affrighted Belvidera following next,
As she stood trembling on the vessel's side,
Was, by a wave, wash'd off into the deep;
When instantly I plung'd into the sea,
And buffetting the billows to her rescue,
Redeem'd her life with half the loss of mine.
Like a rich conquest, in one hand I bore her,
And with the other dash'd the saucy waves,
That throng'd and press'd to rob me of my prize.
I brought her, gave her to your despairing arms:

VENICE PRESERVED;

OR,

A PLOT DISCOVERED,

Is a play evidently the result of acute remark upon the influence of passion on life. The Author seems to have consulted nature in his own mind, and unfortunately his own mind was corrupt.

Hence his characters, except indeed *Belvidera*, excite little sympathy at their fate.—The Traitor to his Country expires upon the wheel, and the Betrayer of his Friend is the *slayer of himself*.

In the works of some dramatists, there is danger lest Vice should wear the wreath of Virtue from the fascination of specious qualities—it is thus in the *School for Scandal*; where the character of Charles is a seducing *poison* to *our blood*.—Otway's Rascals are, however, sufficiently despised—Pierre is sunken by cruel ambition—Jaffier by meanness unmanly and contemptible.. On the side of the *amor patriæ* he is paralytic—he can support the idea of destroying his Country, but poverty, the importunities of a wife, or

the reflections of treachery to a friend, agonize him
with compunction and hurry him to despair.

BELVIDERA, unhappy, duteous, tender, and vir-
tuous, claims our full commiseration, and claims it
alone.

PROLOGUE.

IN these distracted times, when each man dreads
The bloody stratagems of busy heads:
Whence we had fear'd three years we know not what,
'Till witnesses began to die o' th' rot;
What made our poet meddle with a plot?
Was't that he fancy'd for the very sake
And name of plot, his trifling play might take?
For there's not in't one inch-board evidence;
But 'tis, he says, to reason plain and sense;
And that he thinks a plausible defence.
Were truth by sense and reason to be try'd,
Sure all our swearers might be laid aside.
No; of such tools our author has no need,
To make his plot, or make his play succeed;
He of Black Bills has no prodigious tales,
Or Spanish pilgrims cast ashore in Wales:
Here's not one murder'd magistrate, at least,
Kept rank, like ven'son for a city feast,
Grown four days stiff, the better to prepare
And fit his pliant limbs to ride in chair.
Yet here's an army rais'd, tho' under ground,
But no man seen, nor one commission found:
Here is a traitor too, that's very old,
Turbulent, subtle, mischievous, and bold.

Bloody, revengeful, and—to crown his part,
Loves fumbling with a wench with all his heart:
'Till, after having many changes past,
In spite of age (thanks t' heaven) is hang'd at last;
Next is a senator that keeps a whore
In Venice none a higher office bore,
To lewdness ev'ry night the leacher ran;
Shew me, all London, such another man;
Match him at Mother Creswell's, if you can.
O Poland! Poland! had it been thy lot
T' have heard in time of this Venetian plot,
Thou surely chosen hadst one king from thence,
And honour'd them, as thou hast England since.

DRURY-LANE.

DUKE of VENICE	- - -
PRIÚLI	
BEDAMAR	- - -
JAFFIER	- - - - -
PIERRE	- - - - -
RENAULT	
ELLIOTT	} Conspirators {
SPINOSA	
THEODORE	

Woman.

BELVIDERA   - - - -   Mrs. Siddons.

COVENT-GARDEN.

Men.

DUKE of VENICE	Mr. Thompson.
PRIULI - - - - -	Mr. Hull.
BEDAMAR - -	Mr. Davies.
JAFFIER	Mr. Holman.
PIERRE - -	Mr. Harley.
RENAULT	Mr. W. Powell.
ELLIOTT } Conspirators {	Mr. Macready.
SPINOSA	Mr. Cubit.
THEODORE	Mr. Reeves.

Woman.

BELVIDERA   - - -   Mrs. Esten.

Two Women, attendants on Belvidera.
The Council of ten.
Officer, Guard, Friar, Executioner, and Rabble.

Indeed you thank'd me; but a nobler gratitude
Rose in her soul: for from that hour she lov'd me,
'Till for her life she paid me with herself.

     Pri. You stole her from me; like a thief you stole
         her,
At dead of night! that cursed hour you chose
To rifle me of all my heart held dear.
May all your joys in her prove false, like mine;
A sterile fortune, and a barren bed,
Attend you both; continual discord make
Your days and nights bitter and grievous: still
May the hard hand of a vexatious need
Oppress and grind you; till at last you find   60
The curse of disobedience all your portion.

     Jaf. Half of your curse you have bestow'd in vain:
Heav'n has already crown'd our faithful loves
With a young boy, sweet as his mother's beauty:
May he live to prove more gentle than his grandsire,
And happier than his father.

     Pri. Rather live
To bait thee for his bread, and din your ears
With hungry cries; whilst his unhappy mother
Sits down and weeps in bitterness of want.

     Jaf. You talk as if 'twould please you.

     Pri. 'Twould, by heav'n!
" Once she was dear indeed; the drops that fell
" From my sad heart, when she forgot her duty,
" The fountain of my life was not so precious—
" But she is gone, and, if I am a man,
" I will forget her."

Jaf. Would I were in my grave?

Pri. And she too with thee.

For, living here, you're but my curst remembrancers.
I once was happy.   81

   Jaf. You use me thus, because you know my soul
Is fond of Belvidera. You perceive
My life feeds on her, therefore thus you treat me.

   Oh! could my soul ever have known satiety;
Were I that thief, the doer of such wrongs
As you upbraid me with, what hinders me
But I might send her back to you with contumely,
And court my fortune where she would be kinder?

   Pri. You dare not do't.

   Jaf. Indeed, my Lord, I dare not.
My heart, that awes me, is too much my master:
Three years are past, since first our vows were plighted,
During which time, the world must bear me witness,
I've treated Belvidera like your daughter,
The daughter of a senator of Venice:
Distinction, place, attendance, and observance,
Due to her birth, she always has commanded.
Out of my little fortune I've done this;
Because (tho' hopeless e'er to win your nature)
The world might see I lov'd her for herself;
Not as the heiress of the great Priuli.

   Pri. No more.

   Jaf. Yes, all, and then adieu for ever.
There's not a wretch, that lives on common charity,
But's happier than me: for I have known
The luscious sweets of plenty; every night

Have slept with soft content about my head,
And never wak'd, but to a joyful morning :
Yet now must fall, like a full ear of corn,
Whose blossom 'scap'd, yet's wither'd in the ripening.

   Pri. Home, and be humble; study to retrench;
Discharge the lazy vermin of thy hall,
Those pageants of thy folly :
Reduce the glitt'ring trappings of thy wife
To humble weeds, fit for thy little state :
Then, to some suburb cottage both retire ;
Drudge to feed loathsome life; get brats and starve—
Home, home, I say.——————   [*Exit.*

   Jaf. Yes, if my heart would let me——————
This proud, this swelling heart: home I would go,
But that my doors are hateful to my eyes,
Fill'd and damm'd up with gaping creditors.
" Watchful as fowlers when their game will spring."
I've now not fifty ducats in the world,
Yet still I am in love, and pleas'd with ruin.
Oh! Belvidera ! Oh! she is my wife——
And we will bear our wayward fate together,
But ne'er know comfort more.

Enter PIERRE.

   Pier. My friend, good morrow.
How fares the honest partner of my heart?
What, melancholy! not a word to spare me ?
   Jaf. I'm thinking, Pierre, how that damn'd starv-
      ing quality,
Call'd honesty, got footing in the world.

Pier. Why, powerful villany first set it up,
For its own ease and safety.   Honest men
Are the soft easy cushions on which knaves
Repose and fatten.   Were all mankind villains,
They'd starve each other ; lawyers would want prac-
  tice,
Cut-throats rewards: each man would kill his
  brother
Himself; none would be paid or hang'd for murder.
Honesty! 'twas a cheat invented first   142
To bind the hands of bold deserving rogues,
That fools and cowards might sit safe in power,
And lord it uncontroul'd above their betters.
 Jaf. Then honesty is but a notion ?
 Pier. Nothing else ;
Like wit, much talk'd of, not to be defin'd :
He that pretends to most, too, has least share in't.
'Tis a ragged virtue : Honesty! no more on't.
 Jaf. Sure thou art honest ?
 Pier. So, indeed, men think me;
But they're mistaken, Jaffier : I'm a rogue
As well as they;
A fine, gay, bold-fac'd villain as thou seest me.
'Tis true, I pay my debts, when they're contracted ;
I steal from no man; would not cut a throat
To gain admission to a great man's purse,   .
Or a whore's bed ; I'd not betray my friend
To get his place or fortune ; I scorn to flatter   160
A blown-up fool above me, or crush the wretch be-
  neath me ;

Yet, Jaffier, for all this I'm a villain.

Jaf. A villain !

Pier. Yes, a most notorious villain ;

To see the sufferings of my fellow-creatures,

And own myself a man : to see our senators

Cheat the deluded people with a shew

Of liberty, which yet they ne'er must taste of.

They say, by them our hands are free from fetters ;

Yet whom they please they lay in basest bonds ;

Bring whom they please to infamy and sorrow ;

Drive us, like wrecks, down the rough tide of power,

Whilst no hold's left to save us from destruction.

All that bear this are villains, and I one,

Not to rouse up at the great call of nature,

And check the growth of these domestic spoilers,

That make us slaves, and tell us, 'tis our charter.

    Jaf. " Oh, Aquilina ! Friend to lose such beauty.

" The dearest purchase of thy noble labours !

" She was thy right by conquest, as by love.   180

    Pier. " Oh ! Jaffier ! I had so fix'd my heart upon

       her,

" That, wheresoe'er I fram'd a scheme of life,

" For time to come, she was my only joy,

" With which I wish'd to sweeten future cares :

" I fancy'd pleasures ; none but one that loves

" And doats as I did, can imagine like 'em :

" When in th' extremity of all these hopes,

" In the most charming hour of expectation,

" Then, when our eager wishes soar'd the highest,

" Ready to stoop and grasp the lovely game,

" A haggard owl, a worthless kite of prey,

" With his foul wings, sail'd in, and spoil'd my quarry.

    Jaf. " I know the wretch, and scorn him as thou

        hat'st him.

    Pier. " Curse on the common good that's so pro-

        tected,

" Where every slave, that heaps up wealth enough

" To do much wrong, becomes the lord of right!

" I, who believ'd no ill could e'er come near me,

" Found in th' embraces of my Aquilina

" A wretched, old, but itching senator;

" A wealthy fool, that had bought out my title; 200

" A rogue that uses beauty like a lamb-skin,

" Barely to keep him warm; that filthy cuckoo too

" Was, in my absence, crept into my nest,

" And spoiling all my brood of noble pleasure.

    Jaf. " Did'st thou not chase him thence?

    Pier. " I did, and drove

" The rank old bearded Hirco stinking home.

" The matter was complain'd of in the senate,

" I summon'd to appear, and censur'd basely,

" For violating something they call'd privilege——

" This was the recompence of all my service.

" Would I'd been rather beaten by a coward!

" A soldier's mistress, Jaffier, is his religion;

" When that's profan'd, all other ties are broken:

" That even dissolves all former bonds of service;

" And from that hour I think myself as free

" To be the foe, as e'er the friend of Venice—

" Nay, dear revenge, whene'er thou call'st I'm ready."

Jaf. I think no safety can be here for virtue,
And grieve, my friend, as much as thou, to live 220
In such a wretched state as this of Venice,
Where all agree to spoil the public good;
And villains fatten with the brave man's labours.

   Pier. We've neither safety, unity, nor peace,
For the foundation's lost of common good;
Justice is lame, as well as blind, amongst us;
The laws (corrupted to their ends that make 'em)
Serve but for instruments of some new tyranny,
That every day starts up, t' enslave us deeper.
Now could this glorious cause but find out friends
To do it right, Oh, Jaffier! then might'st thou
Not wear these seals of woe upon thy face;
The proud Priuli should be taught humanity,
And learn to value such a son as thou art.
I dare not speak, but my heart bleeds this moment.

   Jaf. Curs'd be the cause, tho' I thy friend be part
            on't:
Let me partake the troubles of thy bosom,
For I am us'd to mis'ry, and perhaps
May find a way to sweeten 't to thy spirit.

   Pier. Too soon 'twill reach thy knowledge——
   Jaf. Then from thee   241
Let it proceed. There's virtue in thy friendship,
Would make the saddest tale of sorrow pleasing;
Strengthen my constancy, and welcome ruin.

   Pier. Then thou art ruin'd!
   Jaf. That I long since knew;
I and ill fortune have been long acquainted.

Pier. I pass'd this very moment by thy doors,
And found them guarded by a troop of villains;
The sons of public rapine were destroying.
They told me, by the sentence of the law,
They had commission to seize all thy fortune:
Nay, more, Priuli's cruel hand had sign'd it.
Here stood a ruffian with a horrid face,
Lording it o'er a pile of massy plate,
Tumbled into a heap for public sale;
There was another making villanous jests
At thy undoing : he had ta'en possession
Of all thy ancient, most domestic ornaments,
Rich hangings intermix'd and wrought with gold;
The very bed, which on thy wedding-night
Receiv'd thee to the arms of Belvidera,
The scene of all thy joys, was violated
By the coarse hands of filthy dungeon villains,
And thrown amongst the common lumber.
  Jaf. Now thank heaven————
  Pier. Thank heaven l for what ?
  Jaf. That I'm not worth a ducat.
  Pier. Curse thy dull stars, and the worse fate of
      Venice,
Where brothers, friends, and fathers, all are false;
Where there's no truth, no trust; where innocence
Stoops under vile oppression, and vice lords it.
Hadst thou but seen, as I did, how at last
Thy beauteous Belvidera, like a wretch
That's doom'd to banishment, came weeping forth,
" Shining thro' tears, like April-suns in showers,

" That labour to o'ercome the cloud that loads 'em ;
Whilst two young virgins, on whose arms she lean'd,
Kindly look'd up, and at her grief grew sad,
As if they catch'd the sorrows that fell from her. 280
Ev'n the lewd rabble, that were gather'd round
To see the sight, stood mute when they beheld her;
Govern'd their roaring throats, and grumbled pity.
I could have hugg'd the greasy rogues : they pleas'd
     me.

  Jaf. I thank thee for this story, from my soul;
Since now I know the worst that can befal me.
Ah, Pierre ! I have a heart that could have borne
The roughest wrong my fortune could have done me;
But when I think what Belvidera feels,
The bitterness her tender spirit tastes of,
I own myself a coward : bear my weakness :
If throwing thus my arms about thy neck,
I play the boy, and blubber in thy bosom.
Oh ! I shall drown thee with my sorrows.

  Pier. Burn,
First, burn and level Venice to thy ruin.
What ! starve, like beggars' brats, in frosty weather,
Under a hedge, and whine ourselves to death !
Thou or thy cause shall never want assistance,
Whilst I have blood or fortune fit to serve thee :
Command my heart, thou'rt every way its master.

  Jaf. No, there's a secret pride in bravely dying.

  Pier. Rats die in holes and corners, dogs run mad ;
Man knows a braver remedy for sorrow :
Revenge, the attribute of gods ; they stamp'd it,

With their great image, on our natures. Die!
Consider well the cause, that calls upon thee:
And, if thou'rt base enough, die then. Remember,
Thy Belvidera suffers; Belvidera!
Die—damn first—What! be decently interr'd
In a church-yard, and mingle thy brave dust
With stinking rogues, that rot in winding-sheets,
Surfeit-slain fools, the common dung o' th' soil!

   Jaf. Oh!
   Pier. Well said, out with 't, swear a little——
   Jaf. Swear! By sea and air; by earth, by Heav'n,
       and hell,
I will revenge my Belvidera's tears.
Hark thee, my friend—Priuli—is—a senator.

   Pier. A dog.
   Jaf. Agreed.   320
   Pier. Shoot him.
   Jaf. With all my heart.
No more; where shall we meet at night?

   Pier. I'll tell thee;
On the Rialto, every night at twelve,
I take my evening's walk of meditation;
There we two will meet, and talk of precious
Mischief——

   Jaf. Farewel.
   Pier. At twelve.
   Jaf. At any hour; my plagues
Will keep me waking.   [*Exit* Pierre.
Tell me why, good Heaven,
Thou mad'st me what I am, with all the spirit,

Aspiring thoughts, and elegant desires,
That fill the happiest man? Ah, rather, why
Didst thou not form me sordid as my fate,
Base-minded, dull, and fit to carry burthens?
Why have I sense to know the curse that's on me?
Is this just dealing, Nature?—Belvidera!

Enter BELVIDERA.

Poor Belvidera!
   Bel. Lead me, lead me, my virgins,
To that kind voice. My lord, my love, my refuge!
Happy my eyes, when they behold thy face!
My heavy heart will leave its doleful beating
At sight of thee, and bound with sprightly joys.
Oh smile! as when our loves were in their spring,
And cheer my fainting soul.
   Jaf. As when our loves
Were in their spring! Has then our fortune chang'd?
Art thou not Belvidera, still the same,
Kind, good, and tender, as my arms first found thee?
If thou art alter'd, where shall I have harbour?
Where ease my loaded heart? Oh! where complain?
   Bel. Does this appear like change, or love decaying,
When thus I throw myself into thy bosom,
With all the resolution of strong truth!
Beats not my heart, as 'twould alarum thine
To a new charge of bliss?—I joy more in thee,
Than did thy mother, when she hugg'd thee first,
And bless'd the gods for all her travail past.

Jaf. Can there in woman be such glorious faith?
Sure all ill stories of thy sex are false!
Oh woman! lovely woman! Nature made thee
To temper man: we had been brutes without you!
Angels are painted fair to look like you:
There's in you all that we believe of Heaven;
Amazing brightness, purity and truth,
Eternal joy, and everlasting love.

Bel. If love be treasure, we'll be wondrous rich:
I have so much, my heart will surely break with 't:
Vows can't express it. When I would declare
How great's my joy, I'm dumb with the big thought;
I swell, and sigh, and labour with my longing.
O! lead me to some desart wide and wild,
Barren as our misfortunes, where my soul
May have its vent; where I may tell aloud
To the high Heavens, and ev'ry list'ning planet,
With what a boundless stock my bosom's fraught;
Where I may throw my eager arms about thee,   380
Give loose to love, with kisses kindling joy,
And let off all the fire that's in my heart.

Jaf. Oh, Belvidera! doubly I'm a beggar:
Undone by fortune, and in debt to thee.
Want, worldly want, that hungry meagre fiend,
Is at my heels, and chaces me in view.
Canst thou bear cold and hunger? Can these limbs,
Fram'd for the tender offices of love,
Endure the bitter gripes of smarting poverty?
When banish'd by our miseries abroad
(As suddenly we shall be) to seek out
In some far climate, where our names are strangers,

For charitable succour; wilt thou then,   .
When in a bed of straw we shrink together,
And the bleak winds shall whistle round our heads;
Wilt thou then talk thus to me ? Wilt thou then
Hush my cares thus, and shelter me with love ?

 Bel. Oh ! I will love thee, even in madness love
  thee ;

Tho' my distracted senses should forsake me,
I'd find some intervals, when my poor heart   400
Should 'swage itself, and be let loose to thine.
Tho' the bare earth be all our resting-place,
Its roots our food, some clift our habitation, -
I'll make this arm a pillow for thine head ;
And, as thou sighing ly'st, and swell'd with sorrow,
Creep to thy bosom, pour the balm of love
Into thy soul, and kiss thee to thy rest ;
Then praise our God, and watch thee till the morning.

 Jaf. Hear this, you Heav'ns ! and wonder how you
  made her :

Reign, reign, ye monarchs that divide the world,
Busy rebellion ne'er will let you know
Tranquillity and happiness like mine !
Like gaudy ships th' obsequious billows fall,
And rise again to lift you in your pride ;
They wait but for a storm, and then devour you ;
I, in my private bark already wreck'd,
Like a poor merchant driven to unknown land,
That had by chance pack'd up his choicest treasure
In one dear casket, and sav'd only that ;   419
Since I must wander farther on the shore,

Thus hug my little, but my precious store,
Resolv'd to scorn and trust my fate no more. [*Exeunt.*

ACT II. SCENE I.

" *Enter* PIERRE *and* AQUILINA.

" *Aquilina.*

" By all thy wrongs, thou'rt dearer to my arms
Than all the wealth of Venice. Pr'ythee stay,
" And let us love to night."
Pier. No: there's fool,
" There's fool about thee. When a woman sells
" Her flesh to fools, her beauty's lost to me ;
" They leave a taint, a sully—where they've pass'd ;
" There's such a baneful quality about 'em,
" E'en spoils complexions with their nauseousness ;
" They infect all they touch : I cannot think
" Of tasting any thing a fool has pall'd.
    " *Aqui.* I loath and scorn that fool thou mean'st, as
       much
" Or more than thou canst; but the beast has gold,
" That makes him necessary ; power too,
" To qualify my character, and poise me
" Equal with peevish virtue, that beholds
" My liberty with envy. In their hearts,
" They're loose as I am ; but an ugly power
" Sits in their faces, and frights pleasure from them,

" *Pier.* Much good may't do you, madam, with
     your senator.   20

" *Aqui.* My senator! Why, canst thou think that
     wretch

" E'er fill'd thy Aquil'na's arms with pleasure ?

" Think'st thou, because I sometimes give him leave

" To foil himself at what he is unfit for ;

" Because I force myself t'endure and suffer him,

" Think'st thou, I love him ? No, by all the joys

" Thou ever gav'st me, his presence is my penance.

" The worst thing an old man can be 's a lover,

" A mere *memento mori* to poor woman.

" I never lay by his decrepid side,

" But all that night I ponder on my grave.

" *Pier.* Would he were well sent thither.

" *Aqui.* That's my wish too :

" For then, my Pierre, I might have cause, with
     pleasure,

" To play the hypocrite. Oh ! how I could weep

" Over the dying dotard, and kiss him too,

" In hopes to smother him quite ; then, when the time

" Was come to pay my sorrows at his funeral,

" (For he has already made me heir to treasures

" Would make me out-act a real widow's whining)

" How could I frame my face to fit my mourning !

" With wringing hands attend him to his grave ;

" Fall swooning on his hearse ; take mad possession

" E'en of the dismal vault, where he lay buried ;

" There, like th' Ephesian matron, dwell, till thou,

" My lovely soldier, com'st to my deliverance ;

" Then, throwing up my veil, with open arms
" And laughing eyes, run to new-dawning joy.
 " *Pier.* No more : I've friends to meet me here to-
  night,
" And must be private. As you prize my friendship,
" Keep up your coxcomb; let him not pry, nor listen,
" Nor frisk about the house, as I have seen him,
" Like a tame mumping squirrel with a bell on ;
" Curs will be abroad to bite him, if you do.
 " *Aqui.* What friends to meet! Mayn't I be of
  your council ?
 " *Pier.* How ! a woman ask questions out of bed !
" Go to your senator ; ask him what passes
" Amongst his brethren ; he'll hide nothing from you :
" But pump me not for politics. No more !
" Give order, that whoever in my name   60
" Comes here, receive admittance. So good night.
 " *Aqui.* Must we ne'er meet again! embrace no
  more ?
" Is love so soon and utterly forgotten ?
 " *Pier.* As you henceforward treat your fool, I'll
  think on't.
 " *Aqui.* Curs'd be all fools—I die, if he forsakes me ;
" And how to keep him, Heaven or hell instruct me."
          [*Exeunt.*

SCENE II.

The Rialto.   *Enter* JAFFIER.

Jaf. I'm here; and thus, the shades of night around
    - me,
I look as if all hell were in my heart,
And I in hell.   Nay surely 'tis so with me!——
For every step I tread, methinks some fiend
Knocks at my breast, and bids me not be quiet.
I've heard how desperate wretches, like myself,
Have wander'd out at this dead time of night,
To meet the foe of mankind in his walk.
Sure I'm so curs'd that, tho' of Heaven forsaken,
No minister of darkness cares to tempt me.
Hell, hell! why sleep'st thou?

Enter PIERRE.

Pier. Sure I've staid too long:
The clock has struck, and I may lose my proselyte.
Speak, who goes there?
 - *Jaf.* A dog, that comes to howl
At yonder moon.   What's he, that asks the question?
    Pier. A friend to dogs, for they are honest crea-
        tures,
And ne'er betray their masters : never fawn
On any that they love not.   Well met, friend :
Jaffier!
    Jaf. The same. "O Pierre, thou'rt come in season,
" I was just going to pray.

Pier. " Ah ; that's mechanic ;
" Priests make a trade on't, and yet starve by't, too.
" No praying ; it spoils business, and time's precious.
Where's Belvidera ?——

Jaf. For a day or two
I've lodg'd her privately, till I see farther
What fortune will do for me   Pr'ythee, friend,
If thou would'st have me fit to hear good counsel,
Speak not of Belvidera——

Pier. Not of her !

Jaf. Oh, no !

Pier. Not name her ? May be I wish her well. 100

Jaf. Whom well ?

Pier. Thy wife ; thy lovely Belvidera.
I hope a man may wish his friend's wife well,
And no harm done.

Jaf. Y' are merry, Pierre.

Pier. I am so :
Thou shalt smile too, and Belvidera smile :
We'll all rejoice.   Here's something to buy pins ;
Marriage is chargeable.   [*Gives him a purse.*

Jaf. I but half wish'd
To see the devil, and he's here already.   Well !
What must this buy ? Rebellion, murder, treason ?
Tell me, which way I must be damn'd for this.

Pier. When last we parted, we'd no qualms like
          these,
But entertain'd each other's thoughts like men
Whose souls were well acquainted.   Is the world
Reform'd since our last meeting ? What new miracles

Have happen'd ? Has Friuli's heart relented ?
Can he be honest ?

Jaf. Kind Heav'n, let heavy curses
Gall his old age; cramps, aches rack his bones,
And bitterest disquiet ring his heart.
" Oh ! let him live, till life become his burden :
" Let him groan under 't long, linger an age
" In the worst agonies and pangs of death,
" And find its ease, but late."

Pier. Nay, could'st thou not
As well, my friend, have stretch'd the curse to all
The senate round, as to one single villain ?

Jaf. But curses stick not: could I kill with cursing,
By Heaven I know not thirty heads in Venice
Should not be blasted.   Senators should rot
Like dogs on dunghills : " But their wives and
          daughters
" Die of their own diseases."   Oh ! for a curse
To kill with !

Pier. Daggers, daggers are much better.

Jaf. Ha !

Pier. Daggers.

Jaf. But where are they ?

Pier. Oh ! a thousand   140
May be dispos'd of, in honest hands, in Venice.

Jaf. Thou talk'st in clouds.

Pier. But yet a heart, half wrong'd
As thine has been, would find the meaning, Jaffier.

Jaf. A thousand daggers, all in honest hands!
And have not I a friend will stick one here !

Pier. Yes, if I thought thou wert not be cherish'd
T'a nobler purpose, I would be thy friend;
But thou hast better friends; friends whom thy
        wrongs
Have made thy friends; friends worthy to be call'd so.
I'll trust thee with a secret: There are spirits
This hour at work.—But as thou art a man,
Whom I have pick'd and chosen from the world,
Swear that thou wilt be true to what I utter;
And when I've told thee that which only gods,
And men like gods, are privy to, then swear
No chance or change shall wrest it from thy bosom.

    Jaf. When thou would'st bind me, is there need
        of oaths?
" Green-sickness girls lose maidenheads with such
        counters."
For thou'rt so near my heart, that thou may'st see
Its bottom, sound its strength and firmness to thee.
Is coward, fool, or villain in my face?
If I seem none of these, I dare believe
Thou would'st not use me in a little cause,
For I am fit for honour's toughest task,
Nor ever yet found fooling was my province;
And for a villanous, inglorious enterprize,
I know thy heart so well, I dare lay mine
Before thee, set it to what point thou wilt.

    Pier. Nay, 'tis a cause thou wilt be fond of, Jaffier;
For it is founded on the noblest basis;
Our liberties, our natural inheritance.
There's no religion, no hypocrisy in't;

We'll do the business, and ne'er fast and pray for't;
Openly act a deed the world shall gaze
With wonder at, and envy when 'tis done.

  Jaf. For liberty !

  Pier. For liberty, my friend.

Thou shalt be freed from base Priuli's tyranny,
And thy sequester's fortunes heal'd again-:   180
I shall be free from those opprobrious wrongs
That press me now, and bend my spirit downward;
All Venice free, and every growing merit
Succeed to its just right : fools shall be pull'd
From wisdom's seat: those baleful unclean birds,
Those lazy owls, who, perch'd near fortune's top,
Sit only watchful with their heavy wings
To cuff down new-fledg'd virtues, that would rise
To nobler heights, and make the grove harmonious.

  Jaf. What can I do?

  Pier. Canst thou not kill a senator ?

  Jaf. Were there one wise or honest, I could kill
      him,

or herding with that nest of fools and knaves.
y all my wrongs, thou talk'st as if revenge
Vere to be had ; and the brave story warms me.

  Pier. Swear then !

  Jaf. I do, by all those glittering stars,
nd yon great ruling planet of the night ;
y all good pow'rs above, and ill below ;
y love and friendship, dearer than my life,   200
o pow'r or death shall make me false to thee.

D

Pier. Here we embrace, and I'll unlock my heart.
council's held hard by, where the destruction
this great empire's hatching : there I'll lead thee.
t be a man ! for thou'rt to mix with men
. to disturb the peace of all the world,
id rule it when it's wildest——
Jaf. I give thee thanks
r this kind warning. Yes, I'll be a man ;
id charge thee, Pierrè, whene'er thou see'st my
     fears
tray me less, to rip this heart of mine
it of my breast, and shew it for a coward's.
ime, let's be gone, for from this hour I chase
ll little thoughts, all tender human follies
it of my bosom : Vengeance shall have room :
evenge!
Pier. And liberty!
Jaf. Revenge ! revenge———   [*Exeunt.*

SCENE III.

Changes to Aquilina's *House, the Greek Courtezan.*

Enter RENAULT.

Ren. Why was my choice ambition ? the worst
     ground
wretch can build on ! It's, indeed, at distance, 220
goodly prospect, tempting to the view ;
he height delights us, and the mountain top

Looks beautiful, because it's nigh to Heav'n.
But we ne'er think how sandy's the foundation,
What storm will batter, and what tempest shake us.
Who's there?

Enter SPINOSA.

Spin. Renault, good-morrow, for by this time
I think the scale of night has turn'd the balance,
And weighs up morning? Has the clock struck
    twelve?
Ren. Yes: Clocks will go as they are set; but man,
Irregular man's ne'er constant, never certain :
I've spent at least three precious hours of darkness
In waiting dull attendance; 'tis the curse
Of diligent virtue to be mix'd, like mine,
With giddy tempers, souls but half resolv'd.
    Spin. Hell seize that soul amongst us it can frighten.
    Ren. What's then the cause that I am here alone?
Why are we not together?

Enter ELIOT.

O, Sir, welcome!
You are an Englishman: when treason's hatching,
One might have thought you'd not have been behind-
    hand.   241
In what whore's lap have you been lolling?
Give but an Englishman his whore and ease,
Beef, and a sea-coal fire, he's yours for ever.
    Eli. Frenchman, you are saucy.
    Ren. How!

VEIL, DURAND, BRABE, REVILLIDO, MEZZANA, TERNON, RETROSI, *Conspirators.*

Bed. At difference; fie!
Is this a time for quarrels? Thieves and rogues
Fall out and brawl: should men of your high calling,
Men separated by the choice of Providence
From the gross heap of mankind, and set here
In this assembly as in one great jewel,
T'adorn the bravest purpose it e'er smil'd on;
Should you, like boys, wrangle for trifles?
   Ren. Boys!
   Bed. Renault, thy hand.
   Ren. I thought I'd given my heart
Long since to every man that mingles here;
But grieve to find it trusted with such tempers,
That can't forgive my froward age its weakness.
   Bed. Eliot, thou once had'st virtue. I have seen
Thy stubborn temper bent with god-like goodness,
Not half thus courted: 'Tis thy nation's glory
To hug the foe that offers brave alliance.
One more embrace, my friends—we'll all embrace.
United thus, we are the mighty engine
Must twist this rooted empire from its basis.
Totters not it already?
   Eli. Would 'twere tumbling.
   Bed. Nay, it shall down; this night we seal its
     ruin.

Enter PIERRE.

Oh, Pierre! thou art welcome.
Come to my breast, for by its hopes thou look'st
Lovelily dreadful, and the fate of Venice
Seems on thy sword already. Oh, my Mars!
The poets that first feign'd a god of war,
Sure prophesy'd of thee.
    Pier. Friend, was not Brutus,
(I mean that Brutus, who in open senate
Stabb'd the first Cæsar that usurp'd the world)
A gallant man?   280
    Ren. Yes, and Catiline too;
Tho' story wrong his fame: for he conspir'd
To prop the reeling glory of his country:
His cause was good.
    Bed. And our's as much above it,
As, Renault, thou'rt superior to Cethegus,
Or Pierre to Cassius.
    Pier. Then to what we aim at.
When do we start? or must we talk for ever?
    Bed. No, Pierre, the deed's near birth; fate seems
        to have set
The business up, and given it to our care;
I hope there's not a heart or hand amongst us,
But is firm and ready.
    All. All.
We'll die with Bedamar.
    Bed. O men
Matchless! as will your glory be hereafter.

The game is for a matchless prize, if won,
If lost, disgraceful ruin.

  " *Ren.* What can lose it?

" The public stock's a beggar; one Venetian
" Trusts not another. Look into their stores
" Of general safety; empty magazines,
" A tatter'd fleet, a murmuring unpaid army,
" Bankrupt nobility, a harass'd commonalty,
" A factious, giddy, and divided senate,
" Is all the strength of Venice: let's destroy it;
" Let's fill their magazines with arms to awe them;
" Man out their fleet, and make their trade maintain
     it;
" Let loose the murmuring army on their masters,
" To pay themselves with plunder; lop their nobles
" To the base roots whence most of 'em first sprung;
" Enslave the rout, whom smarting will make humble;
" Turn out their droning senate, and possess
" That seat of empire which our souls were fram'd
     for."

  Pier. Ten thousand men are armed at your nod,
Commanded all by leaders fit to guide
A battle for the freedom of the world:
This wretched state has starv'd them in its service;
And, by your bounty quicken'd, they're resolved
To serve your glory, and revenge their own:
They've all their different quarters in this city,
Watch for th' alarm, and grumble 'tis so tardy.

  Bed. I doubt not, friend, but thy unwearied dili-
    gence

Has still kept waking, and it shall have ease;
After this night it is resolv'd we meet
No more, till Venice owns us for her lords.

 Pier. How lovelily the Adriatic whore,
Dress'd in her flames, will shine? Devouring flames!
Such as shall burn her to the watery bottom,
And hiss in her foundation.

 Bed. Now if any
Amongst us, that owns this glorious cause,
Have friends or interest he'd wish to save,
Let it be told : the general doom is seal'd;
But I'd forego the hopes of a world's empire,
Rather than wound the bowels of my friend.

 Pier. I must confess, you there have touch'd my
   weakness,
I have a friend; hear it! such a friend,
My heart was ne'er shut to him. Nay, I'll tell you :
He knows the very business of this hour;
But he rejoices in the cause, and loves it :
We've chang'd a vow to live and die together,
And he's at hand to ratify it here.

 Ren. How! all betray'd!

 Pier. No—I've nobly dealt with you;
I've brought my all into the public stock :
I've but one friend, and him I'll share amongst you :
Receive and cherish him ; or if, when seen
And search'd, you find him worthless ; as my tongue
Has lodg'd this secret in his faithful breast,
To ease your fears, I wear a dagger here

Shall rip it out again, and give you rest.
Come forth, thou only good I e'er could boast of.

Enter JAFFIER, *with a Dagger.*

Bed. His presence bears the shew of manly virtue.
Jaf. I know you'll wonder all, that thus uncall'd,
I dare approach this place of fatal councils;
But I'm amongst you, and by heav'n it glads me
To see so many virtues thus united
To restore justice, and dethrone oppression.
Command this sword, if you would have it quiet,
Into this breast; but, if you think it worthy
To cut the throats of reverend rogues in robes,
Send me into the curs'd assembled senate :
It shrinks not, tho' I meet a father there.
Would you behold this city flaming? here's
A hand shall bear a lighted torch at noon
To th' arsenal, and set its gates on fire.
Ren. You talk this well, Sir.
Jaf. Nay——by Heaven I'll do this.
Come, come, I read distrust in all your faces:
You fear me a villain, and, indeed, it's odd
To hear a stranger talk thus, at first meeting,
Of matters that have been so well debated;
But! I come ripe with wrongs, as you with councils.
I hate this senate; am a foe to Venice;
A friend to none, but men resolv'd like me
To push on mischief. Oh! did you but know me,
I need not talk thus!

Bed. Pierre, I must embrace him.   380
My heart beats to this man, as if it knew him.

Ren. I never lov'd these huggers.

Jaf. Still I see
The cause delights ye not. Your friends survey me
As I were dangerous————But I come arm'd
Against all doubts, and to your trust will give
A pledge, worth more than all the world can pay for.
My Belvidera. Hoa; my Belvidera!

Bed. What wonder's next?

Jaf. Let me entreat you,
As I have henceforth hopes to call you friends,
That all but the ambassador, and this
Grave guide of councils, with my friend that owns me,
Withdraw a while, to spare a woman's blushes.

                 [*Exeunt all but* BED. REN. JAF. PIER.

            Enter BELVIDERA.

Bed. Pierre, whither will this ceremony lead us?

Jaf. My Belvidera! Belvidera!

Bel. Who,
Who calls so loud at this late peaceful hour?
That voice was wont to come in gentle whispers,
And fill my ears with the soft breath of love.   400
Thou hourly image of my thoughts, where art thou?

Jaf: Indeed 'tis late.

Bel. Oh! I have slept and dreamt;
" And dreamt again. Where hast thou been, thou
      loiterer?
" Tho' my eyes clos'd, my arms have still been open'd:
" Stretch'd every way-betwixt my broken slumbers,

    8

" To search if thou wert come to crown my rest :
" There's no repose without thee : Oh ! the day
" Too soon will break, and wake us to our sorrow.
" Come, come to bed, and bid thy cares good night.

    Jaf. " Oh Belvidera ! we must change the scene,
" In which the past delights of life were tasted :
" The poor sleep little ; we must learn to watch
" Our labours late, and early every morning ;
" 'Midst winter frosts, thin clad, and fed with sparing,
" Rise to our toils, and drudge away the day."

    Bel. Alas ! where am I ! whither is't you lead me ?
Methinks I read distraction in your face,
Something less gentle than the fate you tell me.
You shake and tremble too ! your blood runs cold !
Heav'ns guard my love, and bless his heart with pa-
        tience.   421

    Jaf. That I have patience, let our fate bear witness,
Who has ordain'd it so, that thou and I,
(Thou, the divinest good man e'er possess'd,
And I, the wretched'st of the race of man)
This very hour without one tear, must part.

    Bel. Part ! must we part ? Oh, am I then forsaken ?
" Will my love cast me off ? Have my misfortunes
" Offended him so highly, that he'll leave me ?"
Why drag you from me ; Whither are you going,
My dear ! my life ! my love !

    Jaf. Oh, friends !

    Bel. Speak to me.

    Jaf. Take her from my heart,
She'll gain such hold else, I shall ne'er get loose.

I charge thee take her, but with tender'st care
Relieve her troubles, and assuage her sorrows.

   Ren. Rise, Madam, and command amongst your
      servants.

   Jaf. To you, Sirs, and your honours, I bequeath her,
And with her this; when I prove unworthy——

                                        [*Gives a Dagger.*

You know the rest————Then strike it to her heart;
And tell her, he who three whole happy years
Lay in her arms, and each kind night repeated
The passionate vows of still increasing love,
Sent that reward for all her truth and sufferings.

   Bel. Nay, take my life, since he has sold it cheaply;
   " Or send me to some distant clime your slave;
   " But let it be far off, lest my complainings
   " Should reach his guilty ears, and shake his peace.

   Jaf. " No, Belvidera, I've contriv'd thy honour.
   " Trust to my faith, and be but fortune kind
   " To me, as I'll preserve that faith unbroken;
   " When next we meet, I'll lift thee to a height
   " Shall gather all the gazing world about thee,
   " To wonder what strange virtue plac'd thee there.
   " But if we ne'er meet more."

   Bel. O! thou unkind one;
Ne'er meet more! have I deserv'd this from you;
Look on me, tell me, speak, thou fair deceiver.
Why am I separated from thy love?   460
If I am false, accuse me, but if true,
Don't, pr'ythee don't, in poverty forsake me,
But pity the sad heart that's torn with parting.

Jaf. Oh! " my eyes,
" Look not that way, but turn yourselves a while
" Into my heart, and be wean'd altogether."
My friend; where art thou?

    Pier. Here, my honour's brother.

    Jaf. Is Belvidera gone?

    Pier. Renault has led her
Back to her own apartment; but by Heav'n,
Thou must not see her more, till our work's over.

    Jaf. No!

    Pier. Not for your life.

    Jaf. Oh, Pierre, wert thou but she,
How I would pull thee down into my heart,
Gaze on thee, till my eye-strings crack'd with love
" Till all my sinews, with its fire extended,
" Fix'd me upon the rack of ardent longing:"   4
Then, swelling, sighing, raging to be blest,
Come, like a panting turtle to thy breast;
On thy soft bosom hovering, bill and play,
Confess the cause why last I fled away;
Own 'twas a fault, but swear to give it o'er,
And never follow false ambition more.   [*Exeu.*

ACT III. SCENE I.

" *Enter* Aquilina *and her Maid.*

" *Aquilina.*

" Tell him I am gone to bed; tell him I am not at
" home; tell him I've better company with me, or
" any thing; tell him, in short, I will not see him,
" the eternal troublesome vexatious fool: He's worse
" company than an ignorant physician———I'll not be
" disturb'd at these unseasonable hours.

" *Maid.* But, madam! He's here already, just en-
" ter'd the doors.

" *Aqui.* Turn him out again, you unnecessary,
" useless, giddy-brain'd ass: If he will not be gone,
" set the house a fire, and burn us both: I'd rather
" meet a toad in my dish, than that old hideous ani-
" mal in my chamber to-night.   13

Enter Antonio.

" ———you little puss——Purre, Tuzzy——I am a
" senator.

" *Aqui.* You are a fool, I am sure

" *Ant.* May be so too, sweet-heart: never the
" worse senator for all that. Come, Nacky, Nacky,
" let's have a game at romps, Nacky.

" *Aqui.* You would do well, Signor, to be trouble-
" some here no longer, but leave me to myself; be
" sober, and go home, Sir.

" *Ant.* Home, Madona!

" *Aqui.* Ay, home, Sir. Who am I?   32

" *Ant.* Madona, as I take it, you are my—you are
" —thou art my little Nacky, Nacky——that's all.

" *Aqui.* I find, you are resolv'd to be troublesome;
" and so, to make short of the matter in few words, I
" hate you, detest you, loath you, I am weary of you,
" sick of you—hang you, you are an old, silly, imper-
" tinent, impotent, solicitous coxcomb; crazy in your
" head, and lazy in your body; love to be meddling
" with every thing, and, if you had not money, you
" are good for nothing.

" *Ant.* Good for nothing! Hurry, durry, I'll try
" that presently. Sixty-one years old, and good for
" nothing: that's brave: [*To the Maid*] Come, come,
" come Mrs. Fiddle-faddle, turn you out for a season:
" Go, turn out, I say, it is our will and pleasure to be
" private some moments——out, out, when you are
" bid to——[*Puts her out and locks the door*] Good for
" nothing, you say?

" *Aqui.* Why, what are you good for?

" *Ant.* In the first place, Madam, I am old, and
/ " consequently very wise, very wise, Madona, d'ye
" mark that ? In the second place, take notice, if you
" please, that I am a senator; and, when I think fit,
" can make speeches, Madona. Hurry durry, I can
" make a speech in the senate-house, now and then—
" would make your hair stand an end, Madona.

" *Aqui.* What care I for your speeches in the se-
" nate-house ? if you would be silent here, I should
" thank you.

" *Ant.* Why I can make speeches to thee too, my
" lovely Madona; for example :—

" My cruel Fair one, since it is my fate,
" That you should with your servant angry
    prove,
" Though late at night, I hope 'tis not too late
" With this to gain reception for my Love.

[*Takes out a purse of Gold, and at every pause shakes it*]

" —There's for thee, my little Nicky Nacky—take it,
" here take it——I say take it, or I'll throw it at your
" head—how now, rebel ?   70

" *Aqui.* Truly, my illustrious senator, I must con-
" fess, your honour is at present most profoundly
" eloquent indeed.

" *Ant.* Very well : Come, now let's sit down, and
" think upon't a little—come, sit, I say——sit down
" by me a little, my Nicky Nacky. A—[*sits down.*]
" Hurry durry—good for nothing——

" *Aqui.* No, Sir, if you please, I can know my dis-
" tance, and stand

" *Ant.* Stand! How, Nacky up, and I down?
" Nay, then, let me exclaim with the poet,
 " Shew me a case more pitiful who can,
 " A standing woman and a falling man. 40
" Hurry durry—not sit down—see this, ye gods!
" You won't sit down?

" *Aqui.* No, sir.

" *Ant.* Then look you now; suppose me a bull, a
" Basan-bull, the bull of bulls, or any bull. Thus
" up I get, and with my brows, thus bent——I broo,
" I say, I broo, I broo, I broo. You won't sit down,
" will you—I broo————

  " [*Bellows like a bull, and drives her about.*

" *Aqui.* Well, Sir, I must endure this. [*She sits
" down.*] Now your honour has been a bull, pray
" what beast will your worship please to be next?

" *Ant.* Now, I'll be a senator again, and thy lover,
" little Nicky Nacky. [*He sits by her.*] Ah! toad,
" toad, toad, toad! Spit in my face a little, Nacky, spit
" in my face, pr'ythee, spit in my face never so little:
" Spit but a little bit—spit, spit, spit—spit—when you
" are bid, I say—do, pr'ythee spit,——now, now,
" now, spit; what you won't spit, will you? then I'll
" be a dog. 60

" *Aqui.* A dog, my Lord!

" *Ant.* Ay, a dog—and I'll give thee this t'other
" purse, to let me be a dog—and use me like a dog a

" little. Hurry durry—I will—here 'tis——

[*Gives the purse.*

" *Aqui.* Well, with all my heart. But let me be-
" seech your dogship to play your tricks over as fast
" as you can, that you may come to stinking the soon-
" er, and be turn'd out of doors, as you deserve.

" *Ant.* Ay, ay—no matter for that—that shan't
" move me—[*He gets under the table*] Now, bough,
" waugh, waugh, waugh, bough, waugh.—[*Barks*
" *like a dog.*

" *Aqui.* Hold, hold, hold, Sir, I beseech you :
" What is't you do ? If curs bite, they must be kick'd,
" Sir : Do you see, kick'd thus.

" *Ant,* Ay, with all my heart : Do, kick, kick on !
" now I am under the table, kick again——kick
" harder——harder yet, bough, waugh, waugh,
" waugh, bough—odd, I'll have a snap at thy shins
" —bough, waugh, waugh, waugh, bough——odd,
" she kicks bravely——   122

" *Aqui.* Nay, then I'll go another way to work with
" you : And I think here's an instrument fit for the
" purpose ? [*Fetches a whip and a bell*] What, bite
" your mistress, sirrah ? out of door, you dog, to ken-
" nel, and be hang'd—bite your mistress by the legs,
" you rogue——   [*She whips him.*

" *Ant.* Nay, pr'ythee Nacky, now thou art too
" loving : Hurry durry, odd, I'll be a dog no longer.

" *Aqui.* Nay, none of your fawning and grinning :
" But, begone, or here's the discipline. What, bite

" your mistress by the leg, you mungrel? Out of'
" door's————hout, hout, to kennel, sirrah, go.

" *Ant.* This is very barbarous usage, Nacky, very
" barbarous: look you, I will not go————I will
" not stir from the door, that I resolve————hurry
" durry, what, shut me out?   [*She whips him out.*

" *Aqui.* Ay, and if you come here any more to-
" night, I'll have my footmen lug you, you cur?
What bite your poor mistress, Nacky, sirrah?   100

Enter Maid.

" Heav'ns! Madam, what's the matter?
                  [*He howls at the door like a dog.*
" *Aqui.* Call my footmen hither presently.

Enter two Footmen,

" *Maid.* They're here already, Madam; the house
" is all alarm'd with a strange noise, that no body
" knows what to make of.

" *Aqui.* Go, all of you, and turn that troublesome
" beast in the next room out of my house————If I
" ever see him within these walls again, without my
" leave for his admittance, you sneaking rogues————
" I'll have you poison'd, all poison'd like rats; every
" corner of the house shall stink of one of you; go,
" and learn hereafter to know my pleasure. So; now
" for my Pierre.

" Thus, when the god-like lover is displeas'd,
" We sacrifice our fool, and he's appeas'd.
                              [*Exeunt.*

SCENE IV.

A Chamber.   Enter BELVIDERA.

Bel. I'm sacrific'd! I'm sold! betray'd to shame!
Inevitable ruin has enclos'd me!
" No sooner was I to my bed repair'd
" To weigh and (weeping) ponder my condition;
" But the old hoary wretch, to whose false care
" My peace and honour was entrusted, came,
" (Like Tarquin) ghastly, with infernal lust.
" Oh, thou Roman Lucrecè,
" Thou could'st find friends, to vindicate thy wrong!
" I never had but one, and he's prov'd false:
He that should guard my virtue has betray'd it;
Left me! Undone me! Oh, that I could hate him!
Where shall I go? Oh, whither, whither, wander?

Enter JAFFIER.

Jaf. Can Belvidera want a resting-place,
When these poor arms are ready to receive her?
" Oh! 'tis in vain to struggle with desires,
" Strong is my love to thee; for, every moment
" I'm from thy sight, the heart within my bosom
" Mourns like a tender infant in its cradle,
" Whose nurse had left it. Come, and with the songs
" Of gentle love, persuade it to its peace.
   " *Bel.* I fear the stubborn wanderer will not own
      me;
" 'Tis grown a rebel, to be rul'd no longer;

Or look'd but sad——there was indeed a time,
When Jaffier would have ta'en her in his arms,
Eas'd her declining head upon his breast,
And never left her, till he found the cause.
But let her now weep seas;
Cry, till she rend the earth; sigh, till she burst
Her heart asunder; still he bears it all
Deaf as the winds, and as the rocks unshaken.
   " *Jaf.* Have I been deaf? Am I that rock unmov'd?
" Against whose root, tears beat, and sighs are sent
" In vain? have I beheld thy sorrows calmly?
" Witness against me, Heavens, have I done this?
" Then bear me in a whirlwind back again,
" And let that angry dear one ne'er forgive me. 200
" Oh! thou too rashly censurest of my love;
" Could'st thou but think, how I have spent this night
" Dark, and alone, no pillow to my head,
" Rest in my eyes, nor quiet in my heart,
" Thou would'st not, Belvidera, sure thou would'st
        not
" Talk to me thus; but like a pitying angel,
" Spreading thy wings, come settle on my breast,

" And hatch warm comforts there, ere sorrows freeze
　　it.

　" *Bel.* Why then, poor mourner, in what baleful
　　corner　　　.

" Hast thou been talking, with that witch, the night?
" On what cold stone hast thou been stretch'd along,
" Gathering the grumbling winds about thy head,
" To mix with theirs, the accents of thy woes?
" Oh! now I find the cause my love forsakes me;
" I am no longer fit to bear a share
" In his concernments—My weak female virtue
" Must not be trusted : 'tis too frail and tender."

　Jaf. Oh, Portia, Portia! What a soul was thine?

　Bel. That Portia was a woman; and when Brutus,
Big with the fate of Rome, (Heav'n guard thy safety!)
Conceal'd from her the labours of his mind;
She let him see her blood was great as his,
Flow'd from a spring as noble, and a heart
Fit to partake his troubles as his love.
Fetch, fetch that dagger back, the dreadful dower,
Thou gav'st last night in parting with me; strike it
Here to my heart; and as the blood flows from it,
Judge if it run not pure, as Cato's daughter's.

　" *Jaf.* Thou art too good, and I indeed unworthy;
" Unworthy so much virtue　Teach me how
" I may deserve such matchless love as thine,
" And see with what attention I'll obey thee.

　" *Bel.* Do not despise me : that's the all I ask.

　" *Jaf.* Despise thee! Hear me——

　" *Bel.* Oh! Thy charming tongue,

" Is but too well acquainted with my weakness ;
" Knows, let it name but love, my melting heart
" Dissolves within my breast ; till with clos'd eyes
" I reel into thy arms, and all's forgotten.
　　" *Jaf.* What shall I do ?
　　" *Bel.* Tell me ; be just, and tell me,
" Why dwells that busy cloud upon thy face ?
" Why am I made a stranger ? Why that sigh,
" And I not know the cause ? Why, when the world
" Is wrapp'd in rest, why chooses then my love
" To wander up and down in horrid darkness,
" Loathing his bed, and these desiring arms ?
" Why are these eyes blood-shot with tedious watch-
　　　　ing ?
" Why starts he now, and looks as if he wish'd
" His fate were finish'd ? Tell me, ease my fear ; 250
" Lest, when we next time meet, I want the power
" To search into the sickness of thy mind,
" But talk as wildly then as thou look'st now.
　　Jaf. Oh, Belvidera !
　　Bel. Why was I last night deliver'd to a villain ?
　　Jaf. Ha ! a villain ?
　　Bel. Yes, to a villain ! Why at such an hour
Meets that assembly, all made up of wretches,
" That looks as hell had drawn them into league ?"
Why, I in this hand, and in that a dagger,
Was I deliver'd with such dreadful ceremonies ?
To you, Sirs, and to your honours, I bequeath her,
And with her this : Whene'er I prove unworthy—
You know the rest—then strike it to her heart.

Oh! why's that rest conceal'd from me? Must I
Be made the hostage of a hellish trust?
For such I know I am; that's all my value.
But, by the love and loyalty I owe thee,
I'll free thee from the bondage of the slaves;
Straight to the senate, tell 'em all I know,   270
All that I think, all that my fears inform me.

Jaf. Is this the Roman virtue; this the blood
That boasts its purity with Cato's daughter?
Would she have e'er betray'd her Brutus?

Bel. No:
For Brutus trusted her. Wert thou so kind,
What would not Belvidera suffer for thee?

Jaf. I shall undo myself, and tell thee all.

" *Bel.* Look not upon me as I am, a woman:
" But as a bone, thy wife, thy friend; who long
" Has had admission to thy heart, and there
" Study'd the virtues of thy gallant nature.
" Thy constancy, thy courage, and thy truth,
" Have been my daily lesson: I have learn'd 'em,
" And, bold as thou, can suffer or despise
" The worst of fates for thee, and with thee share
        'em."

Jaf. Oh, you divinest Powers look down and hear
" My prayers! instruct me to reward this virtue '"
Yet think a little, ere thou tempt me further;
Think I've a tale to tell will shake thy nature,   290
Melt all this boasted constancy thou talk'st of
Into vile tears and despicable sorrows:

7

But as thou hop'st to see me live my days,
And love thee long, lock this within thy breast:
I've bound myself, by all the strictest sacraments,
Divine and human————

    Bel. Speak!

    Jaf. To kill thy father————

    Bel. My father!

    Jaf. Nay, the throats of the whole senate
Shall bleed, my Belvidera. He, amongst us,
That spares his father, brother, or his friend,
Is damn'd. " How rich and beauteous will the face
" Of ruin look, when these wide streets run blood!
" I, and the glorious partners of my fortune,
" Shouting, and striding o'er the prostrate dead,
" Still to new waste; whilst thou, far off in safety,
" Smiling, shalt see the wonders of our daring;
" And when night comes, with praise and love receive
       me.

    Bel. Oh!

    Jaf. Have a care, and shrink not even in thought:
For if thou dost————————

    Bel. I know it; thou wilt kill me.
Do, strike thy sword into this bosom: lay me

Has persecuted me to my undoing;
Driven me to basest wants; can I behold him,
With smiles of vengeance, butcher'd in his age?
The sacred fountain of my life destroy'd?
And can'st thou shed the blood that gave me being?
Nay, be a traitor too, and sell thy country?
Can thy great heart descend so vilely low,
Mix with hir'd slaves, bravoes, and common stabbers,
"Nose-slitters, alley-lurking villains!" join
With such a crew, and take a ruffian's wages,
To cut the throats of wretches as they sleep?

   Jaf. Thou wrong'st me, Belvidera! I've engag'd
With men of souls; fit to reform the ills
Of all mankind: there's not a heart amongst them
But's stout as death, yet honest as the nature
Of man first made, e'er fraud and vice were fashion.

   Bel. What's he, to whose curst hands last night
           thou gav'st me?
Was that well done? Oh! I could tell a story,
Would rouse thy lion heart out of its den,
And make it rage with terrifying fury.   340

   Jaf. Speak on, I charge thee.

   Bel. O my love! If e'er
Thy Belvidera's peace deserv'd thy care,
Remove me from this place. Last night, last night!

   Jaf. Distract me not, but give me all the truth.

   Bel. No sooner wert thou gone, and I alone,
Left in the pow'r of that old son of mischief;
No sooner was I lain on my sad bed,

F

But that vile wretch approach'd me, " loose, unbut-
   ton'd,
" Ready for violation:" Then my heart
Throbb'd with its fears : Oh, how I wept and sigh'd,
And shrunk and trembled ! wish'd in vain for him
That should protect me! Thou, alas ! wert gone.
 Jaf. Patience, sweet Heav'n, 'till I make vengeance
   sure.
 Bel. He drew the hideous dagger forth, thou gav'st
   him,
And with upbraiding smiles, he said, *Behold it :*
This is the pledge of a false husband's love :
And in my arms, then press'd, and would have clasp'd
   me ;
But with my cries, I scar'd his coward heart,
Till he withdrew, and mutter'd vows to hell. 360
These are thy friends! with these thy life, thy honour,
Thy love, all stak'd, and all will go to ruin.
 Jaf. No more : I charge thee keep this secret close.
Clear up thy sorrows; look as if thy wrongs
Were all forgot, and treat him like a friend,
As no complaint were made. No more ; retire,

Jaf. Anon, at twelve
I'll steal myself to thy expecting arms :
Come like a travell'd dove, and bring thee peace.
  Bel. Indeed !
  Jaf. By all our loves.
  Bel. 'Tis hard to part :
But sure no falsehood ever look'd so fairly.   '380
Farewel ; remember twelve.   [*Exit.*
  Jaf. Let Heav'n forget me,
When I remember not thy truth, thy love.
" How curs'd is my condition, toss'd and jostled
" From every corner ; fortune's common fool,
" The jest of rogues, an instrumental ass,
" For villains to lay loads of shame upon,
" And drive about just for their ease and scorn."

Enter PIERRE.

  Pier. Jaffier.
  Jaf. Who calls ?
  Pier. A friend, that could have wish'd
T: have found thee otherwise employed. What, hunt
A wife, on the dull soil ! Sure a staunch husband
Of all hounds is the dullest. Wilt thou never,
Never be wean'd from caudles and confections ?
What feminine tales hast thou been list'ning to,
Of unair'd shirts, catarrhs and tooth ach, got
By thin-sol'd shoes ? Damnation ! that a fellow,
Chosen to be a sharer in the destruction
Of a whole people, should sneak thus into corners
To ease his fulsome lusts, and fool his mind.   421
                  F ij

Jaf. May not a man then trifle out an hour
ith a kind woman, and not wrong his calling?

Pier. Not in a cause like ours.

Jaf. Then, friend, our cause
in a damn'd condition: for I'll tell thee,
iat canker-worm, call'd Lechery, has touch'd it;
is tainted vilely. Would'st thou think it? Renault
hat mortify'd old wither'd winter rogue)
ves simple fornication like a priest;
ound him out for watering at my wife;
　visited her last night, like a kind guardian:
ith! she has some temptation, that's the truth
　　　on't.

Pier. He durst not wrong his trust.

Jaf. 'Twas something late, though,
, take the freedom of a lady's chamber.

Pier. Was she in bed?

Jaf. Yes, faith, in virgin sheets,
hite as her bosom, Pierre, dish'd neatly up,
ght tempt a weaker appetite to taste.　　　420
　! how the old fox stunk, I warrant thee,
hen the rank fit was on him!

Jaf. Ay, so say I: but hush, no more on't.
All hitherto is well, and I believe
Myself no monster yet: " tho' 'no man knows
" What fate he's born to." Sure it is near the hour
We all should meet for our concluding orders:
Will the ambassador be here in person ?

    Pier. No, he has sent commission to that villain
         Renault,
To give the executing charge:
I'd have thee be a man, if possible,
And keep thy temper; for a brave revenge
Ne'er comes too late.   440

    Jaf. Fear not, I am cool as patience.
" Had he completed my dishonour, rather
" Than hazard the success our hopes are ripe for,
" I'd bear it all with mortifying virtue."

    Pier. He's yonder, coming this way thro' the hall;
His thoughts seem full.

    Jaf. Pr'ythee retire, and leave me
With him alone: I'll put him to some trial;
See how his rotten part will bear the touching.

    Pier. Be careful, then.   *[Exit.*

    Jaf. Nay, never doubt, but trust me.
What ! be a devil, take a damning oath
For shedding native blood! Can there be a sin
In merciful repentance ? Oh, this villain !

        Enter RENAULT.

    Ren. Perverse and peevish: What a slave is man
To let his itching flesh thus get the better of him!

Jaf. Sir, are you sure of that?
Stands she in perfect health? Beats her pulse even;
Neither too hot nor cold?

Ren. What means that question?

Jaf. Oh! women have fantastic constitutions,
Inconstant in their wishes, always wavering,
And never fix'd. Was it not boldly done,
Even at first sight, to trust the thing I lov'd
(A tempting treasure too) with youth so fierce
And vigorous as thine? but thou art honest.

Ren. Who dares accuse me?

Jaf. Curs'd be he that doubts
Thy virtue! I have try'd it, and declare,
Were I to choose a guardian of my honour,
I'd put it in thy keeping; for I know thee.

Ren. Know me!

Jaf. Ay, know thee. There's no falsehood in thee:
Thou look'st just as thou art. Let us embrace.
Now would'st thou cut my throat, or I cut thine.   480

Ren. You dare not do't.

Jaf. You lie, Sir.

Ren. How!

Jaf. No more,

Enter SPINOSA, THEODORE, ELIOT, REVILLIDO, DURAND, BROMVEIL, *and the rest of the Conspirators.*

Ren. Spinosa, Theodore!
Spin. The same.
Ren. You are welcome.
Spin. You are trembling, Sir.
Ren. 'Tis a cold night, indeed, and I am aged;
Full of decay and natural infirmities: [*Pier. re-enters.*
We shall be warm, my friends, I hope, to-morrow.
  Pier. 'Twas not well done; thou should'st have
      stroak'd him,
And not have gall'd him.
  Jaf. Damn him, let him chew on't.
Heav'n! Where am I? beset with cursed fiends,
That wait to damn me! What a devil's man,
When he forgets his nature——hush, my heart.
  Ren. My friends, 'tis late; are we assembled all?
" Where's Theodore?   500
  Theod. " At hand.
  Ren. " Spinosa.
  Spin. " Here.
  Ren. " Bromveil.
  Brom. " I'm ready.
  Ren. " Durand and Brahe.
  Dur. " Command us.
We are both prepar'd"
  Omnes. All; all.
  Ren. " Mezzano, Revillido;
" Ternon, Retrosi! Oh! you're men, I find

Fit to behold your fate, and meet her summons.
To-morrow's rising sun must see you all
Deck'd in your honours.   Are the soldiers ready?
  Pier. All, all.
  Ren. You, Durand, with your thousand must possess
St. Mark's; you, Captain, know your charge already,
'Tis to secure the ducal palace: '" You,
" Brabe, with an hundred more, must gain the Secque:
" With the like number, Bromveil, to the Procurale;"
Be all this done with the least tumult possible,   521
'Till in each place you post sufficient guards:
Then sheathe your swords in every breast you meet.
  Jaf. Oh! reverend cruelty! damn'd bloody villain!
  Ren. During this execution, Durand, you
Must in the midst keep your battalia fast;
And, Theodore, be sure to plant the cannon
That may command the streets; " whilst Revillido,
" Messano, Ternon, and Retrosi guard you."
This done, we'll give the general alarm,
Apply petards, and force the ars'nal gates;
Then fire the city round in several places,
Or with our cannon (if it dare resist)
Batter to ruin.   But above all I charge you,
Shed blood enough; spare neither sex nor age,
Name nor condition; if there live a senator
After to-morrow, though the dullest rogue
That e'er said nothing, we have lost our ends.
If possible, let's kill the very name
Of senator, and bury it in blood.   540
  Jaf. Merciless, horrid slave—Ay, blood enough!

Shed blood enough, old Renault! how thou charm'st
    –me!

  Ren. But one thing more, and then farewell, till
    fate

Join us again, or sep'rate us for ever:
First let's embrace. Heav'n knows who next shall thus
Wing ye together; but let's all remember,
We wear no common cause upon our swords:
Let each man think that on his single virtue
Depends the good and fame of all the rest;
Eternal honour, or perpetual infamy.
" Let us remember through what dreadful hazards
" Propitious fortune hitherto has led us:
" How often on the brink of some discovery
" Have we stood tottering, yet still kept our ground
" So well, that the busiest searchers ne'er could fol-
    low
" Those subtle tracts, which puzzled all suspicion?"
You droop, Sir.

  Jaf. No; With most profound attention
I've heard it all, and wonder at thy virtue.

  Ren. " Tho' there be yet few hours 'twixt them
    and ruin,
" Are not the senate lull'd in full security,   561
" Quiet and satisfy'd, as fools are always?
" Never did so profound repose fore-run
" Calamity so great. Nay, our good fortune
" Has blinded the most piercing of mankind,
" Strengthen'd the fearfullest, charm'd the most sus-
    pectful,

" Confounded the most subtle : for we live,
" We live, my friends, and quickly shall our life
" Prove fatal to these tyrants." Let's consider,
That we destroy oppression, avarice,
A people nurs'd up equally with vices
And loathsome lusts, which nature most abhors,
And such as without shame she cannot suffer.

    Jaf. Oh, Belvidera! take me to thy arms,
And shew me where's my peace, for I have lost it.
                                  [*Exit.*

    Ren. Without the least remorse then, let's resolve
With fire and sword t'exterminate these tyrants ;
" And when we shall behold those curs'd tribunals
" Stain'd by the tears and sufferings of the innocent,
" Burning with flames rather from Heav'n than ours,
" The raging, furious, and unpitying soldier   581
" Pulling his reeking dagger from the bosoms
" Of gasping wretches; death in every quarter;
" With all that sad disorder can produce
" To make a spectacle of horror; then,
" Then let us call to mind, my dearest friends,
" That there is nothing pure upon the earth ;
" That the most valu'd things have most allays,
" And that in change of all these vile enormities,"
Under whose weight this wretched country labours,
The means are only in our hands to crown them.

    Pier. And may those pow'rs above that are pro-
        pitious
To gallant minds, record this cause and bless it.

    Ren. Thus happy, thus secure of all we wish for,

Should there, my friends, be found among us one
False to this glorious enterprize, what fate,
What vengeance were enough for such a villain?
 Eli. Death here without repentance, Hell hereafter.
 Ren. Let that be my lot, if as here I stand,
Listed by fate among her darling sons   600
Tho' I had one only brother, dear by all
The strictest ties of nature; "tho' one hour
" Had given us birth, one fortune fed our wants,
" One only love, and that but of each other,
" Still fill'd our minds;" could I have such a friend
Join'd in this cause, and had but ground to fear
He mean't foul play; may this right hand drop from
   me,
If I'd not hazard all my future peace,
And stab him to the heart before you. Who,
Who would do less? Would'st thou not, Pierre, the
   same?
 Pier. You've singled me, Sir, out for this hard
   question.
As if 'twere started only for my sake?
Am I the thing you fear! Here, here's my bosom,
Search it with all your swords. Am I a traitor?
 Ren. No: but I fear your late commended friend
Is little less. Come, Sirs, 'tis now no time
To trifle with our safety. Where's this Jaffier?
 Spin. He left the room just now, in strange disorder.
 Ren. Nay, there is danger in him: I observ'd him;
During the time I took for explanation,   620
He was transported from most deep attention

To a confusion which he could not smother,
" His looks grew full of sadness and surprise,
" All which betray'd a wavering spirit in him,
" That labour'd with reluctancy and sorrow."
What's requisite for safety, must be done
With speedy execution; he remains
Yet in our power: I, for my own part, wear
A dagger————

 Pier. Well.
 Ren. And I could wish it———
 Pier. Where?
 Ren. Buried in his heart
 Pier. Away; we're yet all friends,   ▴
No more of this, 'twill breed ill blood among us.
 Spin. Let us all draw our swords, and search the
   house,
Pull him from the dark hole where he sits brooding
O'er his cold fears, and each man kill his share of him.
 Pier. Who talks of killing? Who's he'll shed the
   blood
That's dear to me? is't you, or you, or you, Sir! 640
What, not one speak! how you stand gaping all
On your grave oracle, your wooden god there!
Yet not a word! Then, Sir, I'll tell you a secret;
Suspicion's but at best a coward's virtue. [*To* Ren.
 Ren. A coward!   [*Handles his sword.*
 Pier. Put up thy sword, old man;
Thy hand shakes at it. Come, let's heal this breach;
I am too hot, we yet may all live friends.
 Spin. Till we are safe, our friendship cannot be so.

Pier. Again! Who's that?   650

Spi. 'Twas I.

The. And I.

Ren. And I.

Om. And all.

Ren. " Who are on my side?

Spi. " Every honest sword.

Let's die like men, and not be sold like slaves.

 Pier. One such word more, by Heav'n I'll to the
   senate,

And hang ye all, like dogs, in clusters.

Why weep your coward swords half out their shells?

Why do you not all brandish them like mine?

You fear to die, and yet dare talk of killing.

 Ren. Go to the senate, and betray us! haste!

Secure thy wretched life; we fear to die

Less than thou dar'st be honest.

 Pier. That's rank falsehood.

Fear'st not thou death! Fie, there's a knavish itch

In that salt blood, an utter foe to smarting.

Had Jaffier's wife prov'd kind, he'd still been true.

Faugh, how that stinks! thou die, thou kill my friend?

Or thou! or thou! with that lean wither'd face.

Away, disperse all to your several charges,

And meet to-morrow where your honour calls you.

I'll bring that man, whose blood you so much thirst
   for,

And you shall see him venture for you fairly—

Hence! hence, I say.   [*Exit* Renault *angrily.*

Spi. I fear we've been to blame,
And done too much.

   The. " 'Twas too far urg'd against the man you
      lov'd.

   Rev. " Here, take our swords, and crush them with
      your feet."

   Spi. Forgive us, gallant friend.

   Pier. Nay, now you've found
The way to melt, and cast me as you will.
" I'll fetch this friend, and give him to your mercy
" Nay, he shall die, if you will take him from me.
" For your repose, I'll quit my heart's best jewel;
" But would not have him torn away by villains,
" And spiteful villany.

   Spi. " No, may you both
" For ever live, and fill the world with fame.   220

   Pier. " Now y' are too kind." Whence rose all this
      discord?
Oh, what a dangerous precipice have we 'scap'd!
How near a fall was all we'd long been building!
What an eternal blot had stain'd our glories,
If one, the bravest and the best of men,
Had fall'n a sacrifice to rash suspicion,
Butcher'd by those, whose cause he came to cherish!
" Oh! could you know him all, as I have known him;
" How good he is, how just, how true, how brave,
" You would not leave this place till you had seen
     him;
" Humbled yourselves before him, kiss'd his feet,
" And gain'd remission for the worst of follies."

Come but to-morrow, all your doubts shall end,
And to your loves, me better recommend,
That I've preserv'd your fame, and sav'd my friend.

[*Exeunt.*

ACT IV. SCENE, I.

The Rialto,   *Enter* JAFFIER *and* BELVIDERA.

Jaffier.

WHERE dost thou lead me? Every step I move,
Methinks I tread upon some mangled limb
Of a rack'd friend.   Oh, my charming ruin!
Where are we wandering?
  Bel. To eternal honour.
To do a deed shall chronicle thy name
Among the glorious legends of those few
That have sav'd sinking nations.   Thy renown
Shall be the future song of all the virgins,
Who by thy piety have been preserv'd
From horrid violation.   Every street
Shall be adorn'd with statues to thy honour;
And at thy feet this great inscription written,
Remember him that propp'd the fall of Venice.
  Jaf. Rather, remember him, who, after all
The sacred bonds of oaths, and holier friendship,
In fond compassion to a woman's tears,
Forgot his manhood, virtue, truth, and honour,
To sacrifice the bosom that reliev'd him.
Why wilt thou damn me?   20

G ij

Bel. Oh, inconstant man!
How will you promise; how will you deceive!
Do, return back, replace me in my bondage,
Tell all thy friends how dangerously thou lov'st me,
And let thy dagger do its bloody office.
" Oh! that kind dagger, Jaffier, how 'twill look
" Struck thro' my heart, drench'd in my blood to
        th' hilt;
" Whilst these poor dying eyes shall with their tears
" No more torment thee, then thou wilt be free:"
Or if thou think'st it nobler, let me live,
Till I'm a victim to the hateful lust,
Of that infernal devil, " that old fiend,
" That's damn'd himself, and would undo mankind."
Last night, my love!
    Jaf. Name it not again:
It shews a beastly image to my fancy,
Will wake me into madness. " Oh, the villain!
" That durst approach such purity as thine
" On terms so vile:" Destruction, swift destruction
Fall on my coward head, " and make my name   40
" The common scorn of fools," if I forgive him
" If I forgive him! If I not revenge
" With utmost rage, and most unstaying fury,
" Thy sufferings, thou dear darling of my life.
    Bel. Delay no longer then, but to the senate,
And tell the dismal'st story ever utter'd:
Tell 'em what bloodshed, rapines, desolations,
Have been prepar'd: how near's the fatal hour.
Save thy poor country, save the reverend blood

Of all its nobles, which to-morrow's dawn
Must else see shed.   " Save the poor tender lives
" Of all those little infants, which the swords
" Of murderers are whetting for, this moment.
" Think thou already hear'st their dying screams;
" Think that thou see'st their sad distracted mothers,
" Kneeling before thy feet, and begging pity:
" With torn dishevel'd hair, and streaming eyes,
" Their naked mangled breasts, besmear'd with blood;
" And even the milk, with which their fondled babes
" Softly they hush'd, dropping in anguish from 'em:
" Think thou seest this, and then consult thy heart.
    " *Jaf.* Oh!
    " *Bel.* Think too, if you lose this present minute,
" What miseries the next day brings upon thee:
" Imagine all the horrors of that night;
" Murder and rapine, waste and desolation,
" Confus'dly raging:" Think what then may prove
My lot; the ravisher may then come safe,
And, 'midst the terror of the public ruin,
Do a damn'd deed; " perhaps may lay a train
" To catch thy life: Then where will be revenge,
" The dear revenge that's due to such a wrong?"
    Jaf. By all Heaven's powers, prophetic truth dwells
        in thee;
For every word thou speak'st, strikes thro' my heart,
" Like a new light, and shews it, how 't has wan-
        der'd,"
Just what thou'st made me, take me, Belvidera,
And lead me to the place where I'm to say

G iij

This bitter lesson; where I must betray
My truth, my virtue, constancy, and friends.
Must I betray my friend? Ah! take me quickly:
Secure me well before that thought's renew'd;   81
If I relapse once more, all 's lost for ever,

   Bel. Hast thou a friend more dear than Belvidera?

   Jaf. No; thou'rt my soul itself; wealth, friend-
     ship, honour,
All present joys, and earnest of all future,
Are summ'd in thee. " Methinks, when in thy arms,
" Thus leaning on thy breast, one minute 's more
" Than a long thousand years of vulgar hours.
" Why was such happiness not given me pure?
" Why dash'd with cruel wrongs, and bitter warn-
     ings?"
Come, lead me forward, now, like a tame lamb
To sacrifice. Thus, in his fatal garlands
Deck'd fine and pleas'd, the wanton skips and plays,
Trots by th' enticing flatt'ring priestess' side,
And much transported with its little pride,
Forgets his dear companions of the plain;
Till, by her bound, he's on the altar lain,
Yet then too hardly bleats, such pleasure's in the pain.

   Enter Officer and six Guards.

   Offi. Stand! who goes there?

   Bel. Friends.   100

   " *Jaf.* Friends, Belvidera! Hide me from my
     friends:

" By Heav'n, I'd rather see the face of hell,
" Than meet the man I love."
 Off. But what friends are you?
 Bel. Friends to the senate, and the state of Venice.
 Off. My orders are to seize on all I find
At this late hour, and bring 'em to the council,
Who are now sitting.
 Jaf. Sir, you shall be obey'd.
" Hold, brute, stand off! none of your paws upon
  me."
Now the lot's cast, and, fate, do what thou wilt.
       [*Exeunt guarded.*

SCENE II.

The Senate-House, where appear sitting the Duke of VE-
NICE, PRIULI, ANTONIO, *and eight other Senators.*

 Duke. Antony, Priuli, senators of Venice,
Speak, why are we assembled here this night?
What have you to inform us of, concerns
The state of Venice' honour, or its safety?
 Pri. Could words express the story I've to tell you,
Fathers, these tears were useless, these sad tears
That fall from my old eyes; but there is cause
We all should weep, tear off these purple robes, 120
And wrap ourselves in sackcloth, sitting down
On the sad earth, and cry aloud to Heav'n:
Heav'n knows, if yet there be an hour to come
·Ere Venice be no more.
 All Sen. How!
 4

Pri. Nay, we stand
Upon the very brink of gaping ruin.
Within this city's form'd a dark conspiracy
To massacre us all, our wives and children,
Kindred and friends, our palaces and temples
To lay in ashes: nay, the hour too fix'd;
The swords, for ought I know, drawn e'en this mo-
       ment,
And the wild waste begun. From unknown hands
I had this warning; but, if we are men,
Let's not be tamely butcher'd, but do something
That may inform the world, in after ages,
Our virtue was not ruin'd, tho' we were.
                    [*A noise without.*
Room, room, make room for some prisoners—
  " *Sen.* Let's raise the city."

Enter Officer and Guards.

Duke. Speak, there. What disturbance?
Off. Two prisoners have the guards seiz'd in the
      street,   140
Who say, they come t' inform this reverend senate
About the present danger.

Enter JAFFIER *and Officer.*

All. Give 'em entrance—Well, who are you?
Jaf. A villain.
  " *Ant.* Short and pithy:"
The man speaks well.

Jaf. Would every man, that hears me,
Would deal so honestly, and own his title.

Duke. 'Tis rumour'd, that a plot has been contriv'd
Against this state; and you've a share in't too.
If you are a villain, to redeem your honour
Unfold the truth, and be restor'd with mercy.

Jaf. Think not, that I to save my life came hither;
I know its value better; but in pity
To all those wretches whose unhappy dooms
Are fix'd and seal'd. You see me here before you,
The sworn and covenanted foe of Venice:
But use me as my dealings may deserve,
And I may prove a friend.

Duke. The slave capitulates,   160
Give him the tortures.

Jaf. That you dare not do:
Your fear won't let you, not the longing itch
To hear a story which you dread the truth of:
Truth, which the fear of smart shall ne'er get from
        me.
Cowards are scar'd with threat'nings; boys are whipt
Into confessions: but a steady mind
'Acts of itself, ne'er asks the body counsel.
Give him the tortures! Name but such a thing
Again, by heav'n I'll shut these lips for ever.
Not all your racks, your engines, or your wheels,
Shall force a groan away, that you may guess at.

" *Ant.* A bloody-minded fellow, I'll warrant;
" A damn'd bloody-minded fellow."

Duke. Name your conditions.

Jaf. For myself full pardon,
Besides the lives of two and twenty friends,
Whose names are here enroll'd—Nay, let their crimes
Be ne'er so monstrous, I must have the oaths
And sacred promise of this reverend council,   180
That, in a full assembly of the senate
The thing I ask be ratify'd.   Swear this,
And I'll unfold the secret of your danger.

   " *All.* We'll swear."

Duke. Propose the oath.

Jaf. By all the hopes
Ye have of peace and happiness hereafter,
Swear.

   " *All.* We all swear.

   " *Jaf.* To grant me what I've ask'd,"
Ye swear?

   All. We swear.

Jaf. And, as ye keep the oath,
May you, and your posterity be bless'd,
Or curs'd for ever.

   All. Else be curs'd for ever.

Jaf. Then here's the list, and with 't the full dis-
         close
Of all that threatens you.   ' [*Delivers a paper.*
Now, fate, thou hast caught me.   199

   " *Ant.* Why; what a dreadful catalogue of cut-
" throats is here! I'll warrant you, not one of these
" fellows but has a face like a lion. I dare not so
" much as read their names over."

Duke. Give order that all diligent search be made
To seize these men, their characters are public;
The paper intimates their rendezvous
To be at the house of a fam'd Grecian courtezan,
Call'd Aquilina; see that place secur'd.

    " *Ant.* What, my Nicky Nacky! Hurry, durry!
" Nicky Nacky, in the plot—I'll make a speech:
" Most noble senators,
" What headlong apprehensions drive you on,
" Right, noble, wise, and truly solid senators,
" To violate the laws and rights of nations?
" The lady is a lady of renown;
   'Tis true, she holds a house of fair reception,
" And, tho' I say't myself, as many more
" Can say, as well as I—
    " *2 Sen.* My lord, long speeches
" Are frivolous here, when dangers are so near us.
" We all well know your interest in that lady;   221
" The world talks loud on't.   .
    " *Ant.* Verily I have done;
" I say no more.
    " *Duke.* But, since he has declar'd
" Himself concern'd, pray, Captain, take great caution
" To treat the fair-one as becomes her character;
" And let her bed-chamber be search'd with de-
      cency."
You, Jaffier, must with patience bear till morning
To be our prisoner. -

    Jaf. Would the chains of death
Had bound me safe, ere I had known this minute.

" I've done a deed will make my story hereafter
" Quoted in competition with all ill ones :
" The history of my wickedness shall run
" Down thro' the low traditions of the vulgar,
" And boys be taught to tell the tale of Jaffier."

Duke. Captain, withdraw your prisoner.

Jaf. Sir, if possible,　-　　　　　　　　239
Lead me where my own thoughts themselves may lose
　　me ;
Where I may doze out what I've left of life,
Forget myself, and this day's guilt and falsehood.
Cruel remembrance, how shall I appease thee ?

　　　　　　　　　　　　　[*Exit guarded.*

Off. [*Without.*] More traitors ; room, room, room,
　　make room there.

Duke. How's this ? guards !
Where are our guards ? Shut up the gates, the trea-
　　son's
Already at our doors.

　　　　　　Enter Officer.

Off. My lords, more traitors,
Seiz'd in the very act of consultation ;
Furnish'd with arms and instruments of mischief.
Bring in the prisoners.

Enter PIERRE, RENAULT, THEODORE, ELIOT,
　　REVELLIDO, *and other Conspirators, in fetters.*

Pier. You, my lords, and fathers,
(As you are pleas'd to call yourselves) of Venice ;
If you sit here to guide the course of justice,

Why these disgraceful chains upon the limbs
That have so often labour'd in your service?
Are these the wreaths of triumph ye bestow
On those, that · bring you conquest home, and
　　honours?
　　Duke. Go on; you shall be heard, Sir.
　　" *Ant.* And be hang'd too, I hope."　　260
　　Pier. Are these the trophies I've deserv'd for fighting
Your battles with confederated powers?
When winds and seas conspir'd to overthrow you;
And brought the fleets of Spain to your own harbours;
When you, great Duke, shrunk trembling in your
　　palace,
And saw your wife, the Adriatic, plough'd,
Like a lewd whore, by bolder prows than yours,
Stepp'd not I forth, and taught your loose Venetians
The task of honour, and the way to greatness?
Rais'd you from your capitulating fears
To stipulate the terms of su'd-for peace?
And this my recompence! if I'm a traitor,
Produce my charge; or shew the wretch that's base
And brave enough, to tell me I'm a traitor.
　　Duke. Know you one Jaffier?　　[*Consp. murmur.*
　　Pier. Yes, and know his virtue.
His justice, truth, his general worth, and sufferings
From a hard father, taught me first to love him.

Enter JAFFIER *guarded.*

　　Duke. See him brought forth.
　　Pier. My friend too bound! nay then　　280

H

Our fate has conquer'd us, and we must fall.
Why droops the man whose welfare's so much mine,
They're but one thing? These reverend tyrants, Jaffier,
Call us traitors.   Art thou one, my brother?

Jaf. To thee, I am the falsest, veriest slave,
That e'er betray'd a generous, trusting friend,
And gave up honour to be sure of ruin.
All our fair hopes, which morning was t' have
      crown'd,
Has this curs'd tongue o'erthrown.

Pier. So, then all's over:
Venice has lost her freedom, I my life.
No more! Farewel!

Duke. Say; will you make confession
Of your vile deeds, and trust the senate's mercy?

Pier. Curs'd be your senate: curs'd your constitu-
      tion:
The curse of growing factions and divisions,
Still vex your councils, shake your public safety,
And make the robes of government you wear
Hateful to you, as these base chains to me.

Duke. Pardon, or death?

Pier. Death! honourable death!   300

Ren. Death's the best thing we ask, or you can
      give,
No shameful bonds, but honourable death.

Duke. Break up the council.   Captain, guard your
      prisoners.
Jaffier, you're free, but these must wait for judgment.

              [*Ex. all the Senators.*

Pier. Come, where's my dungeon? Lead me to my
    straw:
It will not be the first time I've lodg'd hard
To do the senate service.

    Jaf. Hold, one moment.

    Pier. Who's he disputes the judgment of the senate?
Presumptuous rebel—on—   [*Strikes* Jaffier.

    Jaf. By Heav'n, you stir not!
I must be heard; I must have leave to speak.
Thou hast disgrac'd me, Pierre, by a vile blow:
Had not a dagger done thee nobler justice?
But use me as thou wilt, thou can'st not wrong me,
For I am fallen beneath the baset injuries:
Yet look upon me with an eye of mercy,
With pity and with charity behold me;
" Shut not thy heart against a friend's repentance;"
But, as there dwells a godlike nature in thee,   320
Listen with mildness to my supplications.

    Pier. What whining monk art thou? what holy
    cheat,
That would'st incroach upon my credulous ears,
And cant'st thus vilely? Hence! I know thee not;
" Dissemble and be nasty." Leave, hypocrite.

    Jaf. Not know me, Pierre!

    Pier. No, I know thee not! What art thou?

    Jaf. Jaffier, thy friend, thy once lov'd valu'd friend!
Tho' now deserv'dly scorn'd, and us'd most hardly.

    Pier. Thou Jaffier! thou, my once lov'd valu'd
    friend!
By Heav'ns thou ly'st; the man so call'd, my friend,

Was generous, honest, faithful, just, and valiant;
Noble in mind, and in his person lovely;
Dear to my eyes, and tender to my heart:
But thou, a wretched, base, false, worthless coward,
Poor, even in soul, and loathsome in thy aspect;
All eyes must shun thee, and all hearts detest thee.
Pr'ythee avoid; nor longer cling thus round me,
Like something baneful, that my nature's chill'd at.

> *Jaf.* I have not wrong'd thee, by these tears I
>   have not,   340
" But still am honest, true, and, hope too, valiant;
" My mind still full of thee, therefore still noble.
" Let not thy eyes then shun me, nor thy heart
" Detest me utterly.   Oh! look upon me,
" Look back, and see my sad, sincere submission!
" How my heart swells, as e'en 'twould burst my bo-
    som;
" Fond of its goal, and labouring to be at thee.
" What shall I do? what say, to make thee hear me?

> *Pier.* Hast thou not wrong'd me? Dar'st thou call
>   thyself

That once lov'd, valu'd friend of mine,
And swear thou hast not wrong'd me? Whence these
    chains?
Whence the vile death which I may meet this moment?
Whence this dishonour, but from thee, thou false one?

> *Jaf.* All's true; yet grant one thing, and I've done
>   asking.

> *Pier.* What's that?

Jaf. To take thy life, on such conditions
The council have propos'd : thou, and thy friends,
May yet live long, and to be better treated.

Pier. Life! ask my life! Confess! record myself
A villain, for the privilege to breathe!   360
And carry up and down this cursed city,
A discontented and repining spirit,
Burthensome to itself, a few years longer;
To lose it, may be, at last, in a lewd quarrel
For some new friend, treacherous and false as thou art!
No, this vile world and I have long been jangling,
And cannot part on better terms than now,
When only men, like thee, are fit to live in't.

Jaf. By all that's just————

Pier. Swear by some other powers,
For thou hast broke that sacred oath too lately.

Jaf. Then, by that hell I merit, I'll not leave thee,
Till, to thyself, at least thou'rt reconcil'd,
However thy resentment deal with me.

Pier. Not leave me!

Jaf. No; thou shalt not force me from thee.
Use me reproachfully, and like a slave;
Tread on me, buffet me, heap wrongs on wrongs
On my poor head; I'll bear it all with patience
Shall weary out thy most unfriendly cruelty: 380
Lie at thy feet, and kiss 'em, tho' they spurn me;
Till wounded by my sufferings, thou relent,
And raise me to thy arms, with dear forgiveness.

Pier. Art thou not————

Jaf. What?

Pier. A traitor?

Jaf. Yes.

Pier. A villain.

Jaf. Granted.

Pier. A coward, a most scandalous coward;
Spiritless, void of honour; one who has sold
Thy everlasting fame, for shameless life!

    Jaf. All, all, and more, much more: my faults
        are numberless.

    Pier. And would'st thou have me live on terms
        like thine?
Base, as thou'rt false————

    Jaf. No; 'tis to me that's granted:
The safety of thy life was all I aim'd at,
In recompence for faith and trust so broken.

    Pier. I scorn it more, because preserv'd by thee;
And, as when first my foolish heart took pity   400
On thy misfortunes, sought thee in thy miseries,
Reliev'd thy wants, and rais'd thee from the state
Of wretchedness, in which thy fate had plung'd thee,
To rank thee in my list of noble friends;
All I receiv'd, in surety for thy truth,
Were unregarded oaths, and this, this dagger,
Giv'n with a worthless pledge, thou since hast stol'n:
So I restore it back to thee again;
Swearing by all those pow'rs which thou hast violated,
Never from this curs'd hour to hold communion,
Friendship, or interest, with thee, tho' our years
Were to exceed those limited the world.
Take it—farewel—for now I owe thee nothing.

Jaf. Say thou wilt live then.

Pier. For my life, dispose it

Just as thou wilt, because 'tis what I'm tir'd with.

Jaf. Oh, Pierre !

Pier. No more.

Jaf. My eyes won't lose the sight of thee,

But languish after thee, and ache with gazing.   420

    Pier. Leave me—Nay, then thus, thus I throw thee

       from me ;

And curses, great as is thy falsehood, catch thee. [*Ex.*

   Jaf. Amen.

He's gone, my father, friend, preserver,

And here's the portion he has left me :

                  [*Holds the dagger up.*

This dagger.   Well remember'd ! with this dagger,

I gave a solemn vow of dire importance ;

Parted with this, and Belvidera together.

Have a care, mem'ry, drive that thought no farther :

No, I'll esteem it, as a friend's last legacy ;

Treasure it up within this wretched bosom,

Where it may grow acquainted with my heart,

That when they meet, they start not from each other.

So now for thinking—A blow, call'd traitor, villain,

Coward, dishonourable coward ; fough !

" Oh ! for a long sound sleep, and so forget it."

Down, busy devil !

Enter BELVIDERA.

Bel. Whither shall I fly ?

Where hide me and my miseries together ?

Where's now the Roman constancy I boasted?   440
Sunk into trembling fears and desperation,
Not daring to look up to that dear face
Which us'd to smile, ev'n on my faults; but, down,
Bending these miserable eyes on earth,
Must move in penance, and implore much mercy.

    Jaf. Mercy! kind Heav'n has surely endless stores,
Hoarded for thee, of blessings yet untasted:
" Let wretches, loaded hard with guilt, as I am,
" Bow with the weight, and groan beneath the bur-
        then,
" Creep with a remnant of that strength they've left
" Before the footstool of that Heav'n they've injur'd.
Oh, Belvidera! I'm the wretched'st creature
E'er crawl'd on earth. " Now, if thou'st virtue, help
        me;
" Take me into thy arms, and speak the words of
        peace
" To my divided soul, that wars within me,
" And raises every sense to my confusion:
" By Heav'n, I'm tottering on the very brink
" Of peace, and thou art all the hold I've left.

    " *Bel.* Alas! I know thy sorrows are most mighty:
" I know thou'st cause to mourn, to mourn, my
        Jaffier,   460
" With endless cries, and never-ceasing wailing:
" Thou'st lost———

    " *Jaf.* Oh! I have lost what can't be counted;"
My friend too, Belvidera, that dear friend,
Who, next to thee, was all my health rejoic'd in,

Has us'd me like a slave, shamefully us'd me :
'Twould break thy pitying heart to hear the story.
" What shall I do ? Resentment, indignation,
" Love, pity, fear, and mem'ry how I've wrong'd him,
" Distract my quiet with the very thought on't,
" And tear my heart to pieces in my bosom.
    Bel. What has he done ?
    " *Jaf.* Thou'dst hate me, should I tell thee.
    " *Bel.* Why ?
    " *Jaf.* Oh ! he has us'd me ! yet, by Heav'n, I bear
       it ;
" He has us'd me, Belvidera—but first swear,
" That when I've told thee, thou wilt not loath me
       utterly,
" Tho' vilest blots, and stains appear upon me ;
" But still, at least, with charitable goodness,
" Be near me in the pangs of my affliction ;   480
" Nor scorn me, Belvidera, as he has done.
    " *Bel.* Have I then e'er been false, that now I'm
       doubted ?
" Speak, what's the cause I'm grown into distrust ?
" Why thought unfit to hear my love's complaining ?
    " *Jaf.* Oh !
    " *Bel.* Tell me.
    " *Jaf.* Bear my failings, for they're many.
" Oh, my dear angel ! in that friend, I've lost
" All my soul's peace ; for every thought of him
" Strikes my sense hard, and deads it in my brains ?
" Would'st thou believe it ?
    " *Bel.* Speak.

" *Jaf.* Before we parted,
Ere yet his guards had led him to his prison,
Full of severest sorrows for his sufferings,
With eyes o'erflowing, and a bleeding heart,
" Humbling myself, almost beneath my nature,
As at his feet I kneel'd and su'd for mercy,
" Forgetting all our friendship, all the dearness,
" In which we've liv'd so many years together,   500
With a reproachful hand he dash'd a blow :
He struck me, Belvidera! by Heav'n, he struck me!
Buffeted, call'd me traitor, villain, coward.
Am I a coward? Am I a villain? Tell me :
Thou'rt the best judge, and mad'st me, if I am so?
Damnation! Coward!
    Bel. Oh! forgive him, Jaffier;
And, if his sufferings wound thy heart already,
What will they do to-morrow?
    Jaf. Ah!
    Bel. To-morrow,
When thou shalt see him stretch'd in all the agonies
Of a tormenting and a shameful death ;
His bleeding bowels, and his broken limbs,
Insulted o'er, by a vile butchering villain ;
What will thy heart do then? Oh! sure 'twill stream,
Like my eyes now.
    Jaf. What means thy dreadful story?
Death, and to-morrow! Broken limbs and bowels!
" Insulted o'er by a vile butchering villain!   520
" By all my fears, I shall start out to madness

" With barely guessing, if the truth's hid longer."

Bel. The faithless senators, 'tis they've decreed it:
They say, according to our friends' request,
They shall have death, and not ignoble bondage:
Declare their promis'd mercy all as forfeited:
False to their oaths, and deaf to intercession,
Warrants are pass'd for public death to-morrow.

Jaf. Death! doom'd to die! condemn'd unheard!
     unpleaded!

Bel. Nay, cruel'st racks and torments are preparing
To force confession from their dying pangs.
Oh! do not look so terribly upon me!
How your lips shake, and all your face disorder'd!
What means my love?

Jaf. Leave me, I charge thee, leave me——Strong
     temptations
Wake in my heart.

Bel. For what?

Jaf. No more, but leave me.

Bel. Why?

Jaf. Oh! by Heav'n, I love thee with that fondness,
I would not have thee stay a moment longer
Near these curs'd hands: Are they not cold upon thee?
               [*Pulls the Dagger half out of his Bosom,*
                         and puts it back again.

Bel. No, everlasting comfort's in thy arms.
To lean thus on thy breast, is softer ease
Than downy pillows, deck'd with leaves of roses.

Jaf. Alas! thou think'st not of the thorns 'tis fill'd
     with:

Fly, ere they gall thee.   There's a lurking serpent
Ready to leap, and sting thee to the heart:
Art thou not terrify'd?

    Bel. No.

    Jaf. Call to mind
What thou hast done, and whither thou hast brought
    me.

    Bel. Hah!

    Jaf. Where's my friend? my friend, thou smiling
    mischief!
Nay, shrink not, now 'tis too late; " thou should'st
    have fled
" When thy guilt first had cause;" for dire revenge
Is up, and raging for my friend.   He groans!
Hark, how he groans! his screams are in my ears
Already; see, they've fix'd him on the wheel,
And now they tear him—Murder! Perjur'd senate!
Murder—Oh!—Hark thee, traitress, thou hast done
    this!
Thanks to thy tears, and false persuading love.
How her eyes speak! Oh, thou bewitching creature!
                      [*Fumbling for his dagger.*
Madness can't hurt thee.   Come, thou little trembler,
Creep even into my heart, and there lie safe;
'Tis thy own citadel—Hah—yet stand off.
Heav'n must have justice, " and my broken vows
" Will sink me else beneath its reaching mercy."
I'll wink, and then 'tis done——

    Bel. What means the lord
Of me, my life, and love? What's in thy bosom,

Thou grasp'st at so? " Nay, why am I thus treated?
      [*Draws the dagger and offers to stab her.*
`" What wilt thou do?" Ah! do not kill me, Jaffier:
" Pity these panting breasts, and trembling limbs,
" That us'd to clasp thee when thy looks were milder,
" That yet hang heavy on my unpurg'd soul;
" And plunge it not into eternal darkness.

    Jaf. Know, Belvidera, when we parted last,
I gave this dagger with thee, as in trust,
To be thy portion if I e'er prov'd false.   530
On such condition, was my truth believ'd:
But now 'tis forfeited, and must be paid for.
      [*Offers to stab her again.*

    Bel. Oh! Mercy!   [*Kneeling.*
    Jaf. Nay, no struggling.
    Bel. Now then, kill me.

      [*Leaps on his neck, and kisses him.*
While thus I cling about thy cruel neck,
Kiss thy revengeful lips, and die in joys
Greater than any I can guess hereafter.

    Jaf. I am, I am a coward, witness Heav'n,
Witness it, earth, and every being witness:
'Tis but one blow! yet by immortal love,
I cannot longer bear a thought to harm thee.

      [*He throws away the dagger, and embraces her.*
The seal of Providence is sure upon thee;
And thou wert born for yet unheard-of wonders.
Oh! thou wert either born to save or damn me.
By all the power that's given me o'er my soul,

By thy resistless tears and conquering smiles,
" By the victorious love, that still waits on thee;"
Fly to thy cruel father, save my friend,
Or all our future quiet's lost for ever.   600
Fall at his feet, cling round his rev'rend knees,
Speak to him with thy eyes, and with thy tears,
Melt his hard heart, and wake dead nature in him,
Crush him in th' arms, torture him with thy soft-
        ness;
Nor till thy prayers are granted, set him free,
But conquer him, as thou hast conquer'd me.

[*Exeunt.*

ACT V. SCENE I.

An Apartment in Priuli's *House.   Enter* PRIULI *solus.*

Priuli.

WHY, cruel Heav'n, have my unhappy days
Been lengthen'd to this sad one? Oh! dishonour
And deathless infamy is fallen upon me.
Was it my fault? Am I a traitor? No.
But then, my only child, my daughter wedded;
There my best blood runs foul, and a disease
Incurable has seiz'd upon my memory,
To make it rot and stink to after-ages.
" Curst be the fatal minute when I got her;
" Or wou'd that I'd been any thing but man,

" And rais'd an issue which would ne'er have wrong'd
      me.
" The miserable creatures (man excepted)
" Are not the less esteem'd, tho' their posterity
" Degenerate from the virtues of their fathers:
" The vilest beasts are happy in their offspring,
" While only man gets traitors, whores, and villains.
" Curs'd be the names, and some swift blow from
      fate
" Lay this head deep, where mine may be forgotten."

Enter BELVIDERA, *in a long mourning veil.*

Bel. He's there, my father, my inhuman father,
That for three years has left an only child   20
Expos'd to all the outrages of fate,
And cruel ruin!—oh———
    Pri. What child of sorrow
Art thou, that comest wrapt in weeds of sadness,
And mov'st as if thy steps were tow'rds a grave?
    Bel. A wretch who from the very top of happi-
      ness
Am fall'n into the lowest depths of misery,
And want your pitying hand to raise me up again.
    " *Pri.* Indeed thou talk'st as 'thou hadst tasted
      sorrows;
" Would I could help thee!
    " *Bel.* Tis greatly in your power:
" The world too speaks you charitable; and I,
" Who ne'er ask'd alms before, in that dear hope,
" Am come a begging to you, Sir.
          I ij

" *Pri.* For what?

" *Bel.* Oh! well regard me, is this voice a strange
      one?

" Consider too, when beggars once pretend

" A case like mine, no little will content 'em."

      Pri. What would'st thou beg for?

      Bel. Pity and forgiveness.   [*Throws up her veil.*

By the kind tender names of child and father,   41

Hear my complaints, and take me to your love.

      Pri. My daughter!

      Bel. Yes, your daughter, " by a mother

" Virtuous and noble, faithful to your honour,

" Obedient to your will, kind to your wishes,

" Dear to your arms.   By all the joys she gave you,

" When in her blooming years she was your treasure,

" Look kindly on me? In my face behold

" The lineaments of her's you've kiss'd so often,

" Pleading the cause of your poor cast-off child.

      " *Pri.* Thou art my daughter.

      " *Bel.* Yes"—and you've oft told me,

With smiles of love and chaste paternal kisses,

I'd much resemblance of my mother.

      " *Pri.* Oh!

" Had'st thou inherited her matchless virtues,

" I'ad been too bless'd.

      " *Bel.* Nay, do not call to memory

" My disobedience; but let pity enter   60

" Into your heart, and quite deface th' impression.

" For could you think how mine's perplex'd, what
      sadness,

" Fears and despairs distract the peace within me,

" Oh! you would take me in your dear, dear arms,

" Hover with strong compassion o'er your young one,

" To shelter me with a protecting wing

" From the black gather'd storm, that's just, just
       breaking.

    Pri. Don't talk thus.

    Bel. Yes, I must; and you must hear too.
I have a husband.

    Pri. Damn him.

    Bel. Oh! do not curse him;
He would not speak so hard a word towards you
On any terms, howe'er he deals with me.

    Pri. Ha! what means my child?

   " *Bel.* Oh! there's but this short moment

" 'Twixt me and fate: yet send me not with curses

" Down to my grave; afford me one kind blessing

" Before we part: just take me in your arms,

" And recommend me with a prayer to Heav'n,   80

" That I may die in peace; and when I'm dead—

   " *Pri.* How my soul's catch'd!

   " *Bel.* Lay me, I beg you, lay me

" By the dear ashes of my tender mother.

" She would have pity'd me, had fate yet spar'd her.

   "'*Pri.* By Heav'n, my aching heart forebodes much
      mischief!

" Tell me thy story, for I'm still thy father.

   " *Bel.* No; I'm contented.

   " *Pri.* Speak.

   " *Bel.* No matter.

" *Pri.* Tell me:

" By yon bless'd Heav'n, my heart runs o'er with
        fondness.

" *Bel.* Oh!

" *Pri.* Utter't.

Bel. Oh! my husband, my dear husband,
Carries a dagger in his once kind bosom,
To pierce the heart of your poor Belvidera.

     Pri. Kill thee!

     Bel. Yes, kill me. When he pass'd his faith
And covenant against your state and senate,   100
He gave me up a hostage for his truth:
With me a dagger and a dire commission,
When'er he fail'd, to plunge it thro' this bosom.
I learnt the danger, chose the hour of love
T' attempt his heart, and bring it back to honour.
Great love prevail'd, and bless'd me with success!
He came, confess'd, betray'd his dearest friends
For promis'd mercy. Now they're doom'd to suffer.
Gall'd with remembrance of what then was sworn,
If they are lost, he vows t'appease the gods
With this poor life, and make my blood th' atonement.

     Pri. Heav'ns!

     " *Bel.* Think you saw what pass'd at our last part-
        ing:

" Think you beheld him like a raging lion,
" Pacing the earth, and tearing up his steps,
" Fate in his eyes, and roaring with the pain
" Of burning fury: think you saw his one hand
" Fix'd on my throat, whilst the extended other

" Grasp'd a keen threat'ning dagger : Oh! 'twas thus
" We last embrac'd, when, trembling with revenge
" He dragg'd me to the ground, and at my bosom
" Presented horrid death.   Cry'd out, my friends,
" Where are my friends? swore, wept, rag'd, threat-
     en'd, lov'd,
" For yet he lov'd, and that dear love preserv'd me
" To this last trial of a father's pity.
" I fear not death; but cannot bear a thought
" That that dear hand should do th' unfriendly of-
     fice."
If I was ever then your care, now hear me ;
Fly to the senate, save the promis'd lives
Of his dear friends, ere mine be made the sacrifice.
     Pri. Oh, my heart's comfort!   131
     Bel. Will you not, my father ?
Weep not, but answer me.
     Pri. By Heav'n I will.
Not one of them but what shall be immortal.
Canst thou forgive me all my follies past ?
I'll henceforth be indeed a father ; never,
Never more thus expose, but cherish thee,
Dear as the vital warmth that feeds my life,   139
Dear as these eyes that weep in fondness o'er thee.
Peace to thy heart.   Farewel.
     Bel. Go, and remember,
 'Tis Belvidera's life her father pleads for.
                    [*Exeunt severally.*

Enter ANTONIO.

" Hum, hum, ha!

" Signor Priuli, my lord Priuli, my lord, my lord, my
" lord. Now we lords love to call one another by
" our titles. My lord, my lord, my lord,—Pox on
" him, I am a lord as well as he. And so let him
" fiddle—I'll warrant him he's gone to the senate-
" house, and I'll be there too, soon enough for some-
" body. Odd—here's a tickling speech about the plot ;
" I'll prove there's a plot with a vengeance,—would
" I had it without book ; let me see——

  " Most reverend senators,

" That there is a plot, surely by this time no man
" that hath eyes or understanding in his head, will
" presume to doubt ; 'tis as plain as the light in the
" cucumber—no—hold there—cucumber does not
" come in yet—'tis as plain as the light in the sun, or
" as the man in the moon, even at noon-day. It is,
" indeed, a pumpkin-plot, which, just as it was mel-
" low, we have gathered, and now we have gathered
" it, prepared and dressed it, shall we throw it like a
" pickled cucumber out of the window ? No : that it
" is not only a bloody, horrid, execrable, damnable,
" and audacious plot : but it is, as I may so say, a saucy
" plot : and we all know, most reverend fathers, that
" which is sauce for a goose is sauce for a gander :
" therefore, I say, as those blood-thirsty ganders of
" the conspiracy would have destroyed us geese of
" the senate, let us make haste to destroy them ; so I

" humbly move for hanging—Hah ! hurry durry,—
" I think this will do; though I was something out
" at first, about the sun and the cucumber.

Enter AQUILINA.

" *Aqui.* Good morrow, senator.
" *Ant.* Nacky, my dear Nacky; morrow, Nacky;
" odd, I am very brisk, very merry, very pert, very
" jovial—ha a a a a—kiss me, Nacky ! how dost thou
" do, my little tory rory strumpet ? Kiss me, I say,
" hussy, kiss me.   480
" *Aqui.* Kiss me, Nacky ! hang you, Sir coxcomb;
" hang you, Sir.
" *Ant.* Haity taity, is it so indeed ? With all my
" heart, faith—*Hey, then up go we.* Faith, *hey—then*
" *up go we,* dum dum derum dump.   [*Sings.*
" *Aqui.* Signor.
" *Ant.* Madona.
" *Aqui.* Do you intend to die in your bed ?
" *Ant.* About threescore years hence much may be
" done, my dear.
" *Aqui.* You'll be hang'd, Signor.
" *Ant.* Hang'd, sweet-heart, pr'ythee be quiet;
" hang'd quoth-a; that's a merry conceit with all my
" heart; why thou jok'st, Nacky; thou art given to
" joking, I'll swear. Well, I protest, Nacky, nay I
" must protest, and will protest, that I love joking
" dearly. And I love thee for joking, and I'll kiss
" thee for joking, and towse thee for joking; and
" odd, I have a devilish mind to take thee aside about

" that business for joking too, odd I have; and *Hey,*
" *then up we go,* dum dum derum dump. ` [*Sings.*
　" *Aqui.* See you this, Sir? 　[*Draws a Dagger.*
　" *Ant.* O laud, a dagger! Oh, laud! it is naturally
" my aversion, I cannot endure the sight on't; hide
" it, for Heav'ns sake; I cannot look that way till it
" be gone—hide it, hide it, oh! oh! hide it.
　" *Aqui.* Yes, in your heart I'll hide it.　　'
　" *Ant.* My heart! what hide a dagger in my heart's
　　　blood!　　　　　 '
　" *Aqui.* Yes, in thy heart, thy throat, thou pam-
　　　per'd devil;
" Thou hast help'd to spoil my peace, and I'll have
　　　vengeance
" On thy curs'd life, for all the bloody senate,
" The perjur'd faithless senate.　Where's my lord,
" My happiness, my love, my god, my hero,
" Doom'd by thy accursed tongue, among the rest,
" T' a shameful rack? By all the rage that's in me,
" I'll be whole years in murdering thee.
　" *Ant.* Why, Nacky,
" Wherefore so passionate? What have I done?
" What's the matter, my dear Nacky? Am not I thy
" love, thy happiness, thy lord, thy hero, thy senator,
" and every thing in the world, Nacky?　　　421
　" *Aqui.* Thou! think'st thou, thou art fit to meet
　　　my joys:
" To bear the eager clasps of my embraces?
" Give me my Pierre, or—

" *Ant.* Why he's to be hang'd, little Nacky;

" Truss'd up for treason and so forth, child.

" *Aqui.* Thou ly'st; stop down thy throat that
    hellish sentence,

" Or 'tis thy last: swear that my love shall live,

" Or thou art dead.

" *Ant.* Ah! h h h.

" *Aqui.* Swear to recall his doom;

" Swear at my feet, and tremble at my fury.

" *Ant.* I do! Now if she would but kick a little

" bit: one kick now, Ah! h h h.

" *Aqui.* Swear, or—

" *Ant.* I do by these dear fragrant foots and little

" toes, sweet as e e e e, my Nacky, Nacky, Nacky,

" faith and troth.

" *Aqui.* How !   439

" *Ant.* Nothing but untie thy shoe-strings a little,

" that's all, that's all, as I hope to live, Nacky, that's

" all, all.

" *Aqui.* Nay, then—

" *Ant.* Hold; hold; thy love, thy lord, thy hero,

" shall be preserv'd and safe.

" *Aqui.* Or may this poniard

" Rust in thy heart.

" *Ant.* With all my soul.

" *Aqui.* Farewel.   [*Exit.*

" *Ant.* Adieu. Why, what a bloody-minded, invete-

" rate, termagant strumpet, have I been plagued with!

" Oh! h h! Yet no more! nay, then I die, I die—

" I'm dead already."   [*Stretches himself out.*

SCENE II.

A Garden. Enter JAFFIER.

Jaf. Final destruction seize on all the world.
Bend down ye heav'ns, and shutting round this earth,
Crush the vile globe into its first confusion;
" Scorch it with elemental flames to one curs'd cinder,
" And all us little creepers in't, call'd men,
" Burn, burn to nothing: but let Venice burn,
" Hotter than all the rest: Here kindle hell,   460
" Ne'er to extinguish; and let souls hereafter
" Groan here, in all those pains which mine feels now."

Enter BELVIDERA.

Bel. My life————   [*Meeting him.*
Jaf. My plague————   [*Turning from her.*
Bel. Nay, then I see my ruin.
If I must die!
    " *Jaf.* No, death's this day too busy;
" Thy father's ill-tim'd mercy came too late.
" I thank thee for thy labours though; and him too:
" But all my poor, betray'd, unhappy friends,
" Have summons to prepare for fate's black hour;
" And yet I live.
    " *Bel.* Then be the next my doom;
" I see, thou hast pass'd my sentence in thy heart,
" And I'll no longer weep, or plead against it,
" But with the humblest, most obedient patience,

" Meet thy dear hands and kiss 'em when they wound
     me.
" Indeed I'm willing, but I beg thee do it
" With some remorse; and when thou giv'st the
     blow,
" View me with eyes of a relenting love,   480
" And shew me pity, for 'twill sweeten justice."
   " *Jaf.* Shew pity to thee!
   " *Bel.* Yes; and when thy hands,
" Charg'd with my fate, come trembling to the deed,
" As thou hast done a thousand thousand times
" To this poor breast, when kinder rage hath brought
     thee,
" When our stung hearts have leap'd to meet each
     other,
" And melting kisses seal'd our lips together;
" When joys have left me gasping in thy arms:
" So let my death come now, and I'll not shrink
     from 't."
Jaf. Nay, Belvidera, do not fear my cruelty,
Nor let the thoughts of death perplex thy fancy;
But answer me to what I shall demand,
With a firm temper and unshaken spirit.
   Bel. I will, when I've done weeping—
   Jaf. Fie, no more on't——
How long is't since that miserable day
We wedded first.
   Bel. Oh! h h!
   Jaf. Nay, keep in thy tears,   500
Lest they unman me too.

K

Bel. Heav'n knows I cannot;
The words you utter sound so very sadly,
The streams will follow—
   Jaf. Come, I'il kiss 'em dry then.
   Bel. But was't a miserable day?
   Jaf. A curs'd one.
   Bel. I thought it otherwise; and you've often sworn,
" In the transporting hours of warmest love,
" When sure you spoke the truth, you've sworn,"
    you bless'd it.
   Jaf. 'Twas a rash oath.
   Bel. Then why am I not curs'd too?
   Jaf. No, Belvidera; by th' eternal truth,
I doat with too much fondness.
   Bel. Still so kind!
Still then do you love me?
   Jaf. " Nature in her workings,
" Inclines not with more ardour to creation,
" Than I do now towards thee:" Man ne'er was
    bless'd
Since the first pair met, as I have been.   520
   Bel. Then sure you will not curse me?
   Jaf. No, I'll bless thee.
I came on purpose, Belvidera, to bless thee.
'Tis now, I think, three years, we've liv'd together.
   Bel. And may no fatal minute ever part us,
Till, reverend grown for age and love, we go
Down to one grave, as our last bed, together;
There sleep in peace, till an eternal morning.
   " *Jaf.* When will that be?   [*Sighing.*

" *Bel.* I hope, long ages hence.

" *Jaf.* Have I not hitherto, (I beg thee tell me
" Thy very fears) us'd thee with tender'st love?
" Did e'er my soul rise up in wrath against thee?
" Did I e'er frown when Belvidera smil'd?
" Or by the least unfriendly word, betray
" Abating passion? have I ever wrong'd thee?

" *Bel.* No.

" *Jaf.* Has my heart, or have my eyes, e'er wan-
　　der'd
" To any other woman?

" *Bel.* Never, never—I were the worst of false
　　ones, should I accuse thee.　　　　　　540
" I own, I've been too happy, bless'd above
" My sex's charter."

Jaf. Did I not say, I came to bless thee?

Bel. You did.

Jaf. Then hear me, bounteous Heav'n:
Pour down your blessings on this beauteous head,
Where everlasting sweets are always springing,
With a continual giving hand: let peace,
Honour, and safety, always hover round her;
Feed her with plenty; let her eyes ne'er see
A sight of sorrow, nor her heart know mourning;
Crown all her days with joy, her nights with rest,
Harmless as her own thoughts; and prop her virtue,
To bear the loss of one that too much lov'd;
And comfort her with patience in our parting.

Bel. How! Parting, parting!

Jaf. Yes, for ever parting;

Bel. O! call back
Your cruel blessing; stay with me and curse me.
"*Jaf.* No, 'tis resolv'd.
"*Bel.* Then hear me too, just Heav'n:
" Pour down your curses on this wretched head,
" With never-ceasing vengeance; let despair,
" Danger and infamy, nay all, surround me;
" Starve me with wantings; let my eyes ne'er see
" A sight of comfort, nor my heart know peace:
" But dash my days with sorrow, nights with horrors,
" Wild as my own thoughts now, and let loose fury,
" To make me mad enough for what I lose,
" If I must lose him. If I must? I will not.
" Oh! turn and hear me?"
Jaf. Now hold, heart, or never.
Bel. By all the tender days we've liv'd together,
"By all our charming nights, and joys that crown'd
        'em,"
Pity my sad condition; speak, but speak.
Jaf. Oh! h h!
Bel. By these arms, that now cling round thy neck,
" By this dear kiss, and by ten thousand more,"
By these poor streaming eyes——   582
Jaf. Murder! unhold me:
By th' immortal destiny that doom'd me
                        [*Draws his dagger.*
To this curs'd minute, I'll not live one longer;
Resolve to let me go, or see me fall——
8

" *Bel.* Hold, Sir, be patient."

Jaf. Hark, the dismal bell   [*Passing Bell tolls.*
Tolls out for death! I must attend its call too;
For my poor friend, my dying Pierre, expects me:
He sent a message to require I'd see him
Before he dy'd, and take his last forgiveness.
Farewell, for ever.

Bel. Leave thy dagger with me,
Bequeath me something—Not one kiss at parting;
Oh! my poor heart, when wilt thou break?
                    [*Going out, looks back at him.*

Jaf. Yet stay:
We have a child, as yet a tender infant;
Be a kind mother to him when I'm gone;
Breed him in virtue, and the paths of honour,   600
But never let him know his father's story;
I charge thee, guard him from the wrongs my fate
May do his future fortune, or his name.
Now—nearer yet—   [*Approaching each other.*
Oh! that my arms were rivetted
Thus round thee ever! But my friend! my oath!
This, and no more.   - [*Kisses her.*

Bel. Another, sure another,
For that poor little one you've ta'en such care of.
I'll giv't him truly.

Jaf. So now farewell.

Bel. For ever?

Jaf. Heav'n knows for ever; all good angels guard
          thee.   [*Exit.*

Bel. All ill ones sure had charge of me this moment.

Curs'd be my days, and doubly curs'd my nights,
" Which I must now mourn out in widow'd tears;
" Blasted be every herb, and fruit, and tree;
" Curs'd be the rain that falls upon the earth,
" And may the general curse reach man and beast."
Oh! give me daggers, fire or water: 600
How I could bleed, how burn, how drown, the waves
Huzzing and booming round my sinking head,
Till I descended to the peaceful bottom!
Oh! there's all quiet, here all rage and fury:
The air's too thin, and pierces my weak brain;
I long for thick substantial sleep: Hell! hell!
Burst from the centre, rage and roar aloud,
If thou art half so hot, so mad as I am

" *Enter* PRIULI, *and Servants.*
" Who's there?   [*They seize her.*
    " *Pri.* Run, seize, and bring her safely home;
" Guard her as you would life: Alas, poor creature!
    " *Bel.* What to my husband! then conduct me
        quickly;
" Are all things ready? Shall we die most gloriously?
" Say not a word of this to my old father:
" Murmuring streams, soft shades, and springing
        flowers!
" Lutes, laurels, seas of milk, and ships of amber.
                                    [*Exeunt.*

SCENE III.

Opening, discovers a scaffold, and a wheel prepared for the Execution of PIERRE ; *then enter Officer,* PIERRE, *and Guards, " a Friar," Executioner, and a great Rabble.*

" *Off.* Room, room there—stand all by, make
" room for the prisoner."
-*Pier.* My friend not come yet ?
" *Fri.* Why are you so obstinate ?　　640
" *Pier.* Why you so troublesome, that a poor
　　　　wretch can't die in peace,
" But you, like ravens, will be croaking round him—
" *Fri.* Yet Heav'n——
" *Pier.* I tell thee, Heav'n and I are friends :
" I ne'er broke peace with't yet, by cruel murders,
" Rapine, or perjury, or vile deceiving ;
" But liv'd in moral justice towards all men :
" Nor am a foe to the most strong believers,
" Howe'er my own short-sighted faith confine me.
" *Fri.* But an all-seeing judge——
" *Pier.* You say my conscience
" Must be my accuser ; I have search'd that con-
　　　　science,
" And find no records there of crimes that scare me.
" *Fri.* 'Tis strange, you should want faith.
" *Pier.* You want to lead
" My reason blind-fold, like a hamper'd lion,
" Check'd of it's nobler vigour ; then when baited

" Down, to obedient tameness, make it couch
" And shew strange tricks, which you call signs of
        faith :
" So silly souls are gull'd, and you get money. 660
" Away; no more. Captain, I'd have hereafter
" This fellow write no lies of my conversion,
" Because he has crept upon my troubled hours."

Enter JAFFIER.

Jaf. Hold: eyes be dry;
Heart, strengthen me to bear
This hideous sight, and humble me, to take
The last forgiveness of a dying friend,
Betray'd by my vile falsehood, to his ruin.
Oh, Pierre!
  Pier. Yet nearer.
  Jaf. Crawling on my knees,
And prostrate on the earth, let me approach thee :
How shall I look up to thy injured face,
That always us'd to smile with friendship on me?
It darts an air of so much manly virtue,
That I, methinks, look little in thy sight,
And stripes are fitter for me, than embraces.
  Pier. Dear to my arms, tho' thou'st undone my
        fame,
I can't forget to love thee. Pr'ythee, Jaffier,
Forgive that filthy blow my passion dealt thee;
I'm now preparing for the land of peace,
And fain would have the charitable wishes
Of all good men, like thee, to bless my journey.

Jaf. Good! I am the vilest creature, worse than
     e'er
Suffer'd the shameful fate thou'rt going to taste of,
" Why was I sent for to be us'd thus kindly?
" Call, call me villain, as I am! describe
" The foul complexion of my hateful deeds:
" Lead me to th' rack, and stretch me in thy stead,
" I've crimes enough to give it its full load,
" And do it credit: thou wilt but spoil the use on't,
" And honest men hereafter bear its figure
" About them, as a charm from treacherous friend-
     ship."
  Off. The time grows short, your friends are dead
     already.
  Jaf. Dead!
  Pier. Yes, dead, Jaffier; they've all died like men
     too,
Worthy their character.
  Jaf. And what must I do?
  Pier. Oh, Jaffier!
  Jaf. Speak aloud thy burthen'd soul,
And tell thy troubles to thy tortur'd friend.
  Pier. Friend! Could'st thou yet be a friend, a ge-
     nerous friend,
I might hope comfort from thy noble sorrows.
Heav'n knows, I want a friend.
  Jaf. And I a kind one,
That would not thus scorn my repenting virtue,
Or think when he's to die, my thoughts are idle.
  Pier. No! live, I charge thee, Jaffier.

Jaf. Yes, I will live:

But it shall be to see thy fall reveng'd

At such a rate, as Venice long shall groan for.

   Pier. Wilt thou?

   Jaf. I will, by Heav'n.

   Pier. Then still thou'rt noble,

And I forgive thee.   Oh!—yet—shall I trust thee?

   Jaf. No; I've been false already.

   Pier. Dost thou love me?

   Jaf. Rip up my heart, and satisfy thy doubtings.

   Pier. Curse on this weakness.   [*He weeps.*

   Jaf. Tears! Amazement! Tears!

I never saw thee melted thus before;

And know there's something labouring in thy bosom,

That must have vent: Tho' I'm a villain, tell me.

   Pier. See'st thou that engine? [*Pointing to the Wheel.*

   Jaf. Why?

   Pier. Is't fit a soldier, who has liv'd with honour,

Fought nation's quarrels, and been crown'd with con-

       quest,

Be expos'd a common carcase on a wheel?

   Jaf. Hah!

   Pier. Speak! is't fitting?

   Jaf. Fitting!

   Pier. Yes; is't fitting?

   Jaf. What's to be done?

   Pier. I'd have thee undertake

Something that's noble, to preserve my memory

From the disgrace that's ready to attaint it.

   Off. The day grows late, Sir.

Pier. I'll make haste. Oh, Jaffier!
Tho' thou'st betray'd me, do me some way justice.

Jaf. No more of that : thy wishes shall be satisfied ;
I have a wife, and she shall bleed : my child too,
Yield up his little throat, and all
T' appease thee——

             [*Going away*, Pierre *holds him.*

Pier. No—this—no more.   [*He whispers* Jaffier.

Jaf. Hah! is't then so?

Pier. Most certainly.

Jaf. I'll do it.

Pier. Remember.

Off. Sir.

Pier. Come, now I'm ready.

             [*He and* Jaffier *ascend the scaffold.*

Captain, you should be a gentleman of honour;
Keep off the rabble that I may have room
To entertain my fate, and die with decency.
Come.

     [*Takes off his gown, executioner prepares to bind him.*

" *Fri.* Son.

" *Pier.* Hence, tempter.

" *Off.* Stand off, priest.

" *Pier.* I thank you, Sir."   [*To the Officer.*
You'll think on't?   [*To* Jaffier.

Jaf. 'Twon't grow stale before to-morrow.

Pier. Now, Jaffier! now I'm going. Now—

             [*Executioner having bound him.*

Jaf. Have at thee,
Thou honest heart, then—here   [*Stabs him.*

And this is well too.   [*Stabs himself.*

" *Fri.* Damnable deed!"

Pier. Now thou hast indeed been faithful.

This was done nobly—We have deceiv'd the senate.

Jaf. Bravely.

Pier. Ha, ha, ha——oh! oh!   [*Dies.*

Jaf. Now, ye curs'd rulers,

Thus of the blood y'ave shed, I make libation

And sprinkle it mingling. May it rest upon you,

And all your race. Be henceforth peace a stranger

Within your walls; let plagues and famine waste

Your generation—Oh, poor Belvidera!

Sir, I have a wife, bear this in safety to her,

A token that with my dying breath I bless'd her,

And the dear little infant left behind me.

I'm sick——I'm quiet.   [*Dies.*

" *Off.* Bear this news to the senate,

" And guard their bodies, till there's further orders.

" Heav'n grant I die so well." [*Scene shuts upon them.*

Soft Music. Enter BELVIDERA *distracted, led by two*
of her Women, PRIULI *and Servants.*

  Pri. Strengthen her heart with patience, pitying
   Heav'n.

  Bel. Come, come, come, come, come, nay, come
   to bed.

Pr'ythee, my love. The winds; hark how they
   whistle;

And the rain beats: Oh! how the weather shrinks
   me!

You are angry now, who cares? Pish, no indeed,
Choose then; I say you shall not go, you shall not;
Whip your ill-nature; get you gone then. Oh!
Are you return'd? See, father, here he's come again:
Am I to blame to love him? O, thou dear one,
Why do you fly me? Are you angry still then?
Jaffier, where art thou? father, why do you do thus?
Stand off, don't hide him from me. He's here some-
    where.
Stand off, I say: What gone? Remember't, tyrant:
I may revenge myself for this trick, one day.
I'll do't—I'll do't. " Renault's a nasty fellow;
" Hang him, hang him, hang him."

Enter Officer.

Pri. News, what news?

        [*Officer whispers* PRIULI.

Off. Most sad, Sir;
Jaffier, upon the scaffold, to prevent
A shameful death, stabb'd Pierre, and next himself;
Both fell together.
  Pri. Daughter.
  Bel. Ha! look there!
My husband bloody and his friend too! Murder!
Who has done this? Speak to me, thou sad vision
On these poor trembling knees I beg it. Vanish'd—
Here they went down—Oh, I'll dig, dig the den up:
You shan't delude me thus. Hoa, Jaffier, Jaffier.
Peep up, and give me but a look. I have him!

L

I've got him, father: Oh! " now how I'll smuggle
      him!
My love! my dear! my blessing! help me! help me!
They have hold on me, and drag me to the bottom.
Nay—now they pull so hard—farewell—   [*Dies.*
   " *Maid.* She's dead;
" Breathless and dead."
    Pri. Oh! guard me from the sight on't.
Lead me into some place that's fit for mourning:
Where the free air, light, and the cheerful sun,
May never enter: hang it round with black:
Set up one taper, that may last a day,
As long as I've to live; and there all leave me:
    Sparing no tears, when you this tale relate,
    But bid all cruel fathers dread my fate.
                         [*Exeunt omnes.*

EPILOGUE.

THE Text is done, and now for application,
And when that's ended, pass your approbation.
Though the conspiracy's prevented here,
Methinks I see another hatching there:
And there's a certain faction fain would sway,
If they had strength enough, and damn this play:
But this the author bid me boldly say,
If any take this plainness in ill part,
He's glad on't from the bottom of his heart.
Poets in honour of the truth should write,
With the same spirit brave men for it fight.
And though against him causeless hatreds rise,
And daily where he goes of late he spies
The scowls of sullen and revengeful eyes;
'Tis what he knows, with much contempt, to bear,
And serves a cause too good to let him fear.
He fears no poison from an incens'd drab,
No ruffian's five-foot sword, nor rascal's stab;
Nor any other snares of mischief laid,
Not a Rose-Alley cudgel ambuscade,
From any private cause where malice reigns,
Or general pique all blockheads have to brains;
Nothing shall daunt his pen, when truth does call,
No, not the * picture-mangler at Guildhall.

* He that cut the Duke of York's picture.

As they before had massacred his name,
Durst their base fears but look him in the face,
They'd use his person as they've us'd his fame:
A face in which such lineaments they read
Of that great martyr's, whose rich blood they shed,
That their rebellious hate they still retain,
And in his son would murder him again.
With indignation then let each brave heart
Rouze and unite to take his injur'd part;
'Till royal love and goodness call him home,
And songs of triumph meet him as he come:
'Till Heav'n his honour and our peace restore,
And villains never wrong his virtue more.

THE END.

LADY JANE GRAY

A

TRAGEDY,

BY N. ROWE, ESQ.

ADAPTED FOR

THEATRICAL REPRESENTATION.

AS PERFORMED AT THE

THEATRES-ROYAL,

DRURY-LANE AND COVENT-GARDEN.

REGULATED FROM THE PROMPT-BOOKS,

By Permission of the Managers.

" The lines distinguished by inverted Commas, are omitted in the Representation."

LONDON :

Printed for the Proprietors, under the Direction of
JOHN BELL, British Library, STRAND.
Bookseller to His Royal Highness the Prince of Wales.

M DCC XCI.

TO
HER ROYAL HIGHNESS
THE PRINCESS OF WALES.

A Princess of the same royal blood to which you are so closely and so happily allied, presumes to throw herself at the feet of your Royal Highness for protection. The character of that excellent lady, as it is delivered down to us in history, is very near the same with the picture I have endeavoured to draw of her; and if, in the poetical colouring, I have aim'd at heightening and improving some of the features, it was only to make her more worthy of those illustrious hands to which I always intended to present her.

As the British nation in general is infinitely indebted to your Royal Highness: so every particular person amongst us ought to contribute according to their several capacities and abilities, towards the discharging that public obligation.

We are your debtors, Madam, for the preference you gave us, in choosing to wear the British, rather than the Imperial crown; for giving the best daughter to our king, and the best wife to our prince. It is to your Royal Highness we owe the security that shall be delivered down to our children's children, by a most hopeful and beautiful, as well as a numerous royal issue. These are the bonds of our civil duty: but your Royal Highness has laid us under others, yet more sacred and engaging; I mean those of religion. You are not only the brightest ornament, but the patroness and defender of our holy faith.

Nor is it Britain alone, but the world, but the present and all succeeding ages, who shall bless your royal name, for the greatest example that can be given of a disinterested piety, and unshaken constancy.

This is what we may certainly reckon amongst the benefits your Royal Highness has conferred upon us. Though, at the same time, how partial soever we may be to ourselves, we ought not to believe you declined the first crown of Europe, in regard to Britain only. No, Madam, it is in justice to your Royal Highness that we must confess, you had more excellent motives for so great an action as that was, since you did it in obedience to the dictates of reason and conscience, for the sake of true religion, and for the honour of God. All things that are great have been offered to you; and all things that are good and happy, as well in this world as a better, shall become the reward of such exalted virtue and piety. The blessings of our nation, the prayers of our church, with the faithful service of all good men, shall wait upon your Royal Highness as long as you live; and whenever, for the punishment of this land, you shall be taken from us, your sacred name shall be dear to remembrance, and *Almighty God, who alone is able, shall bestow on you the fulness of recompence.*

Amongst the several offerings of duty which are made to you here, be graciously pleased to accept of this unworthy trifle, which is, with the greatest respect and lowest submission, presented to your Royal Highness, by,

Madam,

Your Royal Highness's

Most obedient, most devoted, and,

Most faithful humble servant,

N.   R O W E.

T HOUGH I have very little inclination to write prefaces before works of this nature; yet, upon this particular occasion, I cannot but think myself obliged to give some account of this Play, as well in justice to myself, as to a very learned and ingenious gentleman, my friend, who is dead. The person I mean, was Mr. Smith, of Christ-Church, Oxon: one, whose character I could, with great pleasure, enter into, if it was not already very well known to the world. As I had the happiness to be intimately acquainted with him, he often told me, that he designed writing a Tragedy upon the story of Lady Jane Gray; and if he had lived, I should never have thought of meddling with it myself: but as he died without doing it, in the beginning of last summer, I resolved to undertake it. And, indeed, the hopes I had of receiving some considerable assistances from the papers he left behind him, were one of the principal motives that induced me to go about it. These papers were in the hands of Mr. Ducket, to whom my friend, Mr. Thomas Burnet, was so kind as to write, and procure them for me. The least return I can make to those gentlemen, is this public acknowledgment of their great civility on this occasion. I must confess, before those papers came to my hand, I had entirely formed the design, or fable, of my own play; and when I came to look them over, I found it was different from that which Mr, Smith intended; the plan of his being drawn after that which is in print of Mr. Banks; at least I thought so, by what I could pick out of his papers. To say the truth, I was a good deal surprised and disappointed at the sight of them. I hoped to have met with great part of the play written to my hand; or, at least, the whole of

the design regularly drawn out. Instead of that, I found the
quantity of about two quires of paper written over in odd pieces,
blotted, interlined, and confused. What was contained in them,
in general, was loose hints of sentiments, and short obscure
sketches of scenes. But how they were to be applied, or in what
order they were to be ranged, I could not, by any diligence of
mine (and I looked them very carefully over more than once),
come to understand. One scene there was, and one only, that
seemed pretty near perfect, in which Lord Guilford singly per-
suades Lady Jane to take the crown. From that I borrowed all
that I could, and inserted it in my own third act. But indeed
the manner and turn of his fable was so different from mine,
that I could not take above five-and-twenty, or thirty lines at
the most; and even in those I was obliged to make some altera-
tion   I should have been very glad to have come into a part-
nership of reputation with so fine a writer as Mr. Smith was;
but in truth, his hints were so short and dark (many of them
marked even in short-hand), that they were of little use or ser-
vice to me. They might have served as indexes to his own
memory, and he might have formed a play out of them; but I
dare say nobody else could. In one part of his design, he seems
to differ from Mr. Banks, whose tale he generally designed to
follow; since I observed in many of those short sketches of
scenes, he had introduced queen Mary. He seemed to intend
her character pitiful, and inclining to mercy; but urged on
to cruelty by the rage and bloody dispositions of Bonner and
Gardiner. This hint I had likewise taken from the late Bishop
of Salisbury's History of the Reformation; who lays, and, I
believe, very justly, the horrible cruelties that were acted at
that time, rather to the charge of that persecuting spirit by
which the clergy were then animated, than to the queen's own
natural disposition.

Many people believed, or, at least said, that Mr. Smith left
a play very near entire behind him.   All that I am sorry for is,
that it was not so in fact ; I should have made no scruple of
taking three, four, or even the whole five acts from him ; but
then I hope I should have had the honesty to let the world know
they were his, and not take another man's reputation to myself.

This is what I thought necessary to say, as well on my own
account, as in regard to the memory of my friend.

For the play, such as it is, I leave it to prosper as it can ; I
have resolved never to trouble the world with any public apolo-
gies for my writings of this kind, as much as I have been pro-
voked to it.   I shall turn this, my youngest child, out into the
world, with no other provision than a saying which I remember
to have seen before one of Mrs. Behn's :

Va ¹ mon énfant, prend ta fortune.

THIS play has the general characteristics of ROWE's Tragedy; suavity, rather than strength, is the mark of his verse, and his thoughts rather swell with pomp than nature, are much more splendid than great.

In pathetic power it is infinitely below his SHORE; yet the resignation of JANE may affect those whose moral rectitude might refuse in the former play their sympathy to the sufferer, stained by illicit conduct, and only expiating ingratitude by penury and pain.

The chief praise of character must however be given to GARDINER—He displays the usual feelings of a Churchman; and we could extend a greater portion of applause to ROWE for the delineation, if we had not latterly been so much more gratified by a fuller development of the sacerdotal mind in the MYSTE-RIOUS MOTHER of Horace Walpole.

B

A PROLOGUE.

WHEN waking terrors rouze the guilty breast,
And fatal visions break the murd'rer's rest ;
When vengeance does ambition's fate decree,
And tyrants bleed, to set whole nations free ;
Tho' the muse saddens each distressed scene,
Unmov'd is ev'ry breast, and ev'ry face serene :
The mournful lines no tender heart subdue ;
Compassion is to suff'ring goodness due.
The poet your attention begs once more,
T' atone for characters here drawn before ;
No royal mistress sighs through ev'ry page,
And breathes her dying sorrows on the stage.
No lovely fair by soft persuasion won,
Lays down the load of life, when honour's gone.
Nobly to bear the changes of our state,
To stand unmov'd against the storms of fate,
A brave contempt of life, and grandeur lost :
Such glorious toils a female name can boast.
Our author draws not beauty's heavenly smile,
T' invite our wishes, and our hearts beguile ;
No soft enchantments languish in her eye,
No blossoms fade, nor sick'ning roses die.
A nobler passion ev'ry breast must move,
Than youthful raptures, or the joys of love,

A mind unchang'd, superior to a crown,
Bravely defies the angry tyrant's frown;
The same, if fortune sinks, or mounts on high,
Or if the world's extended ruins lie:
With gen'rous scorn she lays the sceptre down;
Great souls shine brightest by misfortunes shown.
With patient courage she sustains the blow,
And triumphs o'er variety of woe.
Through ev'ry scene the sad distress is new:
How well feign'd life does represent the true!
Unhappy age! who views the bloody stain,
But must with tears record Maria's reign;
When zeal by doctrine flatter'd lawless will,
Instructed by Religion's voice to kill?
Ye British fair, lament in silent woe;
Let ev'ry eye with tender pity flow;
The lovely form, through falling drops, will seem
Like flow'ry shadows of the silver stream.
Thus beauty, heaven's sweet ornament, shall prove
Enrich'd by virtue, as ador'd by love.
Forget your charms, fond woman's dear delight,
The fops will languish here another night.
No conquest from dissembling smiles we fear;
She only kills, who wounds us with a tear.

PROLOGUE.

To-night the noblest subject swells our scene,
A heroine, a martyr, and a queen ;
And tho' the poet dares not boast his art,
The very theme shall something great impart,
To warm the gen'rous soul, and touch the tender heart.
To you, fair judges, we the cause submit ;
Your eyes shall tell us how the tale is writ.
If your soft pity waits upon our woe,
If silent tears for suff'ring virtue flow ;
Your grief the muse's labour shall confess,
The lively passions, and the just distress.
Oh, could our author's pencil justly paint,
Such as she was in life, the beauteous saint !
Boldly your strict attention might we claim,
And bid you mark and copy out the dame.
No wand'ring glance one wanton thought confess'd,
No guilty wish inflam'd her spotless breast ·
The only love that warm'd her blooming youth,
Was husband, England, liberty, and truth.
For these she fell, while, with too weak a hand,
She strove to save a blind, ungrateful land.
But thus the secret laws of fate ordain ;
William's great hand was doom'd to break that chain,
And end the hopes of Rome's tyrannic reign.
For ever, as the circling years return,

Ye grateful Britons crown the hero's urn;
To his just care you ev'ry blessing owe,
Which, or his own, or following reigns bestow.
Tho' his hard fate a father's name deny'd;
To you a father, he that loss supply'd.
Then while you view the royal line's increase,
And count the pledges of your future peace;
From this great stock while still new glories come,
Conquest abroad, and liberty at home:
While you behold the beautiful and brave,
Bright princesses to grace you, kings to save,
Enjoy the gift, but bless the hand that gave.

Dramatis Personae.

COVENT-GARDEN.

Men.

Duke of NORTHUMBERLAND,	- -
Duke of SUFFOLK,	- - - -
Lord GUILFORD DUDLEY, -	
Earl of PEMBROKE,	- - - -
Earl of SUSSEX, - - - -	- Mr. Thompson.
GARDINER, Bishop of Winchester -	- Mr. Harley.
Sir JOHN GATES, - - -	- Mr. Davies.
Lieutenant of the Tower, - - -	- Mr. Evatt.

Women.

Dutchess of SUFFOLK, - - -	- Mrs. Rock.
Lady JANE GRAY, - - -	- Mrs. Merry.

Lords of the Council, Gentlemen, Guards, Women, and Attendants.

SCENE, London.

LADY JANE GRAY.

ACT I. SCENE I.

The court. Enter the Duke of NORTHUMBERLAND,
Duke of SUFFOLK, *and Sir* JOHN GATES.

Northumberland.

'TIS all in vain; heav'n has requir'd its pledge,
And he must die.

  Suff. Is there an honest heart,
That loves our England, does not mourn for
      Edward?
The genius of our isle is shook with sorrow,
" He bows his venerable head with pain,
" And labours with the sickness of his lord."
Religion melts in ev'ry holy eye;
" All comfortless, afflicted, and forlorn,
" She sits on earth, and weeps upon her cross,
" Weary of man, and his detested ways:

" Ev'n now she seems to meditate her flight,
" And waft her angels to the thrones above."
　North. Ay, there, my lord, you touch our heaviest
　　loss.
With him our holy faith is doom'd to suffer ;
With him our church shall veil her sacred front,
" That late from heaps of Gothic ruins rose,
" In her first native simple majesty ;
" The toil of saints, and price of martyrs' blood,
" Shall sail with Edward, and again Old Rome
" Shall spread her banners ; and her monkish host,"
Pride, ignorance, and rapine, shall return ;
Blind bloody zeal, and cruel priestly power,
Shall scourge the land for ten dark ages more.
　Sir J. G. Is there no help in all the healing art,
No potent juice or drug to save a life
So precious, and prevent a nation's fate ?
　North. What has been left untry'd that art could
　　do ?
" The hoary wrinkled leech has watch'd and toil'd,
" Try'd ev'ry health-restoring herb and gum,
" And weary'd out his painful skill in vain.
" Close, like a dragon folded in his den,
" Some secret venom preys upon his heart ;
" A stubborn and unconquerable flame
" Creeps in his veins, and drinks the streams of life ;"
His youthful sinews are unstrung, cold sweats
And deadly paleness sit upon his visage,
And every gasp we look shall be his last.

Sir *J. G.* Doubt not, your graces, but the Popish
    faction
Will at this juncture urge their utmost force.
All on the princess Mary turn their eyes,
Well hoping she shall build again their altars,
And bring their idol-worship back in triumph.

   " *North.* Good heav'n, ordain some better fate for
     England!

   " *Suff.* What better can we hope, if she should
     reign?

" I know her well, a blinded zealot is she,
" A gloomy nature, sullen and severe.
" Nurtur'd by proud presuming Romish priests,
" Taught to believe they only cannot err,
" Because they cannot err; bred up in scorn
" Of reason, and the whole lay world; instructed
" To hate whoe'er dissent from what they teach,
" To purge the world from heresy by blood,
" To massacre a nation, and believe it
" An act well pleasing to the Lord of Mercy:
" These are thy gods, oh, Rome, and this thy
     faith!"

   North. And shall we tamely yield ourselves to bond-
     age?
Bow down before these holy purple tyrants,
And bid 'em tread upon our slavish necks?
No; let this faithful free-born English hand
First dig my grave in liberty and honour;
And though I found but one more thus resolv'd,
That honest man and I would die together.

Suff. Doubt, not, there are ten thousand and ten
 thousand,
To own a cause so just.
 Sir *J. G.* The list I gave
Into your grace's hand last night, declares
My power and friends at full. [*To* Northumb.
 North. Be it your care,
Good Sir John Gates, to see your friends appointed
And ready for the occasion. Haste this instant,
Lose not a moment's time.
 Sir *J. G.* I go, my lord. [*Exit Sir* J. Gates.
 North. Your grace's princely daughter, lady Jane,
Is she yet come to court?
 Suff. Not yet arriv'd,
But with the soonest I expect her here.
I know her duty to the dying king,
Join'd with my strict commands to hasten hither,
Will bring her on the wing.
 North. Beseech your grace,
To speed another messenger to press her;
For on her happy presence all our counsels
Depend, and take their fate.
 Suff. Upon the instant
Your grace shall be obey'd. I go to summon her.
         [*Exit* Suffolk.
 North. What trivial influences hold dominion
O'er wise men's counsels, and the fate of empire!
 " The greatest schemes that human wit can forge,
 " Or bold ambition dares to put in practice,
 " Depend upon our husbanding a moment,

" And the light lasting of a woman's will;
" As if the lord of nature should delight
" To hang this pond'rous globe upon a hair,
" And bid it dance before a breath of wind."
She must be here, and lodg'd in Guilford's arms,
Ere Edward dies, or all we've done is marr'd.
Ha! Pembroke! that's a bar which thwarts my way?
His fiery temper brooks not opposition,
And must be met with soft and supple arts,
" With crouching courtesy, and honey'd words,"
Such as assuage the fierce, and bend the strong.

Enter the Earl of PEMBROKE.

Good-morrow, noble Pembroke: we have staid
The meeting of the council for your presence.

   Pem. For mine, my lord! you mock your servant
      sure,
To say that I am wanted, where yourself,
The great Alcides of our state, is present.
Whatever dangers menace prince or people,
Our great Northumberland is arm'd to meet 'em:
The ablest head, and firmest heart you bear,
Nor need a second in the glorious task;
Equal yourself to all the toils of empire.

   North. No; as I honour virtue, I have try'd,
And know my strength too well! nor can the voice
Of friendly flattery, like yours, deceive me.
I know my temper liable to passions,
And all the frailties common to our nature;
" Blind to events, too easy of persuasion,

" And often, too, too often, have I err'd ·"
Much therefore have I need of some good man,
Some wise and honest heart, whose friendly aid
Might guide my treading thro' our present dangers;
And, by the honour of my name I swear,
I know not one of all our English peers,
Whom I wou'd choose for that best friend, like Pem‑
       broke.

   Pem. " What shall I answer to a trust so noble,
" This prodigality of praise and honour ?"
Were not your grace too generous of soul,
To speak a language differing from your heart,
How might I think you could not mean this goodness
To one whom his ill-fortune has ordain'd
The rival of your son.

   North. No more; I scorn a thought
So much below the dignity of virtue.
'Tis true, I look on Guilford like a father,
Lean to his side, and see but half his failings:
But on a point like this, when equal merit
Stands forth to make its bold appeal to honour,
And calls to have the balance held in justice;
Away with all the fondnesses of nature!
I judge of Pembroke and my son alike.

   Pem. I ask no more to bind me to your service.

   North. The realm is now at hazard, and bold fac‑
       tions
Threaten change, tumult, and disastrous days.
These fears drive out the gentler thoughts of joy,
Of courtship, and of love.   Grant, Heav'n, the state

To fix in peace and safety once again ;
Then speak your passion to the princely maid,
And fair success attend you.   For myself,
My voice shall go as far for you my lord,
As for my son, and beauty be the umpire.
But now a heavier matter calls upon us ;
The king with life just lab'ring ; and I fear,
The council grow impatient at our stay.
 Pem. One moment's pause, and I attend your
   grace.   [*Exit.* North.
Old Winchester cries to me oft, Beware
Of proud Northumberl'and.   The testy prelate,
Froward with age, with disappointed hopes,
And zealous for old Rome, rails on the duke,
Suspecting him to favour the new teachers :
Yet ev'n in that, if I judge right, he errs.
But were it so, what are these monkish quarrels,
These wordy wars of proud ill-manner'd school-men,
To us and our lay interest ? Let 'em rail
And worry one another at their pleasure.
This duke, of late, by many worthy offices,
Has sought my friendship.   And yet more, his son,
The noblest youth our England has to boast of,
Has made me long the partner of his breast.
" Nay, when he found, in spite of the resistance
" My struggling heart had made, to do him justice,
" That I was grown his rival ; he strove hard,
" And would not turn me forth from out his bosom,
" But call'd me still his friend."   And see ! He
   comes.

Enter Lord GUILFORD.

Oh, Guilford! just as thou wert ent'ring here,
My thought was running all thy virtues over,
And wond'ring how thy soul could choose a partner
So much unlike itself.

   Guil. How cou'd my tongue
Take pleasure and be lavish in thy praise!
How could I speak thy nobleness of nature,
Thy open manly heart, thy courage, constancy,
And in-born truth unknowing to dissemble!
Thou art the man in whom my soul delights,
In whom, next heav'n, I trust.

   Pem. Oh, generous youth;
What can a heart, stubborn and fierce, like mine
Return to all thy sweetness?——Yet I wou'd,
I wou'd be grateful.——Oh, my cruel fortune!
Wou'd I had never seen her, never cast
Mine eyes on Suffolk's daughter!

   Guil. So wou'd I!
Since 'twas my fate to see and love her first.

   Pem. Oh! Why should she, that universal good-
      ness,
Like light, a common blessing to the world,
Rise like a comet fatal to our friendship,
And threaten it with ruin?

   Guil. Heaven forbid!
But tell me, Pembroke, Is it not in virtue
'To arm against this proud imperious passion?
" Does holy friendship dwell so near to envy,

   3

" She cou'd not bear to see another happy,"
If blind mistaken chance, and partial beauty
Should join to favour Guilford?

   Pem. Name it not;
My fiery spirits kindle at the thought,
And hurry me to rage.

   Guil. And yet I think
I shou'd not murmur, were thy lot to prosper,
And mine to be refus'd. Though sure, the loss
Wou'd wound me to the heart.

   Pem. Ha! Couldst thou bear it?
And yet perhaps thou mightst; thy gentle temper
Is form'd with passions mix'd with due proportion,
Where no one overbears nor plays the tyrant,
" But join in nature's business, and thy happiness:"
While mine disdaining reason and her laws,
Like all thou canst imagine wild and furious,
Now drive me headlong on, now whirl me back,
And hurl my unstable flitting soul
To ev'ry mad extreme   Then pity me,
And let my weakness stand————.

Enter Sir JOHN GATES.

   Sir *J. G.* The lords of council
Wait with impatience.————

   Pem. I attend their pleasure.
This only, and no more then. Whatsoever
Fortune decrees, still let us call to mind
Our friendship and our honour. And since love
Condemns us to be rivals for one prize,

C ij

Let us contend, as friends and brave men ought,
With openness and justice to each other;
That he who wins the fair-one to his arms,
May take her as the crown of great desert,
And if the wretched loser does repine,
His own heart and the world may all condemn him.

[*Exit* Pem.

Guil. How cross the ways of life lie! While we
     think
We travel on direct in one high road,
And have our journey's end oppos'd in view,
A thousand thwarting paths break in upon us,
To puzzle and perplex our wand'ring steps;
Love, friendship, hatred, in their turns mislead us,
And ev'ry passion has its separate interest:
Where is that piercing foresight can unfold
Where all this mazy error will have end,
And tell the doom reserv'd for me and Pembroke?
" There is but one end certain, that is——Death:
" Yet ev'n that certainty is still uncertain.
" For of these several tracks which lie before us,
" We know that one leads certainly to death,
" But know not which that one is." 'Tis in vain,
This blind divining; let me think no more on't:
And see the mistress of our fate appear!

    Enter Lady JANE GRAY. *Attendants.*

Hail, princely maid! who with auspicious beauty
Chear'st ev'ry drooping heart in this sad place;
Who, like the silver regent of the night,

Lift'st up thy sacred beams upon the land,
To bid the gloom look gay, dispel our horrors,
And make us less lament the setting sun.

    L. J. Gray. Yes, Guilford; well dost thou com-
           pare my presence
To the faint comfort of the waning moon:
Like her cold orb, a cheerless gleam I bring:
" Silence and heaviness of heart, with dews
" To dress the face of nature all in tears."
But say, how fares the king?

    Guil. He lives as yet,
But ev'ry moment cuts away a hope,
Adds to our fears, and gives the infant saint
Great prospect of his op'ning heaven.

    L. J. Gray. " Descend ye choirs of angels to re-
           ceive him,
" Tune your melodious harps to some high strain,
" And waft him upwards with a song of triumph;
" A purer soul, and one more like yourselves,
" Ne'er enter'd at the golden gates of bliss."
Oh, Guilford! What remains for wretched England,
When he, our guardian angel, shall forsake us?
" For whose dear sake Heav'n spar'd a guilty land,
" And scatter'd not its plagues while Edward reign'd.

    Guil. I own my heart bleeds inward at the thought,
" And rising horrors crowd the op'ning scene."
And yet, forgive me, thou, my native country,
Thou land of liberty, thou nurse of heroes,
Forgive me, if, in spite of all thy dangers,
New springs of pleasure flow within my bosom,

When thus 'tis giv'n me to behold those eyes,
Thus gaze and wonder, " how excelling nature
" Can give each day new patterns of her skill,
" And yet at once surpass 'em."
　　L. J. Gray. Oh, vain flattery!
" Harsh and ill-sounding ever to my ear;
" But on a day like this, the raven's note
" Strikes on my sense more sweetly." But, no
　　　more,
" I charge thee touch the ungrateful theme no
　　　more;"
Lead me, to pay my duty to the king,
To wet his pale cold hand with these last tears,
And share the blessings of his parting breath.
　　Guil. Were I like dying Edward, sure a touch
Of this dear hand would kindle life anew.
But I obey, I dread that gath'ring frown;
And, oh, whene'er my bosom swells with passion,
And my full heart is pain'd with ardent love,
Allow me but to look on you, and sigh;
'Tis all the humble joy that Guilford asks.
　　L. J. Gray. Still wilt thou frame thy speech to this
　　　vain purpose,
" When the wan king of terrors stalks before us,"
When universal ruin gathers round,
And no escape is left us? Are we not
Like wretches in a storm, whom ev'ry moment
The greedy deep is gaping to devour?
" Around us see the pale despairing crew

" Wring their sad hands, and give their labour
     o'er;"
The hope of life has ev'ry heart forsook,
And horror sits on each distracted look;
" One solemn thought of death does all employ,
" And cancels, like a dream, delight and joy;
" One sorrow streams from all their weeping eyes,
" And one consenting voice for mercy cries;"
Trembling, they dread just Heav'n's avenging power,
Mourn their past lives, and wait the fatal hour.

[Exeunt.

ACT II. SCENE I.

Continues.   *Enter the Duke of* NORTHUMBERLAND, *and
     the Duke of* SUFFOLK.

Northumberland.

YET then be cheer'd my heart, amidst thy mourning.
" Though fate hang heavy o'er us, tho' pale fear
" And wild distraction sit on ev'ry face;"
Though never day of grief was known like this,
Let me rejoice, and bless the hallow'd light,
Whose beams auspicious shine upon our union,
And bid me call the noble Suffolk brother.
   Suff. I know not what my secret soul presages,
But something seems to whisper me within,
That we have been too hasty. " For myself,
" I wish this matter had been yet delay'd;

" That we had waited some more blessed time,
" Some better day with happier omens hallow'd,
" For love to kindle up his holy flame.
" But you, my noble brother, wou'd prevail,
" And I have yielded to you."
   North. Doubt not any thing;
Nor hold the hour unlucky, that good heav'n,
" Who softens the corrections of his hand,
" And mixes still a comfort with afflictions,"
Has giv'n to-day a blessing in our children,
To wipe away our tears for dying Edward.
   Suff. In that I trust. Good angels be our guard,
And make my fears prove vain. But see! My wife!
With her, your son, the gen'rous Guilford comes;
She has inform'd him of our present purpose.

Enter the Duchess of SUFFOLK, *and Lord* GUILFORD.

   L. *Guil.* How shall I speak the fulness of my heart?
What shall I say to bless you for this goodness?
Oh, gracious princess! But my life is yours,
And all the business of my years to come,
Is, to attend with humblest duty on you,
And pay my vow'd obedience at your feet.
   Duch. Suff. Yes, noble youth, I share in all thy
      joys,
" In all the joys which this sad day can give.
" The dear delight I have to call thee son,
" Comes like a cordial to my drooping spirits;
" It broods with gentle warmth upon my bosom,

" And melts that frost of death which hung about
     me."
But haste! Inform my daughter of our pleasure:
" Let thy tongue put on all its pleasing eloquence.
" Instruĉt thy love to speak of comfort to her,
" To sooth her griefs, and cheer the mourning
     maid."
North. All desolate and drown'd in flowing tears,
By Edward's bed the pious princess sits;
" Fast from her lifted eyes the pearly drops
" Fall trickling o'er her cheek, while holy ardour
" And fervent zeal pour forth her lab'ring soul;"
And ev'ry sigh is wing'd with pray'rs so potent,
As strive with Heav'n to save her dying lord.
    Duch. Suff. From the first early days of infant life,
A gentle band of friendship grew betwixt 'em;
And while our royal uncle Henry reign'd,
As brother and as sister bred together,
Beneath one common parent's care they liv'd.
    North. A wondrous sympathy of souls conspir'd
To form the sacred union. " Lady Jane
" Of all his royal blood was still the dearest;
" In ev'ry innocent delight they shar'd,
" They sung, and danc'd, and sat, and walk'd toge-
     ther;
" Nay, in the graver business of his youth,
" When books and learning call'd him from his
     sports,
" Ev'n there the princely maid was his companion.
" She left the shining court to share his toil,

Enter Lady JANE GRAY, *weeping.*

L. J. Gray. Wo't thou not break, my heart!——

Suff. Alas! What mean'st thou? '

Guil. Oh! speak! ˜

Duch. Suff. How fares the king?

North. Say, is he dead?

L. J. Gray. The saints and angels have him.

Duch. Suff. When I left him,

He seem'd a little cheer'd, " just as you enter'd——"

   L. J. Gray. As I approach'd to kneel and pay my
     duty,

He rais'd his feeble eyes, and faintly smiling,

Are you then come? he cry'd: I only liv'd,

To bid farewell to thee, my gentle cousin;

" To speak a few short words to thee, and die."

With that he prest my hand, and, oh!—he said,

When I am gone, do thou be good to England,

Keep to that faith in which we both were bred,

And to the end be constant. More I wou'd, ˴

But cannot——There his falt'ring spirits fail'd,

" And turning ev'ry thought from earth at once,

" To that best place where all his hopes were fix'd,

" Earnest he pray'd;——Merciful, great defender!

" Preserve thy holy altars undefil'd,

" Protect this land from bloody men and idols,

" Save my poor people from the yoke of Rome,
" And take thy painful servant to thy mercy."
Then sinking on his pillow, with a sigh,
He breath'd his innocent and faithful soul
Into his hands who gave it.
   " *Guil.* Crowns of glory,
" Such as the brightest angels wear, be on him ·
" Peace guard his ashes here, and paradise
" With all its endless bliss be open to him."
   North. Our grief be on his grave. Our present
        duty
Enjoins to see his last commands obey'd.
I hold it fit his death be not made known
To any but our friends. To-morrow early
The council shall assemble at the Tower.
Mean while, I beg your grace wou'd strait inform
              [*To the duchess of* Suffolk.
Your princely daughter of our resolution;
Our common interest in that happy tie,
Demands our swiftest care to see it finish'd.
   Duch. Suff. My lord, you have determined well.
      Lord Guilford,
Be it your task to speak at large our purpose.
Daughter, receive this lord as one whom I,
Your father, and his own, ordain your husband:
What more concerns our will and your obedience,
We leave you to receive from him at leisure.
   [*Exeunt Duke and Duchess of* Suffolk, *and duke of*
    Northumberland.

Guil. Wo't thou not spare a moment from thy
     sorrows.
" And bid these bubbling streams forbear to flow?
" Wo't thou not give one interval to joy;"
One little pause, while humbly I unfold
The happiest tale my tongue was ever blest with?
    L. *J. Gray.* My heart is dead within me, ev'ry
     sense
Is dead to joy; but I will hear thee, Guilford,
" Nay, I must hear thee, such is her command,
" Whom early duty taught me still t'obey."
Yet, oh! forgive me, if to all the story,
Though eloquence divine attend thy speaking,
" Though ev'ry muse and ev'ry grace do crown
     thee;"
Forgive me, if I cannot better answer,
Than weeping————thus, and thus————
    Guil. If I offend thee,
Let me be dumb for ever: " Let not life
" Inform these breathing organs of my voice,
" If any sound from me, disturb thy quiet.
" What is my peace or happiness to thine?"
No; tho' our noble parents had decreed,
And urg'd high reasons which import the state,
This night to give thee to my faithful arms,
My fairest bride, my only earthly bliss.————
    L. *J. Gray.* How! Guilford! on this night?
    Guil. This happy night:
Yet if thou art resolv'd to cross my fate,
If this my utmost wish shall give thee pain,
   2

Now rather let the stroke of death fall on me,
And stretch me out a lifeless corpse before thee ·
" Let me be swept away with things forgotten,
" Be huddled up in some obscure blind grave,
" Ere thou shouldst say my love has made thee
  wretched,
" Or drop one single tear for Guilford's sake."
 L. *J. Gray.* Alas! I have too much of death
  already,
And want not thine to furnish out new horror.
" Oh! dreadful thought, if thou wert dead indeed,
" What hope were left me then ? Yes, I will own,
" Spite of the blush that burns my maiden cheek,
" My heart has fondly lean'd towards thee long :
" Thy sweetness, virtue, and unblemish'd youth,
" Have won a place for thee within my bosom :
" And if my eyes look coldly on thee now,
" And shun thy love on this disastrous day,
" It is because I would not deal so hardly,
" To give thee sighs for all thy faithful vows,
" And pay thy tenderness with nought but tears.
" And yet 'tis all I have.
 " *Guil.* I ask no more ;"
Let me but call thee mine, confirm that hope,
To charm the doubts which vex my anxious soul ;
For all the rest, do thou allot it for me,
And at thy pleasure portion out my blessings.
" My eyes shall learn to smile or weep from thine,
" Nor will I think of joy while thou art sad.
" Nay, couldst thou be so cruel to command it,

" And sleep far from thee, on th' unwholesome
      earth,

" Where damps arise, and whistling winds blow loud,

" Then when the day returns, come drooping to
      thee,

" My locks still drizzling with the dews of night,

" And cheer my heart with thee as with the morn-
      ing.

    " *L. J. Gray.* Say, wo't thou consecrate this night
      to sorrow,

" And give up every sense to solemn sadness ?

" Wo't thou, in watching, waste the tedious hours,

" Sit silently and careful by my side,

" List to the tolling clocks, the cricket's cry,

" And ev'ry melancholy midnight noise ?

" Say, wo't thou banish pleasure and delight ?

" Wo't thou forget that ever we have lov'd,

" And only now and then let fall a tear,

" To mourn for Edward's loss, and England's fate ?

    " *Guil.* Unweary'd still, I will attend thy woes,

" And be a very faithful partner to thee.

" Near thee I will complain in sighs as numberless

" As murmurs breathing in the leafy grove :

" My eyes shall mix their falling drops with thine,

" Constant, as never-ceasing waters roll,

" Shall cease to tune her lamentable song,

" Ere I give o'er to weep and mourn with thee.

   " *L. J. G.* Here then I take thee to my heart for
        ever.   [*Giving her hand.*

" The dear companion of my future days:

" Whatever Providence allots for each,

" Be that the common portion of us both ;

" Share all the griefs of thy unhappy Jane ;

" But if good Heav'n has any joys in store,

" Let them be all thy own.

   " *Guil.* Thou wondrous goodness !

" Heav'n gives too much at once in giving thee,

" And by the common course of things below,

" Where each delight is temper'd with affliction,

" Some evil terrible and unforeseen,

" Must sure ensue and poise the scale against

" This vast profusion of exceeding pleasure.

" But be it so, let it be death and ruin,

" On any terms I take thee.

   " *L. J. G.* Trust our fate

" To him whose gracious wisdom guides our ways,

" And makes what we think evil turn to good."

Permit me now to leave thee and retire ;

I'll summon all my reason and my duty,

To sooth this storm within, and frame my heart

To yield obedience to my noble parents.

   Guil. Good angels minister their comforts to thee.

And, oh ! " if, as my fond belief wou'd hope,

" If any word of mine be gracious to thee,"

I beg thee, I conjure thee, drive away

Those murd'rous thoughts of grief that kill thy quiet.
Restore thy gentle bosom's native peace,
Lift up the light of gladness in thy eyes,
And cheer thy heaviness with one dear smile.

    L. J. G. Yes, Guilford, I will study to forget
All that the royal Edward has been to me,
" How we have lov'd, even from our very cradles."
My private loss no longer will I mourn,
But ev'ry tender thought to thee shall turn :
With patience I'll submit to Heav'n's decree,
And what I lost in Edward find in thee.
But, oh! when I revolve what ruins wait
Our sinking altars and the falling state :
" When I consider what my native land
" Expected from her pious sov'reign's hand ;
" How form'd he was to save her from distress,
" A king to govern and a saint to bless :"
New sorrow to my lab'ring breast succeeds,
And my whole heart for wretched England bleeds.
                [*Exit Lady* Jane Gray.

    Guil. My heart sinks in me, at her soft complain-
        ing;
And ev'ry moving accent that she breathes
Resolves my courage, slackens my tough nerves,
And melts me down to infancy and tears.
" My fancy palls, and takes distaste at pleasure :
" My soul grows out of tune, it loaths the world,

" And dwells with hoary hermits; there forget my-
  'self,
" There fix my stupid eyes upon the earth,
" And muse away an age in deepest melancholy.''

Enter PEMBROKE.

Pem. Edward is dead; so said the great Northum-
  berland,
As now he shot along by me in haste.
He press'd my hand, and in a whisper begg'd me
To guard the secret carefully as life,
Till some few hours should pass; for much hung on
  it.
Much may indeed hang on it. See my Guilford!
My friend!   [*Speaking to him.*
 Guil. Ha! Pembroke!   [*Starting.*
 Pem. Wherefore dost thou start?
Why sits that wild disorder on thy visage,
Somewhat that looks like passions strange to thee,
The paleness of surprise and ghastly fear?
Since I have known thee first, and call'd thee friend,
I never saw thee so unlike thyself,
So chang'd upon a sudden.
 Guil. How! so changed!
 Pem. So to my eye thou seem'st.
 Guil. The king is dead.
 Pem. I learn'd it from thy father,
Just as I enter'd here. But say, cou'd that,
A fate which ev'ry moment we expected,
Distract thy thought, or shock thy temper thus?

Guil. Oh, Pembroke! 'tis in vain to hide from
      thee!
For thou hast look'd into my artless bosom,
And seen at once the hurry of my soul.
'Tis true thy coming struck me with surprise.
I have a thought———But wherefore said I one?
I have a thousand thoughts all up in arms,
" Like pop'lous towns disturb'd at dead of night,
" That, mix'd in darkness, bustle to and fro,
" As if their business were to make confusion."
    Pem. Then sure our better angels call'd me hither;
For this is friendship's hour, and friendship's office,
To come, when counsel and when help is wanting,
To share the pain of every gnawing care,
To speak of comfort in the time of trouble,
To reach a hand and save thee from adversity.
    Guil. And wo't thou be a friend to me indeed?
And, while I lay my bosom bare before thee,
" Wo't thou deal tenderly, and let thy hand
" Pass gently over ev'ry painful part?"
Wo't thou with patience hear, and judge with tem-
      per?
And if perchance thou meet with something harsh,
Somewhat to rouse thy rage, and grate thy soul,
Wo't thou be master of thyself and bear it?
    Pem. Away with all this needless preparation!
Thou know'st thou art so dear, so sacred to me,
That I can never think thee an offender.
If it were so, that I indeed must judge thee,

I should take part with thee against myself,
" And call thy fault a virtue."
   Guil. But suppose
The thought were somewhat that concern'd our love.
   Pem. No more ; thou know'st we spoke of that to-
      day,
And on what terms we left it. 'Tis a subject,
Of which, if possible, I would not think;
I beg that we may mention it no more.
   Guil. Can we not speak of it with temper?
   Pem. No.
Thou know'st I cannot. Therefore, pr'ythee spare it.
   Guil. Oh! cou'd the secret I wou'd tell thee sleep,
And the world never know it, my fond tongue
Shou'd cease from speaking, ere I would unfold it,
Or vex thy peace with an officious tale.
But since, howe'er ungrateful to thy ear,
It must be told thee once, hear it from me.
   Pem. Speak then, and ease the doubts that shock
      my soul.
   Guil. Suppose thy Guilford's better stars prevail,
And crown his love————
   Pem. Say not, suppose : 'tis done.
Seek not for vain excuse, or soft'ning words;
Thou hast prevaricated with thy friend,
By under-hand contrivances undone me :
And while my open nature trusted in thee,
Thou hast stepp'd in between me and my hopes,
And ravish'd from me all my soul held dear.
Thou hast betray'd me————

Guil. How! betray'd thee, Pembroke?

Pem. Yes, falsely, like a traitor.

Guil. Have a care.

Pem. But think not I will bear the foul play from
    thee;
There was but this which I could ne'er forgive.
My soul is up in arms, my injur'd honour,
Impatient of the wrong, calls for revenge;
And tho' I love thee——fondly——,

Guil. Hear me yet,
And Pembroke shall acquit me to himself.
Hear, while I tell how fortune dealt between us,
And gave the yielding beauty to my arms——

Pem. What, hear it! Stand and listen to thy tri-
    umph!
Thou think'st me tame indeed. No, hold, I charge
    thee,
Lest I forget that ever we were friends,
Lest, in the rage of disappointed love,
I rush at once and tear thee for thy falsehood.

Guil. Thou warn'st me well; and I were rash, as
    thou art,
To trust the secret sum of all my happiness
With one not master of himself. Farewell. [*Going.*

Pem. Ha! art thou going? Think not thus to part,
Nor leave me on the rack of this incertainty.

Guil. What wouldst thou further?

Pem. Tell it to me all;
Say thou art marry'd, say thou hast possess'd her,
And rioted in vast excess of bliss;

That I may curse myself, and thee, and her.
Come, tell me how thou didst supplant thy friend?
How didst thou look with that betraying face,
And smiling plot my ruin?

   Guil. Give me way.
When thou art better temper'd, I may tell thee,
And vindicate at full my love and friendship.

   Pem. And dost thou hope to shun me then, thou
      traitor;
No, I will have it now, this moment from thee,
" Or drag the secret out from thy false heart.

   " *Guil.* Away, thou madman! I would talk to
      winds,
" And reason with the rude tempestous surge,
" Sooner than hold discourse with rage like thine.

   " *Pem.* Tell it, or by my injur'd love I swear,"
                      [*Laying his Hand upon his Sword.*
I'll stab the lurking treason in thy heart.

   Guil. Ha! stay thee there; nor let thy frantic hand
                              [*Stopping him.*
Unsheath thy weapon. If the sword be drawn,
If once we meet on terms like those, farewell
To ev'ry thought of friendship; one must fall.

   Pem. Curse on thy friendship, I would break the
      band.

   Guil. That as you please—Beside, this place is sa-
      cred,
And wo'not be profan'd with brawls and outrage.
You know I dare be found on any summons.

   Pem. 'Tis well. My vengeance shall not loiter long.

Henceforward let the thoughts of our past lives
Be turn'd to deadly and remorseless hate.
Here I give up the empty name of friend,
Renounce all gentleness, all commerce with thee,
To death defy thee as my mortal foe;
And when we meet again, may swift destruction
Rid me of thee, or rid me of myself. [*Exit* Pembroke.

   Guil. The fate I ever fear'd is fall'n upon me;
And long ago my boding heart divin'd
A breach like this from his ungovern'd rage.
Oh, Pembroke! thou hast done me much injustice,
For I have borne thee true unfeign'd affection;
'Tis past, and thou art lost to me for ever.
" Love is, or ought to be, our greatest bliss;
" Since ev'ry other joy, how dear soever,
" Gives way to that, and we leave all for love.
" At the imperious tyrant's lordly call,
" In spite of reason or restraint we come,
" Leave kindred, parents, and our native home.
" The trembling maid, with all her fears he charms,
" And pulls her from her weeping mother's arms:
" He laughs at all her leagues, and in proud scorn
" Commands the bands of friendship to be torn;
" Disdains a partner should partake his throne,
" But reigns unbounded, lawless, and alone." [*Exit.*

The Tower.   *Enter* PEMBROKE *and* GARDINER.

Gardiner.

NAY, by the rood, my lord, you were to blame
To let a hair-brain'd passion be your guide,
And hurry you into such mad extremes.
Marry, you might have made much worthy profit,
By patient hearing; the unthinking lord
Had brought forth ev'ry secret of his soul;
Then when you were the master of his bosom,
That was the time to use him with contempt,
And turn his friendship back upon his hands.

Pem. Thou talk'st as if a madman cou'd be wise.
Oh, Winchester! thy hoary frozen age
Can never guess my pain; can never know
The burning transports of untam'd desire.
" I tell thee, reverend lord, to that one bliss,
" To the enjoyment of that lovely maid,
" As to their centre, I had drawn each hope,
" And ev'ry wish my furious soul cou'd form;
" Still with regard to that my brain forethought,
" And fashion'd ev'ry action of my life.
" Then, to be robb'd at once, and unsuspecting,
" Be dash'd in all the height of expectation!
" It was not to be borne "
    Gar. Have you not heard of what has happen'd
        since ?

Pem. I have not had a minute's peace of mind,
A moment's pause, to rest from rage, or think.
  Gar. Learn it from me then : But ere I speak,
I warn you to be master of yourself.
Though, as you know, they have confin'd me long,
Gra'mercy to their goodness, pris'ner here ;
Yet as I am allow'd to walk at large
Within the Tower, and hold free speech with any,
I have not dreamt away my thoughtless hours,
" Without good heed to these our righteous rulers."
To prove this true, this morn a trusty spy
Has brought me word, that yester ev'ning late,
In spite of all the grief for Edward's death,
Your friends were marry'd.
  Pem. Marry'd ! who ?————Damnation !
  Gar. Lord Guilford Dudley, and the lady Jane.
  Pem. Curse on my stars !
  Gar. Nay, in the name of Grace,
Restrain this sinful passion ; all's not lost
In this one single woman.
  Pem. I have lost
More than the female world can give me back.
I had beheld even her whole sex, unmov'd,
Look'd o'er 'em like a bed of gaudy flowers,
That lift their painted heads, and live a day,
Then shed their trifling glories unregarded :
My heart disdain'd their beauties, till she came,
With ev'ry grace that Nature's hand could give,
And with a mind so great, it spoke its essence
Immortal and divine.

Gar. She was a wonder;
Detraction must allow that.

   Pem. " The virtuous came,
" Sorted in gentle fellowship, to crown her,
" As if they meant to mend each other's work.
" Candour with goodness, fortitude with sweetness,
" Strict piety, and love of truth, with learning,
" More than the schools of Athens ever knew,
" Or her own Plato taught. A wonder, Winches-
     ter!"
Thou know'st not what she was, nor can I speak her,
More than to say, she was that only blessing
My soul was set upon, and I have lost her.

   Gar. Your state is not so bad as you wou'd make it;
Nor need you thus abandon ev'ry hope.

   Pem. Ha! Wo't thou save me, snatch me from de-
     spair,
And bid me live again.

   Gar. She may be yours.
Suppose her husband die.

   Pem. O vain, vain hope!

   Gar. Marry, I do not hold that hope so vain.
These gospellers have had their golden days,
And lorded it at will; with proud despite
Have trodden down our holy Roman faith,
Ransack'd our shrines, and driv'n her saints to exile.
But if my divination fail me not,
Their haughty hearts shall be abas'd e'er long,
And feel the vengeance of our Mary's reign.

       E

 Pem. And wou'dst thou have my fierce impatience
  stay?
Bid me lie bound upon a rack, and wait
For distant joys, whole ages yet behind?
Can love attend on politician's schemes,
Expect the slow events of cautious counsels,
Cold unresolving heads, and creeping time?
 Gar. To-day, or I am ill-inform'd, Northumber-
  land,
With easy Suffolk, Guilford, and the rest,
Meet here in council on some deep design,
Some traiterous contrivance, to protect
Their upstart faith from near approaching ruin.
But there are punishments——halters and axes
For traitors, and consuming flames for hereticks;
The happy bridegroom may be yet cut short,
Ev'n in his highest hope——But go not you;
Howe'er the fawning sire, old Dudley, court you;
No, by the holy rood, I charge you, mix not
With their pernicious counsels.——Mischief waits
  'em,
Sure, certain, unavoidable destruction
 Pem. Ha! join with them! the cursed Dudley's race!
Who, while they held me in their arms, betray'd me;
Scorn'd me for not suspecting they were villains,
And made a mock'ry of my easy friendship.
No, when I do, dishonour be my portion,
" And swift perdition catch me;—join with them!"
 Gar. I wou'd not have you—Hie you to the city,
And join with those that love our ancient faith.

Gather your friends about you, and be ready
T' assert our zealous Mary's royal title,
And doubt not but her grateful hand shall give you
To see your soul's desire upon your enemies.
The church shall pour her ample treasures' forth too,
And pay you with ten thousand years of pardon.

    Pem. No ; keep your blessings back, and give me
          vengeance :
Give me to tell that soft deceiver, Guilford,
Thus, traitor, hast thou done, thus hast thou wrong'd
          me,
And thus thy treason finds a just reward.—

    Gar. But soft! no more! the lords o'the council
          come,
Ha! by the mass, the bride and bridegroom too!
Retire with me, my lord ; we must not meet 'em.

    Pem. 'Tis they themselves, the cursed happy pair!
Haste, Winchester, haste! let us fly for ever,
And drive her from my very thoughts, if possible.
" Oh! love, what have I lost! Oh! reverend lord!
" Pity this fond, this foolish weakness in me!
" Methinks, I go like our first wretched father,
" When from his blissful garden he was driven :
" Like me he went despairing, and like me,
" Thus at the gate stopt short for one last view !
" Then with the cheerless partner of his woe,
" He turn'd him to the world that lay below :

" He try'd to give the sad remembrance o'er;
" The sad remembrance still return'd again,
" And his lost paradise renew'd his pain."

[*Exeunt* Pembroke *and* Gardiner.

Enter Lord GUILFORD *and Lady* JANE.

Guil. What shall I say to thee! What power divine
Will teach my tongue to tell thee what I feel?
To pour the transports of my bosom forth,
And make thee partner of the joy dwells there?
" For thou art comfortless, full of affliction, ·
" Heavy of heart as the forsaken widow,
" And desolate as orphans." Oh! my fair one!
Thy Edward shines amongst the brightest stars,
And yet thy sorrows seek him in the grave.

L. *J. G.* Alas, my dearest lord! a thousand griefs
Beset my anxious heart: and yet, as if
The burthen were too little, I have added
The weight of all thy cares; and, like the miser,
Increase of wealth has made me but more wretched.
" The morning light seems not to rise as usual,
" It draws not to me, like my virgin days,
" But brings new thoughts and other fears upon me;"
I tremble, and my anxious heart is pain'd,
Lest aught but good shou'd happen to my Guilford.

Guil. Nothing but good can happen to thy Guilford,
While thou art by his side, his better angel,
His blessing and his guard.

L. *J. G.* Why came we hither?
" Why was I drawn to this unlucky place,

" This Tower, so often stain'd with royal blood?
" Here the fourth Edward's helpless sons were mur-
      der'd,
" And pious Henry fell by ruthless Gloster:
" Is this the place allotted for rejoicing?
" The bower adorn'd to keep our nuptial feast in?
" Methinks suspicion and distrust dwell here,
" Staring with meagre forms thro' grated windows;
" Death lurks within, and unrelenting punishment:
" Without, grim danger, fear, and fiercest power
" Sit on the rude old tow'rs, and Gothic battlements;
" While horror overlooks the dreadful wall,
" And frowns on all around.
    Guil. " In safety here,
" The lords o' th' council have this morn decreed
" To meet, and with united care support
" The feeble tottering state." To thee, my princess,
Whose royal veins are rich in Henry's blood,
With one consent the noblest heads are bow'd:
From thee they ask a sanction to their counsels,
And from thy healing hand expect a cure,
For England's loss in Edward.
    L. *J. G.* How! from me!
Alas! my lord—But sure thou mean'st to mock me?
    Guil. No; by the love my faithful heart is full of!
But see, thy mother, gracious Suffolk, comes
To intercept my story: she shall tell thee;
For in her look I read the lab'ring thought,
What vast event thy fate is now disclosing.

Enter the Duchess of SUFFOLK.

D. *Suff.* No more complain, indulge thy tears no
    more,
Thy pious grief has giv'n the grave its due :
" Let thy heart kindle with the highest hopes ;
" Expand thy bosom, let thy soul enlarg'd,"
Make room to entertain the coming glory !
For majesty and purple greatness court thee ;
Homage and low subjection wait : a crown,
That makes the princes of the earth like gods ;"
A crown, my daughter, England's crown attends,
To bind thy brows with its imperial wreath.

    L. *J. G.* Amazement chills my veins ! What says
    my mother ?

    D. *Suff.* 'Tis Heav'n's decree ; for our expiring
    Edward,
When now, just struggling to his native skies,
Ev'n on the verge of heav'n, in sight of angels,
That hover'd round to waft him to the stars,
Ev'n then declar'd my Jane for his successor.

    L. *J. G.* Cou'd Edward do this ? cou'd the dying
    saint
Bequeath his crown to me ? Oh, fatal bounty !
To me ! But 'tis impossible ! " We dream.
" A thousand and a thousand bars oppose me,
" Rise in my way, and intercept my passage.
" Ev'n you, my gracious mother, what must you be,
" Ere I can be a queen ?

    D. *Suff.* " That, and that only,

" Thy mother ; fonder of that tender name,
" Than all the proud additions pow'r can give.
" Yes, I will give up all my share of greatness,
" And live in low obscurity for ever,
" To see thee rais'd, thou darling of my heart,
" And fix'd upon a throne." But see : thy father,
Northumberland, with all the council, come
To pay their vow'd allegiance at thy feet,
To kneel, and call thee queen.

    L. J. G. Support me, Guilford ;
Give me thy aid ; stay thou my fainting soul,
And help me to repress this growing danger.

Enter SUFFOLK, NORTHUMBERLAND, *Lords, and
others of the Privy Council.*

    North. Hail, sacred princess ! sprung from ancient
       kings,
Our England's dearest hope, undoubted offspring
Of York and Lancaster's united line ;
" By whose bright zeal, by whose victorious faith,
" Guarded and fenc'd around our pure religion.
" That lamp of truth which shines upon our altars,
" Shall lift its golden head, and flourish long ;
" Beneath whose awful rule, and righteous sceptre,
" The plenteous years shall roll in long succession ;
" Law shall prevail, and ancient right take place,
" Fair liberty shall lift her cheerful head,
" Fearless of tyranny and proud oppression ;
" No sad complaining in our streets shall cry,
" But justice shall be exercised in mercy."

Hail, royal Jane! behold, we bend our knees,

[*They kneel.*

The pledge of homage, and thy land's obedience;
With humblest duty thus we kneel, and own thee
Our liege, our sovereign lady, and our queen.

   L. J. G. Oh, rise!
My father, rise!   [*To* Suff.
And you, my father, too!   [*To* North.
Rise all, nor cover me with this confusion. [*They rise.*
What means this mock, this masquing shew of great-
       ness?
Why do you hang these pageant glories on me,
And dress me up in honours not my own?

   North. The daughters of our late great master
       Henry,
Stand both by law excluded from succession.
To make all firm,
And fix a power unquestion'd in your hand,
Edward, by will, bequeath'd his crown to you
And the concurring lords in council met,
Have ratify'd the gift.

   L. J. G. Are crowns and empire,
" The government and safety of mankind,"
Trifles of such light moment, to be left
Like some rich toy, " a ring, or fancy'd gem,"
The pledge of parting friends? Can kings do thus,
And give away a people for a legacy?

   North. Forgive me, princely lady, if my wonder
Seizes each sense, each faculty of mind,
To see the utmost wish the great can form,

A crown, thus coldly met: A crown, which slighted,
And left in scorn by you, shall soon be sought,
And find a joyful wearer; one, perhaps,
Of blood, unkindred to your royal house,
And fix its glories in another line.

    L. *J. G.* Where art thou now, thou partner of my
        cares?   [*Turning to* Guilford.
" Come to my aid, and help to bear this burthen:
" Oh! save me from this sorrow, this misfortune,
" Which in the shape of gorgeous greatness comes
" To crown, and make a wretch of me for ever.

    Guil. " Thou weep'st, my queen, and hang'st thy
        drooping head,
" Like nodding poppies, heavy with the rain,
" That bow their weary necks and bend to earth."
See, by thy side, thy faithful Guilford stands,
Prepar'd to keep distress and danger from thee,
To wear thy sacred cause upon his sword,
And war against the world in thy defence.

    North. Oh! " stay this inauspicious stream of tears,
" And cheer your people with one gracious smile.
" Nor comes your fate in such a dreadful form
" To bid you shun it. Turn those sacred eyes
" On the bright prospect empire spreads before you."
Methinks I see you seated on the throne;
" Beneath your feet, the kingdom's great degrees
" In bright confusion shine, mitres and coronets,
" The various ermine, and the glowing purple;"
Assembled senates wait with awful dread,
To 'firm your high commands, and make 'em fate.

L. J. G. You turn to view the painted side of
    royalty,
And cover all the cares that lurk beneath.
Is it, to be a queen, to sit aloft,
In solemn, dull, uncomfortable state,
The flatter'd idol of a servile court?
Is it to draw a pompous train along,
A pageant, for the wondring crowd to gaze at?
" Is it, in wantonness of pow'r to reign,
" And make the world subservient to my pleasure.
" Is it not rather, to be greatly wretched,
" To watch, to toil, to take a sacred charge,
" To bend each day before high Heav'n, and own,
" This people hast thou trusted to my hand,
" And at my hand, I know, thou shalt require 'em?"
Alas, Northumberland!—My father!—Is it not
To live a life of care, and when I die,
Have more to answer for before my judge,
Than any of my subjects?
" *D. Suff.* Ev'ry state,
" Allotted to the race of man below,
" Is, in proportion, doom'd to taste some sorrow,
" Nor is the golden wreath on a king's brow
" Exempt from care; and yet, who would not bear it?
" Think on the monarchs of our royal race,
" They liv'd not for themselves . how many blessings,
" How many lifted hands shall pay thy toil,
" If for thy people's good thou happ'ly borrow
" Some portion from the hours of rest, and wake
" To give the world repose!"

d only thou canst save us.   Persecution,
at fiend of Rome and hell, prepares her tortu
where she comes in Mary's priestly train !
l wo't thou doubt ? till thou behold her stalk.
l with the blood of martyrs, and wide wastin
r England's bosom ? " All the mourning yea
Our towns shall glow with unextinguish'd fires
Our youth on racks shall stretch their crack
      bones ;
Our babes shall sprawl on consecrated spears ;
Matrons and husbands, with their new-born infa
Shall burn promiscuous ; a continu'd peal
Of lamentations, groans, and shrieks, shall sou
Through all our purple ways."
ail. Amidst that ruin,
ink thou behold'st thy Guilford's head laid lov
ody and pale————
.. *J. G.* Oh ! spare the dreadful image !
ail. Oh ! wou'd the misery be bounded there,
life were little ; but the rage of Rome
nands whole hecatombs, a land of victims.
With superstition comes that other fiend,
That bane of peace, of arts and virtue, tyran
That foe of justice, scorner of all law ;
That beast, which thinks mankind were born
    one,

To bend our necks beneath a brazen yoke,
And rule o'er wretches with an iron sceptre.

 L. *J. G.* Avert that. judgment, Heav'n!
Whate'er thy providence allots for me,
In mercy spare my country.

 Guil. Oh, my queen!
Does not thy great, thy generous heart relent,
To think this land, for liberty so fam'd,
Shall have her tow'ry front at once laid low,
And robb'd of all its glory? " Oh! my country!
" Oh! fairest Albion, empress of the deep,
" How have thy noblest sons, with stubborn valour,
" Stood to the last, dy'd many a field in blood,
" In dear defence of birth-right and their laws!
" And shall those hands which fought the cause of
   freedom,
" Be manacled in base unworthy bonds:
" Be tamely yielded up, the spoil, the slaves
" Of hair-brain'd zeal, and cruel coward priests?"

 L: *J. G.* Yes, my lov'd lord, my soul is mov'd like
   thine,
At ev'ry danger which invades our England;
My cold heart kindles at the great occasion
And could be more than man in her defence.
But where is my commission to redress?
Or whence my pow'r to save? Can Edward's will,
Or twenty met in council, make a queen?
Can you, my lords, give me the power to canvass
A doubtful title with king Henry's daughters?
Where are the rev'rend sages of the law,

To guide me with their wisdoms, and point out
The paths which right and justice bid me tread?
 North. The judges all attend, and will at leisure
Resolve you ev'ry scruple.
 L. J. G. They expound;
But where are those, my lord, that make the law?
Where are the ancient honours of the realm,
The nobles, with the mitred fathers join'd?
The wealthy commons solemnly assembled?
Where is that voice of a consenting people,
To pledge the universal faith with mine,
And call me justly queen?
 " *North.* Nor shall that long
" Be wanting to your wish. The lords and commons
" Shall, at your royal bidding, soon assemble,
" And with united homage own your title.
" Delay not then to meet the general wish,
" But be our queen, be England's better angel.
" Nor let mistaken piety betray you
" To join with cruel Mary in our ruin:
" Her bloody faith commands her to destroy,
" And yours forbids to save."
 Guil. Our foes, already
High in their hopes, devote us all to death:
" The dronish monks, the scorn and shame of man-
   hood,
" Rouse and prepare once more to take possession,
" To nestle in their ancient hives again:
" Again they furbish up their holy trumpery,

" Whole loads of lumber and religious rubbish,
" In high procession mean to bring them back,
" And place the puppets in their shrines again :
" While those of keener malice, savage Bonner,
" And deep-designing Gard'ner, dream of vengeance;
" Devour the blood of innocents, in hope ;
" Like vultures, snuff the slaughter in the wind,
" And speed their flight to havock and the prey."
Haste then, and save us, while 'tis given to save
Your country, your religion.

    North. Save your friends !

    Suff. Your father !

    D. *Suff.* Mother !

    Guil. Husband !

    L. J. G. Take me, crown me,
Invest me with this royal wretchedness ;
Let me not know one happy minute more ;
Let all my sleepless nights be spent in care,
My days be fix'd with tumults and alarms ;
If only I can save you, if my fate
Has mark'd me out to be the public victim,
I take the lot with joy.   Yes, I will die
For that eternal truth my faith is fix'd on,
And that dear native land which gave me birth.

    Guil. Wake ev'ry tuneful instrument to tell it,
And let the trumpet's sprightly note proclaim
My Jane is England's queen!   " Let the loud cannon
" In peals of thunder speak it to Augusta ;
" Imperial Thames, catch thou the sacred sound,
" And roll it to the subject ocean down :

" Tell the old deep, and all thy brother floods,
" My Jane is empress of the wat'ry world!
" Now with glad fires our bloodless streets shall shine:
" With cries of joy our cheerful ways shall ring;"
Thy name shall echo through the rescu'd isle,
And reach applauding heaven!

　　L. J. G. Oh, Guilford! what do we give up for
　　　　glory!
For glory! that's a toy I would not purchase,
An idle, empty bubble.　But for England!
What must we lose for that? Since then my fate
Has forc'd this hard exchange upon my will,
Let gracious Heav'n allow me one request:
For that blest peace in which I once did dwell,
" For books, retirement, and my studious cell,
" For all those joys my happier days did prove,
" For Plato, and his academic grove;"
All that I ask, is, tho' my fortune frown,
And bury me beneath this fatal crown;
Let that one good be added to my doom,
To save this land from tyranny and Rome.　　[*Exeunt.*

ACT IV. SCENE. I.

Continues. Enter PEMBROKE *and* GARDINER.

Gardiner.

IN an unlucky and accursed hour
Set forth that traitor duke, that proud Northumber-
　　land,

" To draw his sword upon the side of heresy,
" And war against our Mary's holy right:
" Ill fortune fly before, and pave his way
" With disappointments, mischief, and defeat;"
Do thou, O holy Becket, the protector,
The champion, and the martyr of our church,
Appear, and once more own the cause of Rome:
Beat down his lance, break thou his sword in battle,
And cover foul rebellion with confusion.

    Pem. I saw him marching at his army's head;
I mark'd him issuing thro' the city-gate
In harness all appointed, as he pass'd;
And (for he wore his beaver up) cou'd read
Upon his visage, horror and dismay.
No voice of cheerful salutation cheer'd him,
None wish'd his arms might thrive, or bade God speed
      him;
But through a staring ghastly-looking crowd,
Unhail'd, unbless'd, with heavy heart he went:
As if his traitor father's haggard ghost,
And Somerset, fresh bleeding from the axe,
On either hand had usher'd him to ruin.

    Gar. Nor shall the holy vengeance loiter long.
At Farmingham, in Suffolk, lies the queen,
Mary, our pious mistress: where each day
The nobles of the land, and swarming populace,
Gather, and list beneath her royal ensigns.
The fleet, commanded by Sir Thomas Jerningham,
Set out in warlike manner to oppose her,
With one consent have join'd to own her cause:

The valiant Sussex, and Sir Edward Hastings,
With many more of note, are up in arms,
And all declare for her.

    " *Pem.* The citizens,
" Who held the noble Somerset right dear,
" Hate this aspiring Dudley and his race,
" And wou'd upon the instant join t'oppose him;
" Could we but draw some of the lords o'th' council
" T'appear among 'em, own the same design,
" And bring the rev'rend sanction of authority
" To lead 'em into action. For that purpose,
" To thee, as to an oracle, I come,
" To learn what fit expedient may be found,
" To win the wary council to our side.
" Say thou, whose head is grown thus silver-white
" In arts of government, and turns of state,
" How we may blast our enemies with ruin,
" And sink the curs'd Northumberland to hell?
    " *Gar.* In happy time be your whole wish accom-
       plish'd
" Since the proud Duke set out, I have had confer
       ence,
" As fit occasion serv'd, with divers of 'em,
" The Earl of Arundel, Mason, and Cheyney,
" And find 'em all dispos'd as we cou'd ask.
" By holy Mary, if I count aright,
" To-day the better part shall leave this place,
" And meet at Baynard's castle in the city;
" There own our sovereign's title, and defy
" Jane and her gospel-crew. But hie you hence!

" This place is still within our foes command,
" Their puppet-queen reigns here."

Enter an Officer with a Guard.

Off. Seize on 'em both.
[*Guards seize* Pembroke *and* Gardiner.
My lord, you are a pris'ner to the state.

Pem. Ha! by whose order?

Off. By the queen's command,
Sign'd and deliver'd by Lord Guilford Dudley.

Pem. Curse on his traitor's heart!

Gard. Rest you contented:
You have loiter'd here too long; but use your pati-
      ence,
These bonds shall not be lasting.

Off. As for you, Sir,   [*To* Gardiner.
'Tis the queen's pleasure you be close confin'd:
You've us'd that fair permission was allow'd you
To walk at large within the Tower, unworthily.
You're noted for an over-busy meddler,
A secret practiser against the state;
For which, henceforth, your limits shall be straiter.
Hence, to your chamber!

Gar. Farewell, gentle Pembroke;
I trust that we shall meet on blither terms:
Till then, amongst my beads I will remember you,
And give you to the keeping of the saints.
[*Exeunt Part of the Guards with* Gardiner.

Pem. Now, whither must I go?

Off. This way, my lord.   [*Going off.*

Enter GUILFORD.

Guil. Hold, Captain! ere you go, I have a word
    or two
For this your noble pris'ner.
  Off. At your pleasure:
I know my duty, and attend your lordship.
      [*The Officer and Guards retire to the farthest*
          Part of the Stage.
  Guil. Is all the gentleness that was betwixt us
So lost, so swept away from thy remembrance,
Thou canst not look upon me?
  Pem. Ha! not look!
What terrors are there in the Dudley's race,
That Pembroke dares not look upon and scorn?
And yet, 'tis true, I wou'd not look upon thee:
Our eyes avoid to look on what we hate,
As well as what we fear.
  Guil. You hate me, then!
  Pem. I do; and wish perdition may o'ertake
Thy father, thy false self, and thy whole name.
  Guil. And yet, as sure as rage disturbs thy reason,
And masters all the noble nature in thee,
As sure as thou hast wrong'd me, I am come
In tenderness of friendship to preserve thee;
To plant ev'n all the pow'r I have before thee,
And fence thee from destruction with my life.
  Pem. Friendship from thee! But my just soul dis-
    dains thee.
Hence! take the prostituted bauble back,

" Hang it to grace some slavering idiot's neck,
" For none but fools will praise the tinsel toy."
But thou art come, perhaps, to vaunt thy greatness,
And set thy purple pomp to view before me;
To let me know that Guilford is a king,
That he can speak the word, and give me freedom.
Oh, short-liv'd pageant! had'st thou all the pow'r
Which thy vain soul wou'd grasp at, I wou'd die,
Rot in a dungeon, ere receive a grace,
The least, the meanest courtesy, from thee.

Guil. Oh, Pembroke! but I have not time to talk,
For danger presses, danger unforeseen,
And secret as the shaft that flies by night,
Is aiming at thy life.   Captain, a word!

                              [*To the Officer.*
I take your pris'ner to my proper charge;
Draw off your guard, and leave his sword with me.
    '[*The Officer delivers the Sword to Lord* Guilford, *and*
        goes out with his Guard.
        [*Lord* Guilford *offering the Sword to* Pembroke.
Receive this gift, ev'n from a rival's hand;
And if thy rage will suffer thee to hear
The counsel of a man once call'd thy friend,
Fly from this fatal place, and seek thy safety.

Pem. How now! what shew! what mockery is this?
" Is it in sport you use me thus? What means
" This swift fantastic changing of the scene?"

Guil. Oh, take thy sword; and let thy valiant hand
Be ready arm'd to guard thy noble life:
The time, the danger, and the wild impatience,

Forbid me all to enter into speech with thee,
Or I cou'd tell thee———

   Pem. No, it needs not, traitor!
For all thy poor, thy little arts are known.
Thou fear'st my vengeance, and art come to fawn,
To make a merit of that proffer'd freedom,
Which, in despite of thee, a day shall give me.
Nor can my fate depend on thee, false Guilford;
For know, to thy confusion, ere the sun
Twice gild the east, our royal Mary comes
To end thy pageant reign, and set me free.

   Guil. Ungrateful and unjust! Hast thou then
         known me
So little, to accuse my heart of fear?
Hast thou forgotten Musselborough's field?
Did I then fear, when by thy side I fought,
And dy'd my maiden sword in Scottish blood?
But this is madness all.

   Pem. Give me my sword.   [*Taking his sword.*
Perhaps indeed, I wrong thee. Thou hast thought;
And, conscious of the injury thou hast done me,
Art come to proffer me a soldier's justice,
And meet my arm in single opposition.
Lead then, and let me follow to the field.

   Guil. Yes, Pembroke, thou shalt satisfy thy ven-
         geance,
And write thy bloody purpose on my bosom.
But let death wait to-day. By our past friendship,
In honour's name, by ev'ry sacred tie,
I beg thee ask no more, but haste from hence.

Pem. What mystic meaning lurks beneath thy
    words?
What fear is this, which thou wou'dst awe my soul
    with?
Is there a danger Pembroke dares not meet?
    Guil. Oh, spare my tongue a tale of guilt and horror;
Trust me this once: believe me when I tell thee,
Thy safety and thy life is all I seek.
Away.
    Pem. " By Heav'n! I wo'not stir a step."
Curse on this shuffling, dark, ambiguous phrase!
If thou wou'dst have me think thou mean'st me fairly,
Speak with that plainness honesty delights in,
And let thy double tongue for once be true.
    Guil. Forgive me, filial piety and nature,
If thus compell'd, I break your sacred laws,
Reveal my father's crime, and blot with infamy
The hoary head of him who gave me being,
To save the man whom my soul loves, from death.
                      [*Giving a paper.*
Read there the fatal purpose of thy foe,
A thought which wounds my soul with shame and
    horror!
Somewhat that darkness shou'd have hid for ever,
But that thy life—Say, hast thou seen that character?
    Pem. I know it well; the hand of proud Northum-
    berland,
Directed to his minions, Gates and Palmer.
What's this?   '   [*Reads.*
    " Remember, with your closest care, to observe

those whom I nam'd to you at parting; especially
keep your eye upon the earl of Pembroke; as his
power and interest are most considerable, so his op_
position will be most fatal to us. Remember the re_
solution was taken, if you should find him inclined to
our enemies. The forms of justice are tedious, and
delays are dangerous. If he falters, lose not the
sight of him till your daggers have reached his heart."
My heart! Oh, murd'rous villain!

    Guil. Since he parted,
Thy ways have all been watch'd, thy steps been mark'd;
Thy secret treaties with the malecontents   '
That harbour in the city, thy conferring
With Gard'ner here in the Tower; all is known:
And, in pursuance of that bloody mandate,
A set of chosen ruffians wait to end thee:
There was but one way left me to preserve thee;
I took it; and this morning sent my warrant
To seize upon thy person——But begone!

    Pem. 'Tis so—'tis truth——I see his honest heart—

    Guil. I have a friend of well-try'd faith and courage,
Who, with a fit disguise, and arms conceal'd,
Attends without to guide thee hence with safety.

    Pem. What is Northumberland? And what art
       thou?

    Guil. Waste not the time. Away!

    Pem. Here let me fix,
And gaze with everlasting wonder on thee.
What is there good or excellent in man,
That is not found in thee? Thy virtues flash,

They break at once on my astonish'd soul;
" As if the curtains of the dark were drawn,
" To let in day at midnight.
^ " *Guil.* Think me true;
" And tho' ill fortune cross'd upon our friendship—
 " *Pem.* Curse on our fortune!—Think I know thee
  honest."

 Guil. For ever I cou'd hear thee—but thy life,
Oh, Pembroke! linger not————

 Pem. And can I leave thee,
Ere I have clasp'd thee in my eager arms,
And giv'n thee back my sad repenting heart?
Believe me, Guilford, like the patriarch's dove,
        [*Embracing.*
It wander'd forth, but found no resting place,
'Till it came home again to lodge with thee.

 Guil. What is there that my soul can more desire,
Than these dear marks of thy returning friendship?
The danger comes————If you stay longer here,
You die, my Pembroke.

 Pem. Let me stay and die;
For if I go, I go to work thy ruin.
Thou know'st not what a foe thou send'st me forth,
That I have sworn destruction to the queen,
And pledg'd my faith to Mary and her cause ·
My honour is at stake.

 Guil. I know 'tis given.
But go—the stronger thy engagements there,
The more's thy danger here. " There is a Power
" Who sits above the stars; in him I trust:

" All that I have, his bounteous hand bestow'd ;

" And he that gave it, can preserve it to me.

" If his o'er-ruling will ordains my ruin,

" What is there more, but to fall down before him,

" And humbly yield obedience !"——Fly ! begone !

　Pem. Yes, I will go—for, see ! Behold who comes !

Oh, Guilford ! hide me, shield me from her sight ;

Every mad passion kindles up again,

Love, rage, despair—and yet I will be master—

I will remember thee——Oh, my torn heart !

I have a thousand thousand things to say,

But cannot, dare not stay to look on her.

" Thus gloomy ghosts, where'er the breaking morn

" Gives notice of the cheerful sun's return,

" Fade at the light, with horror stand oppress'd,

" And shrink before the purple dawning east ;

" Swift with the fleeting shades they wing their way,

" And dread the brightness of the rising day."

　　　　　　　[*Exeunt* Guilford *and* Pembroke.

　　　Enter Lady JANE, *reading.*

　L. *J. Gray.* " 'Tis false ! The thinking soul is
　　　somewhat more

" Than symmetry of atoms well dispos'd,

" The harmony of matter.　Farewell else

" The hope of all hereafter, that new life,

" That separate intellect, which must survive,

" When this fine frame is moulder'd into dust."

Enter GUILFORD.

Guil. What read'st thou there, my queen?

L. *J. Gray.* 'Tis Plato's Phædon;
Where dying Socrates takes leave of life,
With such an easy, careless, calm indifference,
As if the trifle were of no account,
Mean in itself, and only to be worn
In honour of the giver.

Guil. Shall thy soul
Still scorn the world, still fly the joys that court
" Thy blooming beauty, and thy tender youth?"
Still shall she soar on contemplation's wing,
And mix with nothing meaner than the stars;
" As heaven and immortality alone
" Were objects worthy to employ her faculties?
    " L. *J. Gray.* Bate but thy truth, what is there here
    .   below
" Deserves the least regard? Is it not time
" To bid our souls look out, explore hereafter,
" And seek some better sure abiding place;
" When all around our gathering foes come on,
" To drive, to sweep us from this world at once?
    " *Guil.* Does any danger new——"

L. *J. Gray.* The faithless counsellors
Are fled from hence to join the princess Mary.
The servile herd of courtiers, who so late
In low obedience bent the knee before me;
They, who with zealous tongues, and hands uplifted,
Besought me to defend their laws and faith;

Vent their lewd execrations on·my name,
Proclaim me trait'ress now, and to the scaffold
Doom my devoted head.

   Guil. The changeling villains!
That pray for slavery, fight for their bonds,
And shun the blessing, liberty, like ruin.
" What art thou, human nature, to do thus?
" Does fear or folly make thee, like the Indian,
" Fall down before this dreadful devil, tyranny,
" And worship the destroyer?"
But wherefore do I loiter tamely here?
Give me my arms: I will preserve my country,
Ev'n in her own despite. Some friends I have,
Who will or die or conquer in thy cause,
Thine and religion's, thine and England's cause.

   L. J. Gray. Art thou not all my treasure, all my
        guard?
And wo't thou take from me the only joy,
The last defence is left me here below?
Think not thy arm can stem the driving torrent,
Or save a people, who with blinded rage
Urge their own fate, and strive to be undone.
Northumberland, thy father, is in arms;
And if it be in valour to defend us,
His sword, that long has known the way to conquest,
Shall be our surest safety.

         Enter the Duke of SUFFOLK.

   Suff. Oh, my children!
   L. J. Gray. Alas! what means my father?

Suff. Oh, my son,
Thy father, great Northumberland, on whom
Our dearest hopes were built——

　　Guil. Ha! What of him?

　Suff. Is lost! betray'd!
His army, onward as he march'd, shrunk from him,
Moulder'd away, and melted by his side;
" Like falling hail thick strewn upon the ground,
" Which, ere we can essay to count, is vanish'd."
With some few followers he arriv'd at Cambridge;
But there ev'n they forsook him, and himself
Was forc'd, with heavy heart and wat'ry eye,
To cast his cap up, with dissembled cheer,
And cry, God save queen Mary.　But, alas!
Little avail'd the semblance of that loyalty:
For soon thereafter, by the earl of Arundel,
With treason he was charg'd, and there arrested;
And now he brings him pris'ner up to London.

　　L. J. Gray. Then there's an end of greatness: the
　　　　vain dream
Of empire, and a crown that danc'd before me,
" With all those unsubstantial empty forms:
" Waiting in idle mockery around us;
" The gaudy masque, tedious, and nothing meaning,"
Is vanish'd all at once——Why, fare it well.

　　Guil. And canst thou bear this sudden turn of fate,
With such unshaken temper?

　　L. J. Gray. For myself,
If I could form a wish for Heav'n to grant,
It should have been, to rid me of this crown.

And thou, o'er-ruling, great, all-knowing Power!
Thou, who discern'st our thoughts, who see'st 'em
      rising
And forming in the soul! Oh, judge me, thou,
If e'er ambition's guilty fires have warm'd me,
If e'er my heart inclin'd to pride, to power,
Or join'd in being a queen. I took the sceptre
To save this land, thy people, and thy altars:
And now, behold, I bend my grateful knee, [*Kneeling.*
In humble adoration of that mercy,
Which quits me of the vast unequal task.

     Enter the Duchess of SUFFOLK.

  Duch. *Suff.* Nay, keep that posture still, and let
    us join,
Fix all our knees by thine, lift up our hands,
And seek for help and pity from above,
For earth and faithless man will give us none.
  L. *J. Gray.* What is the worst our cruel fate or-
    dains us?
  Duch. *Suff.* Curs'd be my fatal counsels, curs'd my
    tongue,
That pleaded for thy ruin, and persuaded
Thy guiltless feet to tread the paths of greatness!
My child————I have undone thee!
  L. *J. Gray.* Oh, my mother!
Shou'd I not bear a portion in your sorrows?
  Duch. *Suff.* Alas, thou hast thy own, a double
    portion.
Mary is come, and the revolting Londoners,

Who beat the heav'ns with thy applauded name,
Now crowd to meet, and hail her as their queen.
Sussex is enter'd here, commands the Tower,
Has plac'd his guards around, and this sad place,
So late thy palace, is become our prison.
I saw him bend his knee to cruel Gardiner,
Who, freed from his confinement, ran to meet him,
Embrac'd and bless'd him with a hand of blood,
Each hast'ning moment I expect 'em here,
To seize, and pass the doom of death upon us.

   Guil. Ha! seiz'd! Shalt thou be seiz'd? and shall
       I stand,
And tamely see thee borne away to death?
Then blasted be my coward name for ever.
No, I will set myself to guard this spot,
To which our narrow empire now is shrunk:
Here I will grow the bulwark of my queen;
Nor shall the hand of violence profane thee,
Until my breast have borne a thousand wounds,
Till this torn mangled body sink at once
A heap of purple ruin at thy feet.

   L. J. Gray. And could thy rash distracted rage do
       thus'?
Draw thy vain sword against an armed multitude,
" Only to have my poor heart split with horror,
" To see thee stabb'd and butcher'd here before me?"
Oh, call thy better nobler courage to thee,
And let us meet this adverse fate with patience!
" Greet our insulting foes with equal tempers,
" With even brows, and souls secure of death;

" Here stand unmov'd; as once the Roman senate
" Receiv'd fierce Brennus, and the conquering Gauls,
" Till ev'n the rude Barbarians stood amaz'd
" At such superior virtue." Be thyself,
For see the trial comes!

Enter SUSSEX, GARDINER, *Officers and Soldiers.*

Suss. Guards, execute your orders; seize the trai-
    tors:
Here my commission ends. To you, my lord, [*To* Gar.
So our great mistress, royal Mary, bids,
I leave the full disposal of these pris'ners?
To your wise care the pious queen commends
Her sacred self, her crown, and what's yet more,
The holy Roman church; for whose dear safety,
She wills your utmost diligence be shewn,
To bring rebellion to the bar of justice.
Yet farther, to proclaim how much she trusts
In Winchester's deep thought, and well try'd faith,
The seal attends to grace those rev'rend hands;
And when I next salute you, I must call you
Chief minister and chancellor of England.
    Gar. Unnumber'd blessings fall upon her head,
My ever-gracious lady! to remember
With such full bounty her old humble beadsman!
For these, her foes, leave me to deal with them.
    Suss. The queen is on her entrance, and expects me:
My lord, farewell.
    Gar. Farewell, right noble Sussex:
Commend me to the queen's grace; say her bidding

Shall be observ'd by her most lowly creature.

[*Exit* Sussex.

Lieutenant of the Tower, take hence your pris'ners :
Be it your care to see 'em kept apart,
That they may hold no commerce with each other.

   L. J. Gray. That stroke was unexpected.

   Guil. Wilt thou part us ?

   Gar. I hold no speech with heretics and traitors.
Lieutenant, see my orders are obey'd.   [*Exit* Gar.

   Guil. Inhuman, monstrous, unexampl'd cruelty !
Oh, tyrant ! but the task becomes thee well ;
Thy savage temper joys to do death's office ;
To tear the sacred bands of love asunder,
And part those hands which heav'n itself hath join'd.

   Duch. Suff. To let us waste the little rest of life
Together, had been merciful.

   Suff. Then it had not
Been done like Winchester.

   Guil. Thou stand'st unmov'd ;
Calm temper sits upon thy beauteous brow ;
Thy eyes, that flow'd so fast for Edward's loss,
Gaze unconcern'd upon the ruin round thee ;
As if thou hadst resolv'd to brave thy fate,
And triumph in the midst of desolation.
 " Ha ! see, it swells ; the liquid crystal rises,
 " It starts, in spite of thee,——but I will catch it ;
 " Nor let the earth be wet with dew so rich."

   L. J. Gray. And dost thou think, my Guilford, I
      can see,
My father, mother, and ev'n thee my husband,

   3

Torn from my side without a pang of sorrow ?
How art thou thus unknowing in my heart!
Words cannot tell thee what I feel.   There is
An agonizing softness busy here,
That tugs the strings, that struggles to get loose,
And pour my soul in wailings out before thee.

   Guil. Give way, and let the gushing torrent come
Behold the tears we bring to swell the deluge,
Till the flood rise upon the guilty world,
And make the ruin common.

   L. *J. Gray.* Guilford! no:
The time for tender thoughts and soft endearments
Is fled away and gone : joy has forsaken us ;
Our hearts have now another part to play ;
They must be steel'd with some uncommon fortitude,
That, fearless, we may tread the paths of horror ;
And, in despite of fortune and our foes,
Ev'n in the hour of death, be more than conquerors.

   Guil. Oh, teach me ! say, what energy divine
Inspires thy softer sex, and tender years,
With such unshaken courage ?

   L. *J. Gray.* Truth and innocence;
A conscious knowledge rooted in my heart,
That to have sav'd my country was my duty.
Yes, England, yes, my country, I would save thee ;
But Heav'n forbids, Heav'n disallows my weakness.
And to some dear selected hero's hand
Reserves the glory of thy great deliverance.

   Lieut. My lords, my orders————
   Guil. See! we must—must part.

L. J. Gray. Yet surely we shall meet again.

" *Guil.* Oh! Where?

" *L. J. Gray.* If not on earth, among yon golden
     stars,
" Where other suns arise on other earths,
" And happier beings rest on happier seats·
" Where with a reach enlarg'd, our soul shall view
" The great Creator's never-ceasing hand
" Pour forth new worlds to all eternity,
" And people the infinity of space."

    Guil. Fain wou'd I cheer my heart with hopes like
       these;
But my sad thoughts turn ever to the grave;
To that last dwelling, whither now we haste;
Where the black shade shall interpose betwixt us,
And veil thee from these longing eyes for ever.

    L. *J. Gray.* 'Tis true, by those dark paths our
       journey leads,
And through the vale of death we pass to life.
But what is there in death to blast our hopes? ·
Behold the universal works of nature,
Where life still springs from death. " To us the sun
" Dies ev'ry night, and ev'ry morn revives:
" The flow'rs, which winter's icy hand destroy'd,
" Lift their fair heads, and live again in spring."
Mark, with what hopes upon the furrow'd plain,
The careful plowman casts the pregnant grain;
There hid, as in a grave, a while it lies,
Till the revolving season bids it rise;

" Till nature's genial pow'rs command a birth ;
" And potent call it from the teeming earth :"
Then large increase the bury'd treasures yield,
And with full harvest crown the plenteous field.

[Exeunt severally with guards.

ACT V.   SCENE I.

Continues.   Enter GARDINER, *as Lord Chancellor, and
the Lieutenant of the Tower. Servants with lights before
'em.*

Lieutenant.

GOOD morning to your lordship ; you rise early.

Gar. Nay, by the rood, there are too many sleepers ;
Some must stir early, or the state shall suffer.
Did you, as yesterday our mandate bade,
Inform your pris'ners, Lady Jane and Guilford,
They were to die this day ?

Lieut. My lord, I did.

Gar. 'Tis well. But say, How did your message
like 'em ?

Lieut. My lord, they met the summons with a temper
That shew'd a solemn, serious sense of death,
Mix'd with a noble scorn of all its terrors.
In short, they heard me with the self-same patience
With which they still have borne them in their prison.
In one request they both concurr'd : each begg'd
To die before the other.

Gar. That dispose
As you think fitting.

Lieut. The lord Guilford only
Implor'd another boon, and urg'd it warmly:
That ere he suffer'd he might see his wife,
And take a last farewell.

Gar. That's not much,
That grace may be allow'd him.   See you to it.
How goes the morning?

Lieut. Not yet four, my lord.

Gar. By ten they meet their fate.   Yet one thing
  more.
You know 'twas order'd that the lady Jane
Shou'd suffer here within the Tow'r.   Take care
No crowds may be let in, no maudlin gazers
To wet their handkerchiefs, and make report
How like a saint she ended.   Some fit number,
And those too of our friends, were most convenient:
But, above all, see that good guard be kept:
You know the queen is lodged at present here,
Take care that no disturbance reach her highness.
And so good-morning, good master lieutenant.
       [*Exit Lieutenant.*

How now! What light comes here?

Ser. So please your lordship,
If I mistake not, 'tis the earl of Pembroke.

Gar. 'Pembroke!——'Tis he: What calls him forth
  thus early?
Somewhat he seems to bring of high import;

" Some flame uncommon kindles up his soul,
" And flashes forth impetuous at his eyes."

Enter PEMBROKE ; *a Page with a light before him.*

Good morrow, noble Pembroke! What importunate
And strong necessity breaks on your slumbers,
And rears your youthful head from off your pillow
At this unwholsome hour ; " while yet the night
" Lasts in her latter course, and with her raw
" And rheumy damps infest the dusky air ?"
Pem. Oh, rev'rend Winchester! my beating heart
Exults and labours with the joy it bears :
The news I bring shall bless the breaking morn.
" This coming day the sun shall rise more glorious
" Than when his maiden beams first gilded o'er
" The rich immortal greens, the flow'ry plains,
" And fragrant bow'rs of paradise new-born."
Gar. What happiness is this!
Pem. 'Tis mercy, mercy,
" The mark of Heav'n impress'd on human kind ;
" Mercy, that glads the world, deals joy around ;
" Mercy, that smooths the dreadful brow of power,
" And makes dominion light ; mercy, that saves,
" Binds up the broken heart, and heals despair."
Mary, our royal, ever-gracious mistress,
Has to my services and humblest prayers
Granted the lives of Guilford and his wife ;
Full and free pardon!
Gar. Ha! What said you? Pardon!
But sure you cannot mean it ; cou'd not urge

The queen to such a rash and ill-tim'd grace?
What! save the lives of those who wore her crown!
My lord, 'tis most unweigh'd, pernicious counsel,
And must not be comply'd with.

   Pem. Not comply'd with!
And who shall dare to bar her sacred pleasure,
And stop the stream of mercy!

   Gar. That will I ;
Who wo'not see her gracious disposition
Draw to destroy herself.

   Pem. Thy narrow soul
Knows not the godlike glory of forgiving :
Nor can thy cold, thy ruthless heart conceive,
How large the power, how fix'd the empire is,
Which benefits confer on generous minds :
" Goodness prevails upon the stubborn foes,
" And conquer more then even Cæsar's sword did."

   Gar. These are romantic, light, vain-glorious
     dreams.
Have you consider'd well upon the danger?
How dear to the fond many, and how popular
These are whom you would spare? Have you forgot,
When at the bar, before the seat of judgment,
This lady Jane, this beauteous trait'ress, stood,
With what command she charm'd the whole assembly?
With silent grief the mournful audience sat,
Fix'd on her face, and list'ning to her pleading.
Her very judges wrung their hands for pity ;
Their old hearts melted in 'em as she spoke,
And tears ran down upon their silver beards.

Ev'n I myself was mov'd, and for a moment
Felt wrath suspended in my doubtful breast,
And question'd if the voice I heard was mortal.
But when her tale was done, what loud applause,
Like bursts of thunder, shook the spacious hall!
At last, when sore constrain'd, th' unwilling lords
Pronounc'd the fatal sentence on her life;
A peal of groans ran through the crowded court,
As every heart was broken, and the doom,
Like that which waits the world, were universal.

 Pem. And can that sacred form, that angel's voice,
Which mov'd the hearts of a rude ruthless crowd,
Nay, mov'd ev'n thine, now sue in vain for pity?

 Gar. Alas, you look on her with lover's eyes:
I hear and see through reasonable organs,
Where passion has no part. Come, come, my lord,
You have too little of the statesman in you.

 Pem. And you, my lord, too little of the churchman.
Is not the sacred purpose of our faith
Peace and good-will to man? The hallow'd hand,
Ordain'd to bless, should know no stain of blood.
'Tis true, I am not practis'd in your politics;
'Twas your pernicious counsel led the queen
To break her promise with the men of Suffolk,
To violate, what in a prince should be
Sacred above the rest, her royal word.

 Gar. Yes, and I dare avow it: I advis'd her
To break through all engagements made with heretics,
And keep no faith with such a miscreant crew.

Pem. Where shall we seek for truth, when ev'n
  religion,
The priestly robe and mitred head disclaim it?
" But thus bad men dishonour the best cause."
I tell thee, Winchester, doctrines like thine
Have stain'd our holy church with greater infamy
Than all your eloquence can wipe away.
Hence 'tis, that those who differ from our faith,
Brand us with breach of oaths, with persecution,
With tyranny o'er conscience, and proclaim
Our scarlet prelates men that thirst for blood,
And Christian Rome more cruel than the pagan.
 Gar. Nay, if you rail, farewell. The queen must be
Better advis'd, than thus to cherish vipers,
Whose mortal stings are arm'd against her life.
But while I hold the seal, no pardon passes
For heretics and traitors. [*Exit* Gardiner.
 Pem. 'Twas unlucky
To meet and cross upon this froward priest:
But let me lose the thought on't; let me haste,
Pour my glad tidings forth in Guilford's bosom,
And pay him back the life his friendship sav'd. [*Exit.*

SCENE II.

The Lady JANE *kneeling, as at her devotion; a light, and
a book placed on a table before her.   Enter Lieutenant of
the Tower, Lord* GUILFORD, *and one of Lady* JANE's
women.*

Lieut. Let me not press upon your lordship farther,
But wait your leisure in the antichamber.
    Guil. I will not hold you long.   [*Exit Lieutenant.*
    Wom. Softly, my lord!
For yet, behold she kneels. " Before the night
" Had reach'd her middle space, she left her bed,
" And with a pleasing, sober cheerfulness,
" As for her funeral, array'd herself
" In those sad solemn weeds. Since then her knee
" Has known that posture only, and her eye,
" Or fix'd upon the sacred page before her,
" Or lifted, with her rising hopes, to heav'n."
    Guil. See, with what zeal those holy hands are rear'd!
" Mark her vermilion lip, with fervour trembling;
" Her spotless bosom swells with sacred ardor,
" And burns with ecstasy and strong devotion;
" Her supplication sweet, her faithful vows
" Fragrant and pure, and grateful to high Heaven,
" Like incense from the golden censer rise;
" Or blessed angels minister unseen,
" Catch the soft sounds, and with alternate office,
" Spread their ambrosial wings, then mount with joy,
H iij

" And waft them upwards to the throne of grace."
But she has ended, and comes forward.
[*Lady* JANE *rises, and comes toward the front of the stage.*
　　L. *J. Gray.* Ha!
Art thou my Guilford? Wherefore dost thou come
To break the settled quiet of my soul?
I meant to part without another pang,
And lay my weary head down full of peace.
　　Guil. Forgive the fondness of my longing soul,
That melts with tenderness, and leans toward thee:
" Tho' the imperious, dreadful voice of fate
" Summon her hence, and warn her from the world."
But if to see thy Guilford give thee pain,
Wou'd I had died, and never more beheld thee:
" Tho' my lamenting discontented ghost
" Had wander'd forth unbless'd by those dear eyes,
" And wail'd thy loss in death's eternal shades."
　　L. *J. Gray.* My heart had ended ev'ry earthly care,
And offer'd up its pray'rs for thee and England,
" And fix'd its hopes upon a rock unfailing;"
While all the little bus'ness that remain'd,
Was but to pass the forms of death and constancy,
And leave a life become indifferent to me.
But thou hast waken'd other thoughts within me;
Thy sight, my dearest husband and my lord,
Strikes on the tender strings of love and nature:
My vanquish'd passions rise again, and tell me,
'Tis more, far more than death to part from thee.

Enter PEMBROKE.

Pem. Oh, let me fly, bear me, thou swift impatience,
And lodge me in my faithful Guilford's arms!

                     [*Embracing.*

That I may snatch thee from the greedy grave,
That I may warm his gentle heart with joy,
And talk to him of life, of life and pardon.
    Guil. What means my dearest Pembroke?
    Pem. Oh, my speech
Is choak'd with words that crowd to tell my tidings!
But I have sav'd thee—and—Oh, joy unutterable!
The queen, my gracious, my forgiving mistress,
Has given not only thee to my request,
But she, she too, in whom alone thou liv'st,
The partner of thy heart, thy love is safe.
    Guil. Millions of blessings wait her!—Has she—tell
       me,
Oh, has she spar'd my wife?
    Pem. Both, both are pardon'd.
But haste, and do thou lead me to thy saint,
That I may cast myself beneath her feet,
And beg her to accept this poor amends
For all I've done against her——Thou fair excellence,

                     [*Kneeling.*

Canst thou forgive the hostile hand that arm'd
Against thy cause, and robb'd thee of a crown?
    L. J. Gray. Oh, rise, my lord, and let me take your
       posture.
Life and the world are hardly worth my care,

But you have reconcil'd me to 'em both;
Then let me pay my gratitude, and for
This free, this noble, unexpected mercy,
Thus low I bow to Heav'n, the queen, and you.

    Pem. To me! forbid it goodness! if I live,
Somewhat I will do shall deserve your thanks.
" All discord and remembrance of offence
" Shall be clean blotted out; and for your freedom,
" Myself have underta'en to be your caution."
Hear me, you saints, and aid my pious purpose:
These that deserve so much, this wondrous pair,
Let these be happy: ev'ry joy attend 'em;
A fruitful bed, a chain of love unbroken,
" A good old age, to see their children's children;"
A holy death, and everlasting memory;
" While I resign to them my share of happiness,
" Contented still to wait what they enjoy,
" And singly to be wretched."

        Enter Lieutenant of the Tower.

    Lieut. The Lord Chancellor
Is come with orders from the queen.

        Enter GARDINER, *and Attendants.*

    Pem. Ha! Winchester!
    Gar. The queen, whose days be many,
By me confirms her first accorded grace;
But, as the pious princess means her mercy
Should reach e'en to the soul as well as body,
By me she signifies her royal pleasure,

That thou, Lord Guilford, and the Lady Jane,
Do instantly renounce, abjure your heresy,
And yield obedience to the see of Rome.

   L. J. Gray. What! turn apostate?

   Guil. Ha! forego my faith!

   Gar. This one condition only seals your pardon:
But if, through pride of heart, and stubborn obstinacy,
With wilful hands you push the blessing from you,
" And shut your eyes against such manifest light,"
Know ye, your former sentence stands confirm'd,
And you must die to-day.

   Pem. 'Tis false as hell:
The mercy of the queen was free and full.
Think'st thou that princes merchandize their grace,
As Roman priests their pardons? " Do they barter,
" Screw up, like you, the buyer to a price,
" And doubly sell what was design'd a gift?"

   Gar. My lord, this language ill beseems your noble-
       ness;
Nor come I here to bandy words with madmen.
Behold the royal signet of the queen,
Which amply speaks her meaning. You, the pris'ners,
Have heard, at large, its purport, and must instantly
Resolve upon the choice of life or death.

   Pem. Curse on——But wherefore do I loiter here?
I'll to the queen this moment, and there know
What 'tis this mischief-making priest intends. [*Exit.*

   Gar. Your wisdom points you out a proper course.
A word with you, Lieutenant.

              [*Talks with the Lieutenant aside.*

Guil. Must we part then?
What are those hopes that flatter'd us but now;
Those joys, that, like the spring, with all its flow'rs,
Pour'd out their pleasures ev'ry where around us?　.
In one poor minute gone; " at once they wither'd,
" And left their place all desolate behind them."
　　L. *J. Gray.* Such is this foolish world, and such
　　　　the certainty
Of all the boasted blessings it bestows :
Then, Guilford, let us have no more to do with it;
Think only how to leave it as we ought;
" But trust no more, and be deceiv'd no more."
　　Guil. Yes, I will copy thy divine example,
" And tread the paths are pointed out by thee :"
By thee instructed, to the fatal block
I bend my head with joy, and think it happiness
To give my life a ransom for my faith.
" From thee, thou angel of my heart, I learn
" That greatest, hardest task, to part with thee."
　　L. *J. Gray.* Oh, gloriously resolv'd! " Heav'n is
　　　　my witness,
" My heart rejoices in thee more ev'n now,
" Thus constant as thou art, in death thus faithful,
" Than when the holy priest first join'd our hands,
" And knit the sacred knot of bridal love."
　　Gar. The day wears fast; Lord Guilford, have you
　　　　thought?
Will you lay hold on life?
　　Guil. What are the terms?
　　Gar. Death, or the mass, attend you.

Guil. 'Tis determin'd :
Lead to the scaffold.

Gar. Bear him to his fate.

Guil. Oh, let me fold thee once more in my arms,
Thou dearest treasure of my heart, and print
A dying husband's kiss upon thy lip !
Shall we not live again, ev'n in those forms ?
Shall I not gaze upon thee with these eyes ?

   L. J. Gray. Oh, wherefore dost thou sooth me
      with thy softness ?
Why dost thou wind thyself about my heart,
And make this separation painful to us ?
' Here break we off at once ; and let us now,
' Forgetting ceremony, like two friends
' That have a little business to be done,
' Take a short leave, and haste to meet again.
   " *Guil.* Rest on that hope, my soul—my wife——
   " *L. J. Gray.* No more."

Guil. My sight hangs on thee——Oh, support me,
     Heav'n.
In this last pang—and let us meet in bliss !

          [Guilford *is led off by the guard.*

   " *L. J. Gray.* Can nature bear this stroke ?"

Wom. Alas, she faints !   [*Supporting.*

L. J. Gray. Wo't thou fail now———The killing
     stroke is past,
And all the bitterness of death is o'er.

Gar. Here let the dreadful hand of vengeance stay ;
Have pity on your youth, and blooming beauty ;
" Cast not away the good which Heav'n bestows ;"

Time may have many years in store for you,
All crown'd with fair prosperity.   Your husband
Has perish'd in perverseness.

   L. J. Gray. Cease, thou raven,
Nor violate, with thy profaner malice,
My bleeding Guilford's ghost—'Tis gone, 'tis flown :
But lingers on the wing, and waits for me.

     [*The scene draws, and discovers a scaffold hung with*
       black, Executioner and Guards.
And see my journey's end.

   1 *Wom.* My dearest lady.   [*Weeping.*

   " 2 *Wom.* Oh, misery !"

   L. J. Gray. Forbear my gentle maids,
Nor wound my peace with fruitless lamentations ;
The good and gracious hand of Providence
Shall raise you better friends than I have been.

   1 *Wom.* Oh, never, never !————

   L. J. Gray. Help to disarray,
And fit me for the block : do this last service,
And do it cheerfully.   Now you will see
Your poor unhappy mistress sleep in peace,
And cease from all her sorrows.   These few trifles,
The pledges of a dying mistress' love,
Receive and share among you.   " Thou, Maria,

                      [*To* 1 *Wom.*

" Hast been my old, my very faithful servant :
" In dear remembrance of thy love, I leave thee
" This book, the law of everlasting truth :
" Make it thy treasure still ; 'twas my support,
" When all help else forsook me."

Gar. Will you yet
Repent, be wise, and save your precious life?

   L. J. Gray. Oh, Winchester! has learning taught
       thee that:
To barter truth for life?

   Gar. Mistaken folly!
You toil and travel for your own perdition,
And die for damned errors.

   L. J. Gray. Who judge rightly,
And who persists in error, will be known,
Then, when we meet again. Once more, farewell,
             [*To her women.*
Goodness be ever with you. " When I'm dead,
" Entreat they do no rude, dishonest wrong
" To my cold, headless corpse; but see it shrouded,
" And decent laid in earth."

   Gar. Wo't thou then die?
Thy blood be on thy head.

   L. J. Gray. My blood be where it falls; let the earth
       hide it;
And may it never rise, or call for vengeance.
Oh, that it were the last shall fall a victim
To zeal's inhuman wrath! Thou, gracious **Heaven,**
Hear and defend at length thy suffering people;
Raise up a monarch of the royal blood,
Brave, pious, equitable, wise and good.
" In thy due season let the hero come,
" To save thy altars from the rage of Rome:
" Long let him reign, to bless the rescu'd land,
" And deal out justice with a righteous hand."

And when he fails, oh, may he leave a son,
With equal virtues to adorn his throne ;
To latest times the blessing to convey,
And guard that faith for which I die to-day.

    [*Lady* Jane *goes up to the scaffold. The scene closes.*

Enter PEMBROKE.

    Pem. Horror on horror ! Blasted be the hand
That struck my Guilford ! Oh, his bleeding trunk
Shall live in these distracted eyes for ever !
Curse on thy fatal arts, thy cruel counsels! [*To* Gard.
The queen is deaf, and pitiless as thou art.

    Gar. The just reward of heresy and treason
Is fallen upon 'em both, for their vain obstinacy ;
Untimely death, with infamy on earth,
And everlasting punishment hereafter.

    Pem. And canst thou tell ? Who gave thee to explore
The secret purposes of Heaven, or taught thee
To set a bound to mercy unconfin'd ?
But know, thou proud, perversely-judging Win-
        chester !
Howe'er you hard, imperious censures doom,
And portion out our lot in worlds to come,
Those, who, with honest hearts, pursue the right,
And follow faithfully truth's sacred light, .
Tho' suff'ring here, shall from their sorrows cease,
Rest with the saints, and dwell in endless peace.

                        [*Exeunt.*

EPILOGUE

THE palms of virtue heroes oft have worn;
Those wreaths to-night a female brow adorn.
The destin'd saint, unfortunately brave,
Sunk with those altars which she strove to save.
Greatly she dar'd to prop the juster side,
As greatly with her adverse fate comply'd,
Did all that Heav'n could ask, resign'd, and dy'd;
Dy'd for the land for which she wish'd to live,
And gain'd that liberty she could not give.
Oh, happy people of this fav'rite isle,
On whom so many better angels smile!
For you, kind Heav'n new blessings still supplies,
Bids other saints, and other guardians rise:
For you the fairest of her sex is come,
Adopts our Britain, and forgets her home:
For truth and you the heroine declines
Austria's proud eagles, and the Indian mines.
What sense of such a bounty can be shown!
But Heav'n must make the vast reward its own,
And stars shall join to make her future crown.
Your gratitude with ease may be express'd;
Strive but to be, what she would make you, bless'd.
Let not vile faction vex the vulgar ear
With fond surmise, and false affected fear.

Confirm but to yourselves the given good ;
'Tis all she asks, for all she has bestow'd.
Such was our great example shewn to-day,
And with such thanks our author's pains repay.
If from these scenes, to guard your faith you learn ;
If for our laws you shew a just concern ;
If you are taught to dread a popish reign ;
Our beauteous patriot has not dy'd in vain.

THE END,

Thornthwaite sc.

M.ʳ KEMBLE as ŒDIPUS.

I challenge Fate to find another wretch

OEDIPUS

A

TRAGEDY.

BY DRYDEN AND LEE.

ADAPTED FOR

THEATRICAL REPRESENTATION,

AS PERFORMED AT THE

THEATRE-ROYAL, DRURY-LANE.

REGULATED FROM THE PROMPT-BOOKS,

By Permission of the Managers.

LONDON:

Printed for the Proprietors, under the Direction of
JOHN BELL, British Library, STRAND,
Bookseller to His Royal Highness the Prince of Wales.

MDCCXCI.

Though it be dangerous to raise too great an expectation, especially in works of this nature, where we are to please an unsatiable audience; yet 'tis reasonable to prepossess them in favour of an author, and therefore both the Prologue and Epilogue informed you that Œdious was the most celebrated piece of all antiquity: that Sophocles, not only the greatest wit, but one of the greatest men in Athens, made it for the stage at the public cost, and that it had the reputation of being his masterpiece, not only amongst the seven of his which are still remaining, but of the greater number which are perished. Aristotle has more than once admired it in his book of poetry; Horace has mentioned it; Lucullus, Julius Cæsar, and other noble Romans, have written on the same subject, though their poems are wholly lost; but Seneca's is still preserved In our own age, Corneille has attempted it, and it appears by his preface, with great success: but a judicious reader will easily observe how much the copy is inferior to the original. He tells you himself, that he owes a great part of his success to the happy episode of Theseus and Dirce; which is the same thing as if we should acknowledge, that we were indebted for our good fortune to the underplot of Adrastus, Eurydice, and Creon. The truth is, he miserably failed in the character of his hero. If he desired that Œdipus should be pitied, he should have made him a better man. He forgot that Sophocles had taken care to shew him in his first entrance, a just, a merciful, a successful, a religious prince: and, in short, a father of his

country : instead of these, he has drawn him suspicious, de-
signing, more anxious of keeping the Theban crown, than so-
licitous for the safety of his people ; hectored by Theseus, con-
temned by Dirce, and scarce maintaining a second part in his
own tragedy. This was an error in the first concoction : and
therefore never to be mended in the second or third. He intro-
duced a greater hero than Œdipus himself ; for when Theseus
was once there, that companion of Hercules must yield to
none. The poet was obliged to furnish him with business, to
make him an equipage suitable to his dignity, and, by follow-
ing him too close, to lose his other King of Brentford in the
crowd. Seneca, on the other side, as if there were no such
thing as nature to be minded in a play, is always running after
pompous expression, pointed sentences, and philosophical no-
tions, more proper for the study than the stage. The French-
man followed a wrong scent, and the Roman was absolutely at
cold hunting. All we could gather out of Corneille was, that
an episode must be, but not his way ; and Seneca supplied us
with no new hint, but only a relation which he makes of his Ti-
resias raising the ghost of Laius ; which is here performed in
view of the audience ; the rites and ceremonies so far his, as he
agreed with antiquity, and the religion of the Greeks : but he
himself was beholden to Homer's Tiresias in the Odysses for
some of them, and the rest have been collected from Helio-
dore's Æthiopiques, and Lucan's Erictho. Sophocles, indeed,
is admirable every where ; and therefore we have followed him
as close as possibly we could. But the Athenian theatre (whe-
ther more perfect than ours, is not now disputed) had a per-
fection differing from ours. You see there in every act a sin-
gle scene, (or two at most) which manage the business of the
play, and after that succeeds the chorus, which commonly
takes up more time in singing, than there has been employed
in speaking. The principal person appears almost constantly
through the play ; but the inferior parts seldom above once in

the whole tragedy. The conduct of our stage is much more difficult, where we are obliged never to lose any considerable character which we have once presented. Custom likewise has obtained, that we must form an under-plot of second persons, which must be depending on the first, and their byewalks must be like those in a labyrinth, which all of them lead into the great parterre; or like so many several lodging chambers, which have their outlets into the same gallery. Perhaps, after all, if we could think so, the ancient method, as it is the easiest, is also the most natural, and the best. For variety, as it is managed, is too often subject to breed distraction; and while we would please too many ways, for want of art in the conduct, we please in none. But we have given you more already than was necessary for a preface, and, for aught we know, may gain no more by our instructions, than that politic nation is like to do, who have taught their enemies to fight so long, that at last they are in a condition to invade them.

THERE is a proverb, which says, that two heads are better than one—In designing, perhaps, it may be so; in executing, such a co-operation seems to forbid the proper assimilation of parts.

This Play is written by DRYDEN and LEE, and their several parts of the production are known. To DRYDEN we owe the entire first and third acts, with the plan and arrangement of the whole; LEE furnished out the remainder.

The Fable, if it can ever please, will please from its being ancient—Sophocles presented this subject to the audiences of ancient Greece, and its interest must there have been powerful—But to a modern the whole play is founded upon an ideal criminality—for we consider the heart as indispensably necessary to constitute either crime or merit; and no more affix the imputation of guilt to unconscious offence, than we do of virtue to unintended good.

In the play of OEDIPUS, we behold a man involved by a fatality which he has no power to shun, murdering his father, and incestuously embracing his mother ; whom conviction plunges in despair, whom feeling hurries into phrenzy.—The other in-cidents are arraved with suitable barbarity ; they are such as the mind loaths to imagine, and the sensi-bilities of man shrink from beholding.

With the incurable defects therefore of historic truth to treat, and circumstances too well known to be any way softened, this composition will be found, from its sentiments and language, among the best productions of these authors. It but seldom makes its appearance upon the modern stage, and is hasting, with all its *mythological* brethren, to that repose, which only solitary curiosity disturbs in the silent though classic ground of the library.—

Ibant obscuri sola sub nocte per umbram,
Perque domos ditis vacuas et inania regna.

PROLOGUE.

WHEN Athens all the Grecian states did guide,
And Greece gave laws to all the world beside,
Then Sophocles and Socrates did sit,
Supreme in wisdom one, and one in wit:
And wit from wisdom differ'd not in those,
But as 'twas sung in verse, or said in prose.
Then OEdipus, on crowded theatres,
Drew all admiring eyes, and list'ning ears:
The pleas'd spectator shouted every line,
The noblest, manliest, and the best design!
And every critic of each learned age,
By this just model has reform'd the stage.
Now, should it fail, (as Heav'n avert our fear!)
Damn it in silence, lest the world should hear.
For were it known this poem did not please,
You might set up for perfect savages:
Your neighbours would not look on you as men;
But think the nation all turn'd Picts again.
Faith, as you manage matters, 'tis not fit,
You should suspect yourselves of too much wit.
Drive not the jest too far, but spare this piece:
And, for this once, be not more wise than Greece.
See twice; do not pell-mell to damning fall,
Like true-born Britons, who ne'er think at all.

n pointed cannon do not always run.

ith some respect to ancient wits proceed :

ou take the four first councils for your creed,

ut when you lay tradition wholly by,

nd on the private spirit alone rely,

ou turn fanatics in your poetry.

, notwithstanding all that we can say,

ou needs will have your penn'worths of the play,

nd come resolv'd to damn, because you pay,

ecord it, in memorial of the fact,

he first play bury'd since the woollen act.

Dramatis Personae.

Men.

OEDIPUS,
ADRASTUS,
CREON,
TIRESIAS,
HÆMON,
ALCANDER,

Women.

Priests,   &c.

OEDIPUS.

ACT I. SCENE I.

The Curtain rises to a plaintive tune, representing the mi-
series of Thebes; dead bodies appear at a distance in
the streets; some faintly go over the stage, others drop.
Enter ALCANDER, DIOCLES, *and* PYRACMON.

Alcander.

METHINKS we stand on ruins; nature shakes
About us, and the universal frame
So loose, that it but wants another push
To leap from off its hinges.

   Dioc. " No sun to cheer us; but a bloody globe
" That rolls above; a bald and beamless fire;
" His face o'er-grown with scurf." The sun's sick
      too;
Shortly he'll be an earth.

   Pyr. Therefore the seasons
Lie all confus'd; and, by the Heav'ns neglected,
Forget themselves. " Blind winter meets the summer
" In his mid-way, and, seeing not his livery,

" Has driven him head-long back : and the raw damps
" With flaggy wings fly heavily about,
" Scattering their pestilential colds and rheums
" Through all the lazy air."
Alc. Hence murrains follow'd
On bleating flocks, and on the lowing herds :
At last, the malady
Grew more domestic, and the faithful dog
Dy'd at his master's feet.
Dioc. And next his master :
" For all those plagues which earth and air had
       brooded,
" First on inferior creatures try'd their force ;
" And last they seiz'd on man."
   Pyr. " And then a thousand deaths at once ad-
       vanc'd,
" And every dart took place. All was so sudden,
" That scarce a first man fell—One but began
" To wonder, and straight fell a wonder too;
" A third, who stoop'd to raise his dying friend,
" Dropp'd in the pious act."—Heard you that groan?
                     [*Groan within.*
   Dioc. A troop of ghosts took flight together there :
" Now Death's grown riotous, and will play no more
" For single stakes ; but families and tribes."
How are we sure we breathe not now our last,
And that, next minute,
Our bodies, cast into some common pit,
Shall not be built upon, and overlaid
By half a people ?

Alc. There's a chain of causes
Link'd to effects ; invincible necessity,
That whate'er is, could not but so have been ;
That's my security.

Enter CREON.

Cre. So had it need, when all our streets lie co-
    ver'd
With dead and dying men ;
And Earth exposes bodies on the pavements
More than she hides in graves.
Betwixt the bride and bridegroom have I seen
The nuptial torch do common offices
Of marriage and of death.
  Dioc. Now OEdipus
(If he returns from war, our other plague)
Will scarce find half he left, to grace his triumphs.
  Pyr. A feeble Pæan will be sung before him.
  Alc. He would do well to bring the wives and chil-
    dren
Of conquer'd Argians, to renew his Thebes.
  Cre May funerals meet him at the city gates,
With their detested omen.
  Dioc. Of his children.
  Cre. Nay, though she be my sister, of his wife.
  Alc. Oh, that our Thebes might once again behold
A monarch Theban born !
  Dioc. We might have had one.
  Pyr. Yes, had the people pleas'd.
  Cre. Come, you're my friends—

The queen, my sister, after Laius' death,
Fear'd to lie single, and supply'd his place
With a young successor.

   Dioc. He much resembles
Her former husband too.

   Alc. I always thought so.

   Pyr. When twenty winters more have grizzl'd his
      black locks,
He will be very Laius.

   Cre. So he will:
Mean time she stands provided of a Laius
More young and vigorous too, by twenty springs,
These women are such cunning purveyors!
Mark, where their appetites have once been pleas'd,
The same resemblance in a younger lover
Lies brooding in their fancies the same pleasures,
And urges their remembrance to desire.

   Dioc. Had merit, not her dotage, been consider'd,
Then Creon had been king: but OEdipus!
A stranger!——

   Cre. That word, stranger, I confess,
Sounds harshly in my ears.

   Dioc. We are your creatures.
The people prone, as in all general ills,
To sudden change; the king in wars abroad;
The queen a woman weak and unregarded;
Euridice, the daughter of dead Laius,
A princess young, and beauteous, and unmarried.
Methinks, from these disjointed propositions
Something might be produc'd.

Cre. The gods have done
Their part, by sending this commodious plague.
But, oh, the princess! her hard heart is shut,
By adamantine locks, against my love.
   Alc. Your claim to her is strong; you are be-
     troth'd.
   Pyr. True, in her nonage.
   " *Alc.* But that let's remov'd."
   Dioc. I heard the prince of Argos, young Adrastus,
When he was hostage here——
   Cre. Oh, name him not! the bane of all my hopes;
That hot-brain'd, headlong warrior, has the charms
Of youth, and somewhat of a lucky rashness,
To please a woman yet more fool than he.
That thoughtless sex is caught by outward form,
And empty noise, and loves itself in man.
   Alc. But since the war broke out about our frontiers,
He's now a foe to Thebes
   Cre. But is not so to her. See, she appears;
Once more I'll prove my fortune: you insinuate
Kind thoughts of me into the multitude;
Lay load upon the court; gull them with freedom;
And you shall see them toss their tails, and gad,
As if the breeze had stung them.
   Dioc. We'll about it. [*Exeunt* Alc. Dioc. *and* Pyr.

Enter EURYDICE.

   Cre. Hail, royal maid; thou bright Eurydice!
A lavish planet reign'd when thou wert born;

And made thee of such kindred-mould to heav'n,
Thou seem'st more heav'n's than ours.

   Eur. Cast round your eyes;
Where late the streets were so thick sown with men,
Like Cadmus brood, they jostled for the passage:
Now look for those erected heads, and see them
Like pebbles paving all our public ways:
When you have thought on this, then answer me,
If these be hours of courtship.

   Cre. Yes, they are;
For when the gods destroy so fast, 'tis time
We should renew the race.

   Eur. What; in the midst of horror?

   Cre. Why not then?
There's the more need of comfort.

   Eur. Impious Creon!

   Cre. Unjust Eurydice! can you accuse me
Of love, which is Heav'n's precept, and not fear
That vengeance which you say pursues our crimes,
Should reach your perjuries?

   Eur. Still th' old argument.
I bade you cast your eyes on other men,
Now cast them on your self: think what you are.

   Cre. A man.

   Eur. A man!

   Cre. Why doubt you? I'm a man.

   Eur. 'Tis well you tell me so, I should mistake you
For any other part o' th' whole creation,
Rather than think you man. Hence from my sight,
Thou poison to my eyes.

Cre. 'Twas you first poison'd mine; and yet me-
thinks
My face and person should not make you sport.
　Eur. You force me, by your importunities,
To shew you what you are.
　Cre. A prince, who loves you :
And since your pride provokes me, worth your love,
Ev'n at its highest value.
　Eur. Love from thee!
Why love renounc'd thee ere thou saw'st the light:
Nature herself started back when thou wert born ;
And cry'd, the work's not mine——
The midwife stood aghast ; and when she saw
Thy mountain back, and thy distorted legs,
Thy face itself,
Half-minted with the royal stamp of man,
And half o'ercome with beast, stood doubting long,
Whose right in thee were more ;
And knew not, if to burn thee in the flames,
Were not the holier work.
　Cre. Am I to blame, if nature threw my body
In so perverse a mould ? Yet when she cast
Her envious hand upon my supple joints,
Unable to resist, and rumpled them
On heaps in their dark lodging, to revenge
Her bungled work, she stampt my mind more fair;
And as from chaos, huddled and deform'd,
The god struck fire, and lighted up the lamps
That beautify the sky, so he inform'd

This ill-shap'd body with a daring soul ;
And making less than man, he made me more.

Eur. No ; thou art all one error,　soul and body,
The first young trial of some unskill'd pow'r ;
Rude in the making art, and ape of Jove.
Thy crooked mind within hunch'd out thy back ;
And wander'd in thy limbs : to thy own kind
Make love, if thou canst find it in the world ;
And seek not from our sex to raise an offspring,
Which, mingled with the rest, would tempt the gods
To cut off human kind.

Cre. No ; let them leave
The Argian prince for you ; that enemy
Of Thebes has made you false, and break the vows
You made to me.

Eur. They were my mother's vows,
Made in my nonage.

Cre. But hear me, maid :
This blot of nature, this deform'd, loath'd Creon,
Is master of a sword, to reach the blood
Of your young minion, spoil the gods' fine work,
And stab you in his heart.

Eur. This when thou dost,
Then may'st thou still be curs'd with loving me ;
And, as thou art, be still unpitied, loath'd ;
And let his ghost—No, let his ghost have rest :
But let the greatest, fiercest, foulest fury,
Let Creon haunt himself.　　　　　　[*Exit* Eur.

Cre. 'Tis true, I am

What she has told me, an offence to sight:
My body opens inward to my soul,
And lets in day to make my vices seen
By all discerning eyes, but the blind vulgar.
I must make haste ere OEdipus return,
To snatch the crown and her; for I still love;
But love with malice; as an angry cur
Snarls while he feeds, so will I seize and stanch
The hunger of my love on this proud beauty,
And leave the scraps for slaves.

Enter TIRESIAS, *leaning on a staff, and led by his daughter* MANTO.

What makes this blind prophetic fool abroad!
Would his Apollo had him; he's too holy
For earth and me; I'll shun his walk; and seek
My popular friends.   [*Exit* Creon.

Tir. A little farther; yet a little farther,
Thou wretched daughter of a dark old man,
Conduct my weary steps: and thou, who seest
For me and for thyself, beware thou tread not
With impious steps upon dead corpses;—now stay;
Methinks I draw more open, vital air.
Where are we?

Man. Under covert of a wall:
The most frequented once, and noisy part
Of Thebes, now midnight silence reigns ev'n here;
And grass untrodden springs beneath our feet.

Tir. If there be nigh this place a sunny bank,
There let me rest awhile: a sunny bank!

Alas, how can it be, where no sun shines!
But a dim winking taper in the skies,
That nods, and scarce holds up his drowzy head
To glimmer through the damps!

　　[*A noise within.* Follow, follow, follow! A Creon,
　　　　　a Creon, a Creon!

Hark! a tumultuous noise, and Creon's name
Thrice echo'd.

　Man. Fly! the tempest drives this way.
　Tir. Whither can age and blindness take their
　　　flight?
If I could fly, what could I suffer worse,
Secure of greater ills!

　　　　　[*Noise again,* Creon, Creon, Creon!

Enter CREON, DIOCLES, ALCANDER, PYRACMON;
　　followed by the crowd.

　Cre. I thank ye, countrymen; but must refuse
The honours you intend me; they're too great;
And I am too unworthy; think again,
And make a better choice.

　1st Cit. Think twice! I ne'er thought twice in all
my life: that's double work.

　2d Cit. My first word is always my second; and
therefore I'll have no second word; and therefore
once again, I say, a Creon.

　All. A Creon, a Creon, a Creon!
　Cre. Yet hear me, fellow-citizens.
　Dioc. Fellow-citizens! there was a word of kind-
　　ness.

Alc. When did OEdipus salute you by that fami-
liar name?

1st Cit. Never, never; he was too proud.

Cre. Indeed he could not, for he was a stranger:
But under him our Thebes is half destroy'd.
Forbid it, Heav'n, the residue should perish
Under a Theban born.
'Tis true, the gods might send this plague among you,
Because a stranger rul'd: but what of that,
Can I redress it now?

2d Cit. Yes, you or none.
'Tis certain that the gods are angry with us,
Because he reigns.

Cre. OEdipus may return: you may be ruin'd.

1st Cit. Nay, if that be the matter, we are ruined
already.

2d Cit. Half of us that are here present, were liv-
ing men but yesterday, and we that are absent do
but drop and drop, and no man knows whether he
be dead or living. And therefore while we are sound
and well, let us satisfy our consciences, and make a
new king.

3d Cit. Ha, if we were but worthy to see another
coronation, and then, if we must die, we'll go merrily
together.

All. To the question, to the question.

Dioc. Are you content, Creon should be your king?

All. A Creon, a Creon, a Creon!

Tir. Hear me, ye Thebans, and thou, Creon, hear
me.

1st Cit. Who's that would be heard ? We'll hear no man : we can scarce hear one another.

Tir. I charge you, by the gods, to hear me.

2d Cit. Oh, 'Tis Apollo's priest, we must hear him; 'tis the old blind prophet that sees all things.

3d Cit. He comes from the gods too, and they are our betters ; and in good manners we must hear him. Speak, prophet.

2d Cit. For coming from the gods that's no great matter, they can all say that ; but he's a great scholar ; he can make almanacks, an he were put to't, and therefore, I say, hear him.

Tir. When angry Heav'n scatters its plagues among
           you,
Is it for nought, ye Thebans? Are the gods
Unjust for punishing ? Are there no crimes
Which pull this vengeance down ?

1st Cit. Yes, yes, no doubt there are some sins stirring, that are the cause of all.

3d Cit. Yes, there are sins; or we should have no taxes.

2d Cit. For my part, I can speak it with a safe conscience, I ne'er sinned in all my life.

1st Cit. Nor I.

3d Cit. Nor I.

2d Cit. Then we are all justified, the sin lies not at our doors.

Tir. All justified alike, and yet all guilty;
Were every man's false dealing brought to light,
His envy, malice, lying, perjuries,

its and measures, th' other man's extortions,
at face could you tell offended Heav'n,
not sinn'd ?

  Nay, if these be sins, the case is alter'd;
irt I never thought any thing but murder
  a sin.
nd yet, as if all these were less than nothing,
rebellion to them, impious Thebans !
ι not sworn before the gods to serve
bey this OEdipus, your king
ɔ voice elected ? Answer me,
    true !
  This is true; but it's a hard world, neigh-
bours,
's oath must be his master.
peak, Diocles; all goes wrong.
low are you traitors, countrymen of Thebes ?
y sire, who presses you with oaths,
your first ; were you not sworn before
ɔ and his blood ?
Je were ; we were.
While Laius has a lawful successor,
ιt oath still must bind : Eurydice
ɔ Laius; let her marry Creon :
  Heav'n will never be appeas'd
Edipus pollutes the throne of Laius,
er to his blood.
Je'll no OEdipus, no OEdipus.
  He puts the prophet in a mouse-hole.

2d Cit. I knew it would be so, the last man ever
speaks the best reason.

Tir. Can benefits thus die, ungrateful Thebans!
Remember yet, when after Laius' death,
The monster Sphinx laid your rich country waste,
Your vineyards spoil'd, your labouring oxen slew;
Yourselves for fear mew'd up within your walls,
She, taller than your gates, o'erlook'd your town;
But when she rais'd her bulk to sail above you,
She drove the air around her like a whirlwind,
And shaded all beneath; till stooping down,
She clapp'd her leathern wings against your tow'rs,
And thrust out her long neck, ev'n to your doors.

Dioc. Alc. Pyr. We'll hear no more.

Tir. You durst not meet in temples
T' invoke the gods for aid, the proudest he
Who leads you now, then cower'd, like a dar'd lark:
This Creon shook for fear,
The blood of Laius curdled in his veins;
'Till OEdipus arriv'd.
Call'd by his own high courage and the gods,
Himself to you a god: ye offer'd him
Your queen and crown; (but what was then your crown?)
And Heav'n authoriz'd it by his success.
Speak then, who is your lawful king?

All. 'Tis OEdipus.

Tir. 'Tis OEdipus indeed: your king more lawful
Than yet you dream; for something still there lies
In Heav'n's dark volume, which I read through mists:
'Tis great, prodigious; 'tis a dreadful birth,

Of wondrous fate ; and now, just now disclosing.
I see, I see, how terrible it dawns :
And my soul sickens with it.

   1st Cit. How the god shakes him!

   Tir. He comes ! he comes ! Victory ! Conquest !
      Triumph !

But, oh, guiltless and guilty ! Murder ! Parricide !
Incest ! Discovery ! Punishment——'tis ended,
And all your sufferings o'er.

   A Trumpet within. Enter HÆMON.

   Hæm. Rouse up, you Thebans ; tune your Io
      Pæans !

Your king returns ; the Argians are o'ercome ;
Their warlike prince in single combat taken,
And led in bands by godlike OEdipus.

   All. OEdipus, OEdipus, OEdipus!

   Cre. Furies confound his fortune !——   [*Aside.*

Haste, all haste.   [*To them.*

And meet with blessings our victorious king ;
Decree processions ; bid new holy-days,
Crown all the statues of our gods with garlands ;
And raise a brazen column, thus inscrib'd :
To OEdipus, now twice a conqueror : deliverer of
      his Thebes.
Trust me, I weep for joy to see this day.

   Tir. Yes, Heav'n knows how thou weep'st :—Go,
      countrymen,

And, as you use to supplicate your gods——
So meet your king with bays and olive-branches:

          C iij

An end of all your woes; for only he
Can give it you.   [*Exit* Tiresias, *the people following.*

Enter OEDIPUS *in triumph*; ADRASTUS *prisoner*;
        DYMAS, *train.*

   Cre. All hail, great OEdipus;
Thou mighty conqueror, hail; welcome to Thebes;
To thy own Thebes; to all that's left of Thebes;
For half thy citizens are swept away,
And wanting of thy triumphs:
And we, the happy remnant, only live
To welcome thee, and die.
   OEdip. Thus pleasure never comes sincere to man;
But lent by Heav'n upon hard usury;
And, while Jove holds us out the bowl of joy,
Ere it can reach our lips, it's dash'd with gall
By some left-handed god.   Oh, mournful triumph!
Oh, conquest gain'd abroad, and lost at home!
Oh, Argos! now rejoice, for Thebes lies low;
Thy slaughter'd sons now smile, and think they won;
When they can count more Theban ghosts than theirs.
   Adr. No; Argos mourns with Thebes; you tem-
        per'd so
Your courage while you fought, that mercy seem'd
The manlier virtue, and much more prevail'd.
While Argos is a people, think your Thebes
Can never want for subjects.   Every nation
Will crowd to serve where OEdipus commands.

Cre. [*To* Hæm.] How mean it shows to fawn upon
  the victor!

Hæm. Had you beheld him fight, you had said other-
  wise :

Come, 'tis brave bearing in him, not to envy
Superior virtue.

OEdip. This indeed is conquest,

To gain a friend like you : why were we foes?

Adr. 'Cause we were kings, and each disdain'd an
  equal.

I fought to have it in my pow'r to do
What thou hast done ; and so to use my conquest.
To shew thee, honour was my only motive,
Know this that were my army at thy gates,
And Thebes thus waste, I would not take the gift,
Which, like a toy dropt from the hands of fortune,
Lay for the next chance-comer.

OEdip. [*Embracing.*] No more captive,

But brother of the war : 'tis much more pleasant,
And safer, trust me, thus to meet thy love,
Than when hard gantlets clench'd our warlike hands,
And keep them from soft use.

Adr. My conqueror!

OEdip. My friend! that other name keeps enmity

Adr. I go without a blush, though conquer'd twice,
By you, and by my princess.   [*Exit* Adrastus.
   Cre. [*Aside.*] Then I am conquer'd thrice; by
       OEdipus,
And her, and ev'n by him, the slave of both :
Gods, I'm beholden to you, for making me your
       image,
Would I could make you mine!

Enter the people with branches in their hands, holding them
   up, and kneeling : two priests before them.

Alas, my people !
What means this speechless sorrow, down-cast eyes,
And lifted hands ?   If there be one among you
Whom grief has left a tongue, speak for the rest.
   1st Pr. Oh, father of thy country !
To thee these knees are bent, these eyes are lifted,
As to a visible divinity.
A prince on whom Heav'n safely might repose
The business of mankind : for Providence
Might on thy " careful" bosom sleep secure,
And leave her task to thee.
But where's the glory of thy former acts ?
Ev'n that's destroy'd, when none shall live to speak it.
Millions of subjects shalt thou have ; but mute.
A people of the dead ; a crowded desert ;
A midnight silence at the noon of day.
   OEdip. Oh, were our gods as ready with their pity,
As I with mine, this presence should be throng'd

With all I left alive; and my sad eyes
Not search in vain for friends, whose promis'd sight
Flatter'd my toils of war.

    1st Pr. Twice our deliverer.

    OEdip. Nor are now your vows
Address'd to one who sleeps.
When this unwelcome news first reach'd my ears,
Dymas was sent to Delphos, to enquire
The cause and cure of this contagious ill:
And is this day return'd? But since his message
Concerns the public, I refus'd to hear it,
But in this general presence: let him speak.

    Dym. A dreadful answer from the hallow'd urn,
And sacred Tripos did the priestess give,
In these mysterious words:

    THE ORACLE. " Shed in a cursed hour, by cursed
        hand,
Blood-royal unreveng'd has curs'd the land.
When Laius' death is expiated well,
Your plague shall cease. The rest let Laius tell."

    OEdip. Dreadful indeed! Blood! and a king's blood
        too;
And such a king's, and by his subjects shed!
(Else why this curse on Thebes?) no wonder then
If monsters, wars, and plagues revenge such crimes!
If Heav'n be just, its whole artillery,
All must be empty'd on us: not one bolt
Shall err from Thebes; but more be call'd for, more:
New moulded thunder of a larger size;
Driv'n whole by Jove. What, touch anointed pow'r!

Then, gods, beware; Jove would himself be next,
Could you but reach him too.

 2d Pr. We mourn the sad remembrance.

 OEdip. Well you may:
Worse than a plague infects you: y'are devoted
To mother earth, and to th' infernal pow'rs:
Hell has a right in you: I thank you, gods,
That I'm no Theban born. How my blood curdles!
As if this curse touch'd me, and touch'd me nearer
Than all this presence!——Yes, 'tis a king's blood,
And I, a king, am ty'd in deeper bonds
To expiate this blood——But where, from whom,
Or how must I atone it? Tell me, Thebans,
How Laius fell; for a confus'd report
Pass'd through my ears, when first I took the crown:
But full of hurry, like a morning dream,
It vanish'd in the business of the day.

 1st Pr. He went in private forth; but thinly fol-
  low'd;
And ne'er return'd to Thebes.

 OEdip. Nor any from him? Came there no attend-
  ant?
None to bring the news?

 2d Pr. But one; and he so wounded,
He scarce drew breath to speak some few faint words.

 OEdip. What were they? Something may be learn'd
  from thence.

 1st Pr. He said a band of robbers watch'd their
  passage;
Who took advantage of a narrow way

To murder Laius and the rest : himself
Left too for dead.

   OEdip. Made you no more enquiry,
But took this bare relation ?

   2d Pr. 'Twas neglected :
For then the monster Sphinx began to rage ;
And present cares soon buried the remote ;
So was it hush'd, and never since reviw'd.

   OEdip. Mark, Thebans, mark !
Just then, the Sphinx began to rage among you ;
The gods took hold ev'n of th' offending minute,
And dated thence your woes: thence will I trace
       them.

   1st Pr. 'Tis just thou shouldst.

   OEdip. Hear then this dreadful imprecation; hear it:
'Tis laid on all ; not any one exempt :
Bear witness, Heav'n, avenge it on the perjur'd.
If any Theban born, if any stranger
Reveal this murder, or produce its author,
Ten Attic talents be his just reward :
But, if for fear, for favour, or for hire,
The murd'rer he conceal, the curse of Thebes
Fall heavy on his head: unite our plagues,
Ye gods, and place them there : from fire and water,
Converse, and all things common, be he banish'd.
But for the murderer's self, unfound by man,
Find him, ye pow'rs cœlestial and infernal ;
And the same fate, or worse than Laius met,
Let be his lot: his children be accurst ;

His wife and kindred, all of his be curs'd.
   Both Pr. Confirm it, Heav'n!

        Enter JOCASTA, *attended by Women.*

   Joc. At your devotions! Heav'n succeed your
        wishes;
And bring th' effect of these your pray'rs
On you, on me, and all.
   Pr. Avert this omen, Heav'n?
   OEdip. Oh, fatal sound, unfortunate Jocasta!
What hast thou said? An ill hour hast thou chosen
For these foreboding words! Why, we were cursing!
   Joc. Then may that curse fall only where you laid it.
   OEdip. Speak no more!
For all thou say'st is ominous: we were cursing;
And that dire imprecation hast thou fasten'd
On Thebes, and thee and me, and all of us.
   Joc. Are then my blessings turn'd into a curse?
Oh, unkind OEdipus! My former lord
Thought me his blessing: be thou like my Laius.
   OEdip. What, yet again? The third time hast thou
        curs'd me:
This imprecation was for Laius' death,
And thou hast wish'd me like him.
   Joc. Horror seizes me!
   OEdip. Why dost thou gaze upon me? Pr'ythee,
        love,
Take off thy eye; it burdens me too much.
   Joc. The more I look, the more I find of Laius:

His speech, his garb, his action; nay, his frown;
(For I have seen it;) but ne'er bent on me.

  OEdip. Are we so like?

  Joc. In all things but his love.

  OEdip. I love thee more : so well I love, words
      cannot speak how well.

No pious son e'er lov'd his mother more
Than I my dear Jocasta.

  Joc. I love you too
The self-same way; and when you chid, methought
A mother's love start up in your defence,
And bade me not be angry: be not you .
For I love Laius still, as wives should love :
But you more tenderly; as part of me;
And when I have you in my arms, methinks
I lull my child asleep.

  OEdip. Then we are blest:
And all these curses sweep along the skies
Like empty clouds; but drop not on our heads.

  Joc. I have not joy'd an hour since you departed,
For public miseries, and for private fears;
But this blest meeting has o'er-paid 'em all.
Good fortune that comes seldom comes more wel-
      come.
All I can wish for now, is your consent
To make my brother happy.

  OEdip. How, Jocasta?

  Joc. By marriage with his niece, Eurydice ?

  OEdip. Uncle and niece; they are too near, my
      love :

D

'Tis too like incest : 'tis offence to kind :
Had I not promis'd, were there no Adrastus,
No choice but Creon left her of mankind,
They should not marry ; speak no more of it ;
The thoug⸺ disturbs me.

    Joc. Heav'n can never bless
A vow so broken, which I made to Creon;
Remember he's my brother.

    OEdip. That's the bar ;
And she thy daughter : nature would abhor
To be forc'd back again upon herself,
And, like a whirlpool, swallow her own streams.

    Joc. Be not displeas'd : I'll move the suit no more.

    OEdip. No, do not ; for, I know not why, it
        shakes me
When I but think on incest; move we forward
To thank the gods for my success, and pray
To wash the guilt of royal blood away.   [*Exeunt.*

ACT II. SCENE I.

An open Gallery. A Royal Bed-chamber being supposed
  behind. The Time, Night. Thunder, &c. Enter
  HÆMON, ALCANDER, *and* PYRACMON.

Hæmon.

SURE 'tis the end of all things; fate has torn
The lock of time off, and his head is now
The ghastly ball of round eternity !

Call you these peals of thunder but the yawn
Of bellowing clouds? By jove, they seem to me
The world's last groans; and those vast sheets of
       flame
Are its last blaze! The tapers of the gods
The sun and moon, run down like waxen globes;
The shooting stars end all in purple jellies,
And chaos is at hand.

    Pyr. 'Tis midnight, yet there's not a Theban sleeps,
But such as ne'er must wake. All crowd about
The palace, and implore, as from a god,
Help of the king; who, from the battlement,
By the red lightning's glare, descry'd afar,
Atones the angry pow'rs.   *[Thunder, &c.*

    Hæm. Ha! Pyracmon, look;
Behold, Alcander, from yon' west of Heav'n,
The perfect figures of a man and woman:
A sceptre bright with gems in each right hand,
Their flowing robes of dazzling purple made,
Distinctly yonder in that point they stand,
Just west; a bloody red stains all the place;
And see, their faces are quite hid in clouds.

    Pyr. Clusters of golden stars hang o'er their heads,
And seem so crowded, that they burst upon them:
All dart at once their baleful influence
In leaking fire.

    Alc. Long-bearded comets stick,
Like flaming porcupines, to their left sides,
As they would shoot their quills into their hearts.

Hæm. But see! the king, and queen, and all the
    court!
Did ever day or night shew aught like this?
    [*Thunders again. The Scene draws, and discovers*
       the Prodigies.

Enter OEDIPUS, JOCASTA, EURYDICE, ADRASTUS,
and all coming forward with Amazement.

OEdip. Answer, you Pow'rs divine; spare all this
    noise,
This rack of Heav'n, and speak your fatal pleasure.
Why breaks yon dark and dusky orb away?
Why, from the bleeding womb of monstrous night,
Burst forth such myriads of abortive stars?
Ha! my Jocasta, look! the silver moon!
A settling crimson stains her beauteous face!
She's all o'er blood! and look, behold again,
What mean the mystic heav'ns she journeys on?
A vast eclipse darkens the labouring planet:
Sound there, sound all our instruments of war;
Clarions and trumpets, silver, brass, and iron,
And beat a thousand drums to help her labour.
    Adr. 'Tis vain; you see the prodigies continue;
Let's gaze no more, the gods are humorous.
    OEdip. Forbear, rash man——Once more I ask
    your pleasure!
If that the glow-worm light of human reason
Might dare to offer at immortal knowledge,
And cope with gods, why all this storm of nature?
Why do the rocks split, and why rolls the sea?

Why these portents in Heav'n, and plagues on earth?
Why yon gigantic forms, ethereal monsters?
Alas! is all this but to fright the dwarfs
Which your own hands have made? Then be it so.
Or if the fates resolve some expiation
For murder'd Laius: hear me, hear me, gods!
Hear me thus prostrate: spare this groaning land,
Save innocent Thebes, stop the tyrant death;
Do this, and lo! I stand up an oblation
To meet your swiftest and severest anger.
Shoot all at once, and strike me to the centre.

> [*The Cloud draws that veil'd the Heads of the Figures of the sky, and shews them crowned with the Names of* OEdipus *and* Jocasta *written above in great Characters of Gold.*

Adr. Either I dream, and all my cooler senses
Are vanish'd with that cloud that fleets away,
Or just above those two majestic heads,
I see, I read distinctly in large gold,
OEdipus and Jocasta.

Alc. I read the same.

Adr. 'Tis wonderful; yet ought not man to wade
Too far in the vast deep of destiny.

> [*Thunder, and the Prodigies vanish.*

Joc. My lord, my OEdipus, why gaze you now,
When the whole heav'n is clear, as if the gods
Had some new monsters made? Will you not turn,
And bless your people, who devour each word
You breathe?

OEdip. It shall be so.

Yes, I will die, oh, Thebes, to save thee !
Draw from my heart my blood, with more content
Than e'er I wore thy crown.   Yet, oh, Jocasta!
By all th' endearments of miraculous love,
By all our languishings, our fears in pleasure,
Which oft have made us wonder; here I swear
On thy fair hand, upon thy breast I swear,
I cannot call to mind, from budding childhood
To blooming youth, a crime by me committed,
For which the awful gods should doom my death.
   Joc. 'Tis not you, my lord,
But he who murder'd Laius, frees the land :
Were you, which is impossible, the man,
Perhaps my poignard first should drink your blood ;
But you are innocent, as your Jocasta,
From crimes like those.   This made me violent
To save your life, which you unjust would lose :
Nor can you comprehend, with deepest thought,
The horrid agony you cast me in,
When you resolv'd to die.
   OEdip. Is't possible ?
   Joc. Alas, why start you so ? Her stiff'ning grief,
Who saw her children slaughter'd all at once,
Was dull to mine : methinks I should have made
My bosom bare against the armed god,
To save my OEdipus !
   OEdip. I pray, no more.
   Joc. You've silenc'd me, my lord.
   OEdip. Pardon me, dear Jocasta!
Pardon a heart that sinks with sufferings,

And can but vent itself in sobs and murmurs :
Yet to restore my peace, I'll find him out.
Yes, yes, you gods ! you shall have ample vengeance
On Laius' murderer. O, the traitor's name !
I'll know't, I will ; art shall be conjur'd for it,
And nature all unravell'd.

   Joc. Sacred sir————

   OEdip. Rage will have way, and 'tis but just ; I'll
      fetch him,
Tho' lodg'd in air, upon a dragon's wing,
Tho' rocks should hide him : nay, he shall be dragg'd
From hell, if charms can hurry him along :
His ghost shall be, by sage Tiresias' power,
(Tiresias, that rules all beneath the moon)
Confin'd to flesh, to suffer death once more ;
And then be plung'd in his first fires again.

Enter CREON.

   Cre. My lord,
Tiresias attends your pleasure.

   OEdip. Haste, and bring him in.
O, my Jocasta, Eurydice, Adrastus,
Creon, and all ye Thebans, now the end
Of plagues, of madness, murders, prodigies,
Draws on : this battle of the heav'ns and earth
Shall, by his wisdom, be reduc'd to peace.

Enter TIRESIAS, *leaning on a Staff, led by his Daughter*
MANTO, *followed by other Thebans.*

O thou, whose most aspiring mind

Knows all the business of the courts above,
Opens the closets of the gods, and dares
To mix with Jove himself and fate at council;
O prophet, answer me, declare aloud
The traitor who conspir'd the death of Laius:
Or be they more, who from malignant stars
Have drawn this plague that blasts unhappy Thebes?

   Tir. We must no more than fate commissions us
To tell; yet something, and of moment, I'll unfold,
If that the god would wake; I feel him now,
" Like a strong spirit charm'd into a tree,
" That leaps and moves the wood without a wind:
" The ɩoused god, as all this while he lay,
" Intomb'd alive, starts and dilates himself;"
He struggles, and he tears my aged trunk
With holy fury, " my old arteries burst;
" My rivell'd skin,
" Like parchment, crackles at the hallow'd fire;
" I shall be young again:" Manto, my daughter,
" Thou hast a voice that might have sav'd the bard
" Of Thrace, and forc'd the raging bacchanals,
" With lifted prongs, to listen to thy airs:"
O charm this god, this fury in my bosom,
Lull him with tuneful notes, and artful strings,
With pow'rful strains; " Manto, my lovely child,"
Sooth the unruly godhead to be mild.

SONG *to* APOLLO.

Phœbus, 'god belov'd by men,
At thy dawn, every beast is rous'd in his den;

At thy setting, all the birds of thy absence complain,
And we die, all die till the morning comes again.
   Phœbus, god belov'd by men!
   Idol of the Eastern kings,
   Awful as the god who flings
   His thunder round, and the lightning wings;
   God of songs, and Orphean strings,
   Who to this mortal bosom brings
   All harmonious heav'nly things!
   Thy drowsy prophet to revive,
Ten thousand thousand forms before him drive;
With chariots and horses all o'fire awake him,
Convulsions, and furies, and prophesies shake him.
Let him tell it in groans, tho' he bend with the load,
Tho' he burst with the weight of the terrible god.

   Tir. The wretch, who shed the blood of old Lab-
        dacides,
Lives, and is great;
But cruel greatness ne'er was long:
The first of Laius' blood his life did seize,
And urg'd his fate,
Which else had lasting been and strong.
The wretch, who Laius kill'd, must bleed or fly;
Or Thebes, consum'd with plagues, in ruins lie.
   OEdip. The first of Laius' blood! pronounce the
        person;
May the god roar from thy prophetic mouth,
That even the dead may start up, to behold.
Name him, I say, that most accursed wretch,

For, by the stars, he dies!
Speak, I command thee;
By Phœbus, speak; for sudden death's his doom;
Here shall he fall, bleed on this very spot;
His name, I charge thee once more, speak.

   Tir. 'Tis lost,
Like what we think can never shun remembrance;
Yet of a sudden's gone beyond the clouds.

   Œdip. Fetch it from thence; I'll have it, where-
     e'er it be.

   Cre. Let me intreat you, sacred sir, be calm,
And Creon shall point out the great offender.
'Tis true, respect of nature might enjoin
Me silence at another time; but, oh,
Much more the pow'r of my eternal love!
That, that should strike me dumb: yet, Thebes, my
     country——
I'll break through all to succour thee, poor city.
O, I must speak.

   Œdip. Speak then, if aught thou know'st·
As much thou seem'st to know, delay no longer.

   Cre. O beauty! O illustrious royal maid!
To whom my vows were ever paid till now,
And with such modest, chaste, and pure affection,
The coldest nymph might read 'em without blush-
     ing.
Art thou the murd'ress, then, of wretched Laius?
And I, must I accuse thee? Oh, my tears!
Why will you fall in so abhorr'd a cause?
But that thy beauteous, barbarous hand destroy'd

Thy father (O monstrous aɕt!) both gods
And men at once take notice.

　OEdip. Eurydice!

　Eur. Traitor, go on; I scorn thy little malice,
And knowing more my perfeɕt innocence,
Than gods and men, then how much more than thee,
Who art their opposite, and form'd a liar,
I thus disdain thee! Thou once didst talk of love;
Because I hate thy love,
Thou dost accuse me.

　Adr. Villain, inglorious villain,
And traitor, doubly damn'd, who durst blaspheme
The spotless virtue of the brightest beauty;
Thou dy'st : nor shall the sacred majesty

　　　　　　　　[Draws and wounds him.
That guards this place, preserve thee from my rage.

　OEdip. Disarm them both.　Prince, I shall make
　　you know
That I can tame you twice.　Guards, seize him.

　Adr. Sir,
I must acknowledge in another cause
Repentance might abash me ; but I glory
In this, and smile to see the traitor's blood.

　OEdip. Creon, you shall be satisfy'd at full.

　Cre. My hurt is nothing, sir; but I appeal
To wise Tiresias, if my accusation
Be not most true.　The first of Laius' blood
Gave him his death.　Is there a prince before her?
Then she is faultless, and I ask her pardon.
And may this blood ne'er cease to drop, O Thebes,

　　　　　　　　　1

If pity of thy sufferings did not move me
To shew the cure which Heav'n itself prescrib'd.

Eur. Yes, Thebans, I will die to save your lives,
More willingly than you can wish my fate;
But let this good, this wise, this holy man,
Pronounce my sentence: for to fall by him,
By the vile breath of that prodigious villain,
Would sink my soul, tho' I should die a martyr.

Adr. Unhand me, slaves. O mightiest of kings,
See at your feet a prince not us'd to kneel;
Touch not Eurydice, by all the gods,
As you would save your Thebes, but take my life:
For should she perish, Heav'n would heap plagues on
　　　　plagues,
Rain sulphur down, hurl kindled bolts
Upon your guilty heads.

Cre. You turn to gallantry, what is but justice:
Proof will be easy made. Adrastus was
The robber who bereft th' unhappy king
Of life; because he flatly had deny'd
To make so poor a prince his son-in-law:
Therefore 'twere fit that both should perish.

1 Theb. Both, let both die.

All Theb. Both, both; let them die.

OEdip. Hence, you wild herd! For your ringleader
　　, here,
He shall be made example. Hæmon, take him.

1 Theb. Mercy! O mercy!

OEdip. Mutiny in my presence!
Hence, let me see that busy face no more.

Tir. Thebans, what madness makes you drunk with
     rage ?
Enough of guilty death's already aɛ̃ed ;
Fierce Creon has accused Eurydice,
With prince Adrastus ; which the god reproves
By inward checks, and leaves their fates in doubt.

    OEdip. Therefore instruɛ̃ us what remains to do,
Or suffer ; for I feel a sleep like death
Upon me, and I sigh to be at rest.

    Tir. Since that the pow'rs divine refuse to clear
The mystic deed, I'll to the Grove of Furies ;
There I can force the infernal gods to shew
Their horrid forms ; each trembling ghost shall rise,
And leave their grisly king without a waiter.
For prince Adrastus and Eurydice
My life's engag'd ; I'll guard them in the fane,
Till the dark mysteries of hell are done.
Follow me, princes. Thebans, all to rest.
O, OEdipus, to-morrow—but no more.
If that thy wakeful genius will permit,
Indulge thy brain this night with softer slumbers :
To-morrow, O to morrow !——sleep, my son ;
And in prophetic dreams thy fate be shewn.
         [*Exeunt* Tir. Adr. Eur. Man. *and Thebans.*

    OEdip. To bed, my fair, my dear, my best Jo-
     casta.
After the toils of war, 'tis wondrous strange
Our loves should thus be dash'd. One moment's
     thought,
And I'll approach the arms of my belov'd.

Joc. Consume whole years in care, so now and then
I may have leave to feed my famish'd eyes
With one short passing glance, and sigh my vows:
This and no more, my lord, is all the passion
Of languishing Jocasta.   [*Exit.*

   OEdip. Thou softest, sweetest of the world! good
      night.
Nay, she is beauteous too; yet, mighty love!
I never offer'd to obey thy laws,
But an unusual chillness came upon me;
An unknown hand still check'd my forward joy,
Dash'd me with blushes, tho' no light was near;
That even the act became a violation.

   Pyr. He's strangely thoughtful.

   OEdip. Hark! who was that! Ha! Creon, didst
      thou call me?

   Cre. Not I, my gracious lord, nor any here.

   OEdip. That's strange! methought I heard a dole-
      ful voice
Cry OEdipus—The prophet bad me sleep.
He talk'd of dreams, of visions, and to-morrow!
I'll muse no more, come what will or can.
My thoughts are clearer than unclouded stars;
And with those thoughts I'll rest.   Creon, good
      night.   [*Exit with* Hæm.

   Cre. Sleep seal your eyes up, sir, eternal sleep.
But if he sleep and wake again, O all
Tormenting dreams, wild horrors of the night,
And hags of fancy, wing him through the air:
From precipices hurl him headlong down;

Charybdis' roar, and death be set before him.

    Alc. Your curses have already ta'en effect;
For he looks very sad.

    Cre. May he be rooted where he stands for ever;
His eye-balls never move, brows be unbent,
His blood, his entrails, liver, heart, and bowels,
Be blacker than the place I wish him, hell.

    Pyr. No more ; you tear yourself, but vex not him.
Methinks 'twere brave this night to force the temple,
While blind Tiresias conjures up the fiends,
And pass the time with nice Eurydice.

    Alc. Try promises and threats, and if all fail,
Since hell's broke loose, why should not you be mad?
Ravish, and leave her dead with her Adrastus.

    Cre. Were the globe mine, I'd give a province
        hourly
For such another thought. Lust and revenge!
To stab at once the only man I hate,
And to enjoy the woman whom I love!
I ask no more of my auspicious stars.
The rest as fortune please; so but this night
She play me fair, why, let her turn for ever.

Enter HÆMON.

    Hæm. My lord, the troubled king is gone to rest;
Yet, ere he slept, commanded me to clear
The antichambers: none must dare be near him.

    Cre. Hæmon, you do your duty——   [*Thunder.*
And we obey.—The night grows yet more dreadful!
'Tis just that all retire to their devotions.

F

The gods are angry : but to-morrow's dawn,
If prophets do not lie, will make all clear.

As they go off, OEDIPUS *enters, walking asleep in his
Shirt, with a Dagger in his right-hand, and a Taper
in his left.*

OEdip. O, my Jocasta! 'tis for this the wet
Starv'd soldier lies on the cold ground ;
For this he bears the storms
Of winter camps, and freezes in his arms :
To be thus circled, to be thus embrac'd;
That I could hold thee ever!—Ha! where art thou?
What means this melancholy light, that seems
The gloom of glowing embers?
The curtain's drawn ; and see, she's here again!
Jocasta! Ha! what, fall'n asleep so soon?
How fares my love? This taper will inform me.
Ha! lightning blast me, thunder
Rivet me ever to Prometheus' rock,
And vultures gnaw out my incestuous heart.
By all the gods, my mother Merope!
My sword, a dagger! Ha, who waits there? Slaves,
My sword.   What, Hæmon, dar'st thou, villain,
       stop me :
With thy own poignard perish. Ha! who's this?
Or is't a change of death? By all my honours,
New murder ; thou hast slain old Polybus :
Incest and parricide, thy father's murdered!
Out, thou infernal flame : now all is dark,
All blind and dismal, most triumphant mischief!

And now, while thus I stalk about the room,
I challenge fate to find another wretch
Like OEdipus!   [*Thunder, &c.*

Enter JOCASTA *attended, with Lights, in a Night-gown.*

Night, horror, death, confusion, hell, and furies !
Where am I ? O, Jocasta, let me hold thee :
Thus to my bosom, ages let me grasp thee.
All that the hardest temper'd weather'd flesh,
With fiercest human spirit inspir'd, can dare,
Or do, I dare ; but, O you pow'rs, this was
By infinite degrees too much for man.
Methinks my deafen'd ears
Are burst; my eyes, as if they had been knock'd
By some tempestuous hand, shoot flashing fire.
That sleep should do this!

    Joc. Then my fears were true.
Methought I heard your voice, and yet I doubted,
Now roaring like the ocean, when the winds
Fight with the waves; now, in a still small tone
Your dying accents fell, as racking ships,
After the dreadful yell, sink murm'ring down,
And bubble up a noise.

    OEdip. Trust me, thou fairest, best of all thy kind,
None e'er in dreams was toitur'd so before.
Yet what most shocks the niceness of my temper,
Ev'n far beyond the killing of my father,
And my own death, is that this horrid sleep
Dash'd my sick fancy with an act of incest:

E iij

I dream'd, Jocasta, that thou wert my mother;
Which, tho' impossible, so damps my spirits,
That I could do a mischief on myself,
Lest I should sleep and dream the like again.

Joc. O, OEdipus, too well I understand you!
I know the wrath of Heav'n, the care of Thebes,
The cries of its inhabitants, war's toils,
And thousand other labours of the state,
Are all referr'd to you, and ought to take you
For ever from Jocasta.

OEdip. Life of my life, and treasure of my soul,
Heav'n knows I love thee.

Joc. O, you think me vile,
And of an inclination so ignoble,
That I must hide me from your eyes for ever.
Be witness, gods, and strike Jocasta dead,
If an immodest thought, or low desire,
Inflam'd my breast, since first our loves were lighted.

OEdip. O rise, and add not, by thy cruel kindness,
A grief more sensible than all my torments.
Thou think'st my dreams are forg'd; but by thyself,
The greatest oath I swear, they are most true.
But, be they what they will, I here dismiss them.
Begone, chimæras, to your mother clouds.
Is there a fault in us? Have we not search'd
The womb of Heav'n, examin'd all the entrails
Of birds and beasts, and tired the prophet's art?
Yet what avails? He, and the gods together,
Seem, like physicians, at a loss to help us;
Therefore, like wretches that have linger'd long,

We'll snatch the strongest cordial of our love.—
To bed, my fair.

   Ghost within. OEdipus!

   OEdip. Ha! who calls?
Didst thou not hear a voice?

   Joc. Alas! I did.

   Ghost. Jocasta!

   Joc. O, my love, my lord, support me!

   OEdip. Call louder, till you burst your airy forms.
Rest on my hand. Thus, arm'd with innocence,
I'll face these babbling dæmons of the air:
In spite of ghosts, I'll on.
Tho' round my bed the furies plant their charms,
I'll break them with Jocasta in my arms;
Clasp'd in the folds of love, I'll wait my doom,
And act my joys, tho' thunder shake the room.

                         [Exeunt.

ACT III. SCENE I.

A dark Grove.   Enter CREON *and* DIOCLES.

Creon.

'Tis better not to be, than be unhappy.

   Dioc. What mean you by these words?

   Cre. 'Tis better not to be, than to be Creon.
A thinking soul is punishment enough;
But when 'tis great, like mine, and wretched too,
Then every thought draws blood.

Dioc. You are not wretched.

Cre. I am: my soul's ill-married to my body;
I would be young, be handsome, be belov'd:
Could I but breathe myself into Adrastus——

Dioc. You rave; call home your thoughts.

Cre. I pr'ythee let my soul take air awhile:
Were she in OEdipus, I were a king;
Then I had kill'd a monster, gain'd a battle,
And had my rival pris'ner; brave, brave actions:
Why have not I done these?

Dioc. Your fortune hinder'd.

Cre. There's it. I have a soul to do them all:
But fortune will have nothing done that's great
But by young handsome fools: body and brawn
Do all her work: Hercules was a fool,
And straight grew famous: a mad boist'rous fool:
Nay, worse, a woman's fool.
Fool is the stuff, of which Heav'n makes a hero.

Dioc. A serpent ne'er becomes a flying dragon,
Till he has eat a serpent.

Cre. Goes it there?
I understand thee; I must kill Adrastus.

Dioc. Or not enjoy your mistress.
Eurydice and he are pris'ners here,
But will not long be so: this tell-tale ghost
Perhaps will clear them both.

Cre. Well; 'tis resolv'd.

Dioc. The princess walks this way;
You must not meet her
Till this be done.

I must.

c. She hates your sight;
more since you accus'd her.

. Urge it not.
not stay to tell thee my design,
he's too near.

Enter EURYDICE.

, madam, were your thoughts employ'd ?

r. On death and thee.

e. Then they were not well sorted : life and me
been the better match.

r. No, I was thinking
wo the most detested things in nature :
  they are death and thee.

e. The thought of death to one near death is
      dreadful !
'tis a fearful thing to be no more.
f to be, to wander after death ;
walk as spirits do, in brakes all day ;
l when the darkness comes to glide in paths
it lead to graves ; and in the silent vault,
ere lies your own pale shroud, to hover o'er it,
ving to enter your forbidden corpse ;
l often, often, vainly breathe your ghost
) your lifeless lips :
  n, like a lone benighted traveller,
it out from lodging, shall your groans be answer'd
whistling winds, whose every blast will shake
ur tender form to atoms.

Eur. Must I be this thin being, and thus wander,
No quiet after death?

Cre. None: you must leave
This beauteous body; all this youth and freshness
Must be no more the object of desire,
But a cold lump of clay;
Which then your discontented ghost will leave,
And loath its former lodging.
This is the best of what comes after death,
Ev'n to the best.

Eur. What then shall be thy lot!
Eternal torments, baths of boiling sulphur;
Vicissitudes of fires, and then of frosts:
And an old guardian fiend, ugly as thou art,
To hollow in thy ears at every lash,
This for Eurvdice; these for her Adrastus!

Cre. For her Adrastus!

Eur. Yes, for her Adrastus;
For death shall ne'er divide us. Death! what's death?
" *Dioc.* You seem'd to fear it.
" *Eur.* But I more fear Creon:
" To take that hunch-back'd monster in my arms,
" Th' excrescence of a man.
" *Dioc.* [*To* Cre.] See what you've gain'd.
" *Eur.* Death only can be dreadful to the bad:
" To innocence, 'tis like a bug-bear dress'd
" To frighten children; pull but off his mask,
" And he'll appear a friend."

Cre. You talk too slightly
Of death and hell. Let me inform you better.

Eur. You best can tell the news of your own
country.

Dioc. Nay, now you are too sharp.

Eur. Can I be so to one who has accus'd me
Of murder and of parricide ?

Cre. You provok'd me :
And yet I only did thus far accuse you,
As next of blood to Laius : be advis'd,
And you may live.

Eur. The means ?

Cre. 'Tis offer'd you ;
The fool Adrastus has accus'd himself.

Eur. He has indeed, to take the guilt from me.

Cre. He says he loves you; if he does, 'tis well :
He ne'er could prove it in a better time.

Eur. Then death must be his recompence for love ?

Cre. 'Tis a fool's just reward ;
The wise can make a better use of life :
But 'tis the young man's pleasure ; his ambition :
I grudge him not that favour.

Eur. When he's dead,
Where shall I find his equal ?

Cre. Every where.
Fine empty things, like him,
The court swarms with them.
Fine fighting things ; in camps they are so common,
Crows feed on nothing else; plenty of fools ;
A glut of them in Thebes.
And fortune still takes care they should be seen :
She places them aloft, o' th' topmost spoke

Of all her wheel: fools are the daily work
Of nature; her vocation; if she form
A man, she loses by't, 'tis too expensive;
'Twould make ten fools: a man's a prodigy.

 Eur. That is, a Creon: O thou black detraĉtor,
" Who spitt'st thy venom against gods and men !
" Thou enemy of eyes :"
Thou, who lov'st nothing but what nothing loves,
And that's thyself: who hast conspir'd against
My life and fame, to make me loath'd by all,
And only fit for thee.
But for Adrastus' death, good gods, his death !
What curse shall I invent ?

 Dioc. No more—he's here.

 Eur. He shall be ever here.
He who would give his life, give up his fame——

Enter ADRASTUS.

If all the excellence of woman-kind
Were mine——No, 'tis too little all for him :
Were I made up of endless, endless joys——

 Adr. And so thou art :
The man who loves like me,
Would think ev'n infamy, the worst of ills,
Were cheaply purchas'd, were thy love the price.
Uncrown'd, a captive, nothing left but honour,
'Tis the last thing a prince should throw away :
But when the storm grows loud, and threatens love,
Throw ev'n that over-board; for love's the jewel,
And last it must be kept.

Cre. [*To* Dioc.] Work him, be sure,
To rage—He's passionate ;
Make him th' aggressor.

    Dioc. Oh, false love! false honour!

    Cre. Dissembled both, and false!

    Adr. Dar'st thou say this to me?

    Cre. To you! why, what are you, that I should fear
        you?
I am not Laius.   Hear me, Prince of Argos.
You give what's nothing, when you give your honour;
'Tis gone, 'tis lost in battle.   For your love,
Vows made in wine are not so false as that:
You kill'd her father ; you confess'd you did :
A mighty argument to prove your passion to the
        daughter!

    Adr. [*Aside.*] Gods, must I bear this brand, and
        not retort
The lie to his foul throat!

    Dioc. Basely you kill'd him.

    Adr. [*Aside.*] Oh, I burn inward! my blood's all
        o' fire!
Alcides, when the poison'd shirt sat closest,
Had but an ague-fit to this my fever.
Yet, for Eurydice, ev'n this I'll suffer,
To free my love——Well, then, I kill'd him basely.

    Cre. Fairly, I'm sure, you could not.

    Dioc. Nor alone.

    Cre. You had your fellow thieves about you, prince:
They conquer'd, and you kill'd.

F

Adr. [*Aside.*] Down, swelling heart!

'Tis for thy princess, all—Oh, my Eurydice! [*To her.*

Eur. [*To him.*] Reproach not thus the weakness of
    my sex,

As if I could not bear a shameful death,

Rather than see you burden'd with a crime

Of which I know you free.

Cre. You do ill, madam,

To let your headlong love triumph o'er nature.

Dare you defend your father's murderer?

Eur. You know he kill'd him not.

Cre. Let him say so.

Dioc. See, he stands mute.

Cre. Oh, pow'r of conscience! ev'n in wicked men

It works, it stings, it will not let him utter

One syllable, one No, to clear himself

From the most base, detested, horrid act,

That e'er could stain a villain, not a prince.

Adr. Ha! villain!

Cre. Echo to him, groves, cry villain.

Adr. Let me consider—Did I murder Laius,

Thus like a villain?

Cre. Best revoke your words,

And say, you kill'd him not.

Adr. Not like a villain; pr'ythee, change me that

For any other lye.

Dioc. No, villain, villain.

Cre. You kill'd him not——Proclaim your inno-
    cence,

Accuse the princess: so I knew 'twould be.

Adr. I thank thee; thou instruct'st me.
No matter how I kill'd him.

   Cre. [*Aside.*] Cool'd again!

   Eur. Thou, who usurp'st the sacred name of con-
      science,
Did not thy own self declare him innocent?
To me declare him so? The king shall know it.

   Cre. You will not be believ'd; for I'll forswear it.

   Eur. What's now thy conscience?

   Cre. 'Tis my slave, my drudge, my supple glove,
My upper garment, to put on, throw off,
As I think best: 'tis my obedient conscience.

   Adr. Infamous wretch!

   Cre. My conscience shall not do me the ill office
To save a rival's life: when thou art dead,
(As dead thou shalt be, or be yet more base
Than thou think'st me,
By forfeiting her life, to save thy own)
Know this, and let it grate thy very soul,
She shall be mine: (she is, if vows were binding)
Mark me, the fruit of all thy faith and passion,
Ev'n of thy foolish death, shall all be mine.

   Adr. Thine, say'st thou, monster?
Shall my love be thine?
Oh, I can bear no more!
Thy cunning engines have with labour rais'd
My heavy anger, like a mighty weight,
To fall and strike thee dead.
See here thy nuptials; see, thou rash Ixion, [*Draws.*
Thy promis'd Juno vanish'd in a cloud,

And in her room avenging thunder rolls
To blast thee thus——Come both——   [*Both draw.*
    Cre. 'Tis what I wish'd ——
Now see whose arm can launch the surer bolt,
And who's the better Jove——   [*Fight.*
    Eur. Help, murder, help !

Enter HÆMON *and Guards, run betwixt them, and beat*
down their swords.

    Hæm. Hold, hold your impious hands ?   I think
     the furies,
To whom this grove is hallow'd, have inspir'd you.
Now, by my soul, the holiest earth of Thebes
You have profan'd with war.   Nor tree, nor plant
Grows here, but what is fed with magic juice,
All full of human souls, that cleave their barks
To dance at midnight by the moon's pale beams.
At least two hundred years these reverend shades
Have known no blood, but of black sheep and oxen,
Shed by the priest's own hand to Proserpine.
    Adr. Forgive a stranger's ignorance—I knew not
The honours of the place.
    Hæm. Thou, Creon, didst.
Not OEdipus, were all his foes here lodg'd,
Durst violate the religion of these groves,
To touch one single hair; but must, unarm'd,
Parle, as in truce, or surlily avoid
What most he long'd to kill.
    Cre. I drew not first;
But in my own defence.

Adr. I was provok'd
Beyond man's patience; all reproach could urge
Was us'd to kindle one not apt to bear.

Hæm. 'Tis OEdipus, not I, must judge this act.
Lord Creon, you and Diocles retire;
Tiresias and the brotherhood of priests
Approach the place. None at these rites assist,
But you th' accus'd, who by the mouth of Laius
Must be absolv'd or doom'd.

Adr. I bear my fortune.

Eur. And I provoke my trial.

Hæm. 'Tis at hand:
For see, the prophet comes with vervain crown'd,
The priests with yew; a venerable band.
We leave you to the gods.

        [*Exit* Hæmon, *with* Creon *and* Diocles.

Enter TIRESIAS, *led by* MANTO; *the Priests follow,*
all clothed in long black habits.

Tir. Approach, ye lovers:
Ill-fated pair, whom, seeing not, I know.
This day your kindly stars in heav'n were join'd;
When lo, an envious planet interpos'd,
And threaten'd both with death. I fear, I fear.

Eur. Is there no god so much a friend to love,
Who can controul the malice of our fate?
Are they all deaf? Or have the giants heav'n?

Tir. The gods are just——
But how can finite measure infinite?
Reason! alas, it does not know itself!

Yet man, vain man, would, with his short-lin'd plum_
    met,
Fathom the vast abyss of heav'nly justice.
Whatever is, is in its causes just ;
Since all things are by fate.   But purblind man
Sees but a part o' th' chain ; the nearest links ;
His eyes not carrying to that equal beam
That poises all above.
    Eur. Then we must die !
 / *Tir.* The danger's imminent this day.
    Adr. " Why then there's one day less for human
    ills;
" And who would moan himself for suffering that
" Which in a day must pass? Something or nothing :
" I shall be what I was again, before
" I was Adrastus."
Penurious Heav'n I canst thou not add a night
To our one day? Give me a night with her,
And I'll give all the rest.
    Tir. She broke her vow
First made to Creon.   But the time calls on ;
And Laius' death must now be made more plain.
How loth I am to have recourse to rites
So full of horror, that I once rejoice
I want the use of sight.
    1st Pr. The ceremonies stay.
    Tir. Choose the darkest part o' th' grove,
Such as ghosts at noon-day love.
Dig a trench, and dig it nigh
Where the bones of Laius lie,

Altars rais'd of turf or stone
Will th' infernal pow'rs have none.
Answer me if this be done?
   All Pr. 'Tis done.
   Tir. Is the sacrifice made fit?
Draw her backward to the pit;
Draw the barren heifer back;
Barren let her be, and black.
Cut the curled hair that grows
Full betwixt her horns and brows;
And turn your faces from the sun.
Answer me if this be done?
   All Pr. 'Tis done.
   Tir. Pour in blood, and blood like wine,
To mother Earth and Proserpine;
Mingle milk into the stream;
Feast the ghosts that love the steam;
Snatch a brand from funeral pile,
Toss it in, to make them boil;
And turn your faces from the sun.
Answer me if all be done?
   All. Pr. All is done.
     [*Peals of thunder, and flashes of lightning; then
       groaning below the stage.*
   Man. Oh, what laments are those?
   Tir. The groans of ghosts that cleave the earth
     with pain,
And heave it up; they pant and stick half way.
             [*The stage wholly darkened.*

Man. And now a sudden darkness covers all;
True, genuine night; night added to the groves;
The fogs are blown full in the face of heav'n.

   Tir. Am I but half obey'd? Infernal gods,
Must you have music too? Then tune your voices,
And let them have such sounds as hell ne'er **heard**
Since Orpheus brib'd the shades.

         " *Music first, then sing.*

  " 1. Hear, ye sullen pow'rs below;
       " Hear, ye taskers of the dead:
  " 2. You that boiling cauldrons blow,
       " You that scum the molten lead.
  " 3. You that pinch with red-hot tongs:
  " 1. You that drive the trembling hosts
      " Of poor, poor ghosts,
     " With your sharpen'd prongs.
  " 2. You that thrust them off the brim,
  " 3. You that plunge them when they swim,
  " 1. Till they drown,
      " Till they go,
      " On a row,
     " Down, down, down,
    " Ten thousand, thousand, thousand fathoms low.
  " *Chorus.* Till they drown, *&c.*
  " 1. Music for a while
     " Shall your cares beguile,
     " Wondring how your pains were eas'd;
  " 2. And disdaining to be pleas'd,

" 3. Till Alecto free the dead
    " From their eternal bands;
" Till the snakes drop from her head,
    " And whip from out her hands.
" 1. Come away,
    " Do not stay,
    " But obey,
    " While we play,
    " For hell's broke up, and ghosts have holiday.
" *Chorus.* Come away, &c.
" [*A flash of lightning : the stage is made bright, and*
    " *the ghosts are seen passing betwixt the trees.*
" 1. Laius !   2. Laius !   3. Laius !
" 1. Hear !   2. Hear !   3. Hear !
" *Tir.* Hear and appear.
" By the Fates that spun thy thread,
" *Cho.* Which are three.
" *Tir.* By the Furies fierce and dread,
" *Cho.* Which are three.
" *Tir.* By the Judges of the dead,
" *Cho.* Which are three.
    " Three times three.
" *Tir.* By Hell's blue flame;
    " By the Stygian lake;
" And by Demogorgon's name,
    " At which ghosts quake,
" Hear and appear !"
[*The Ghost of* Laius *rises, armed in his Chariot, as he was slain ; and behind his Chariot sit the three who were murdered with him.*

Ghost of Laius. Why hast thou drawn me from my
       pains below,
To suffer worse above; to see the day,
And Thebes more hated? Hell is heav'n to Thebes.
For pity, send me back, where I may hide,
In willing night, this ignominious head.
In hell I shun the public scorn; and then
They hunt me for their sport, and hoot me as I fly:
Behold, ev'n now, they grin at my gor'd side,
And chatter at my wounds.
    Tir. I pity thee.
Tell but why Thebes is for thy death accurs'd,
And I'll unbind the charm.
    Ghost. Oh, spare my shame!
    Tir. Are these two innocent?
    Ghost. Of my death they are.
But he who holds my crown, oh, must I speak!
Was doom'd to do what nature most abhors.
The gods foresaw it, and forbade his being
Before he yet was born. I broke their laws,
And cloth'd with flesh his pre-existing soul.
Some kinder pow'r, too weak for destiny,
Took pity, and endu'd his new-form'd mass
With temperance, justice, prudence, fortitude,
And every kingly virtue. But in vain;
For fate, that sent him hoodwink'd to the world,
Perform'd its work by his mistaken hands.
Ask'st thou who murder'd me? 'Twas OEdipus.
Who stains my bed with incest? OEdipus.
For whom then are you curs'd, but OEdipus?

He comes! the parricide! I cannot bear him!
My wounds ake at him! Oh, his murd'rous breath
Venoms my airy substance! Hence with him,
Banish him, sweep him out; the plagues he bears
Will blast your fields, and mark his way with ruin.
From Thebes, my throne, my bed, let him be driven;
Do you forbid him earth, and I'll forbid him heav'n.
[*Ghost descends.*

Enter OEDIPUS, CREON, HÆMON, *&c.*

OEdip. What's this? Methought some pestilential
blast
Struck me just entering; and some unseen hand
Struggled to push me backward. Tell me why
My hair stands bristling up, why my flesh trembles?
You stare at me! Then hell has been among ye,
And some lag fiend yet lingers in the grove.
Tir. What omen saws't thou, ent'ring?
OEdip. A young stork,
That bore his aged parent on his back,
Till, weary with the weight, he shook him off,
And peck'd out both his eyes.
Adr. Oh, OEdipus!
Eur. Oh, wretched OEdipus!
Tir. Oh, fatal king!
OEdip. What mean these exclamations on my name?
I thank the gods, no secret thoughts reproach me.
" No, I dare challenge Heav'n to turn me outward,
" And shake my soul quite empty in your sight."
Then wonder not that I can bear unmov'd

These fix'd regards, and silent threats of eyes.
A generous fierceness dwells with innocence;
And conscious virtue is allow'd some pride.

　　Tir. Thou know'st not what thou say'st.

　　OEdip. What mutters he? Tell me, Eurydice—
Thou shak'st—thy soul's a woman. Speak, Adrastus,
And boldly, as thou met'st my arm in fight.
Dar'st thou not speak? Why, then 'tis bad indeed.
Tiresias, thee I summon by thy priesthood;
Tell me what news from hell; where Laius points,
And who's the guilty head?

　　Tir. Let me not answer.

　　OEdip. Be dumb, then, and betray thy native soil
To farther plagues.

　　Tir. I dare not name him to thee.

　　OEdip. Dar'st thou converse with hell, and canst
　　　　thou fear
An human name?

　　Tir. Urge me no more to tell a thing, which,
　　　　known,
Would make thee more unhappy. 'Twill be found,
Tho' I am silent.

　　OEdip. Old and obstinate! Then thou thyself
Art author or accomplice of this murder;
And shunn'st the justice, which, by public ban,
Thou hast incurr'd.

　　Tir. Oh, if the guilt were mine,
It were not half so great! Know, wretched man,
Thou, only thou art guilty; thy own curse
Falls heavy on thyself.

OEdip. Speak this again:
But speak it to the winds when they are loudest,
Or to the raging seas ; they'll hear as soon,
And sooner will believe.

　　Tir. Then hear me, Heav'n,
For, blushing, thou hast seen it : hear me, earth,
Whose hollow womb could not contain this murder,
But sent it back to light: and thou, hell, hear me,
Whose own black seal has 'firm'd this horrid truth :
OEdipus murdered Laius.

　　OEdip. Rot the tongue,
And blasted be the mouth that spoke that lye,
Thou blind of sight, but thou more blind of soul—

　　Tir. Thy parents thought not so.

　　OEdip. Who were my parents ?

　　Tir. Thou shalt know too soon.

　　OEdip. Why seek I truth from thee ?
The smiles of courtiers, and the harlot's tears,
The tradesman's oaths, and mourning of an heir,
Are truths to what priests tell.
Oh, why has priesthood privilege to lye,
And yet to be believ'd !—Thy age protects thee—

　　Tir. Thou canst not kill me ; 'tis not in thy fate,
As 'twas to kill thy father, wed thy mother,
And beget sons, thy brothers.

　　OEdip. Riddles, riddles !

　　Tir. Thou art thyself a riddle, a perplex'd,
Obscure ænigma, which, when thou unty'st,
Thou shalt be found and lost.

　　OEdip. Impossible !

G

Adrastus, speak; and, as thou art a king,
Whose royal word is sacred, clear my fame.

  Adr. Would I could!

  OEdip. Ha! wilt thou not? Can that plebeian vice
Of lying mount to kings? Can they be tainted?
Then truth is lost on earth.

  Cre. The cheat's too gross.
Adrastus is his oracle, and he,
The pious juggler, but Adrastus' organ.

  OEdip. 'Tis plain; the priest's suborn'd to free the
        pris'ner.

  Cre. And turn the guilt on you.

  OEdip. Oh, honest Creon, how hast thou been
        bely'd!

  Eur. Hear me.

  Cre. She's brib'd to save her lover's life.

  Adr. If, OEdipus, thou think'st——

  Cre. Hear him not speak.

  Adr. Then hear these holy men.

  Cre. Priests, priests, all brib'd, all priests!

  OEdip. Adrastus, I have found thee:
The malice of a vanquish'd man has seiz'd thee.

  Adr. If envy, and not truth——

  OEdip. I'll hear no more: away with him.
[Hæmon *takes him off by force*; Creon *and* Eur. *follow.*
[*To* Tir.] Why stand'st thou here, impostor?
So old and yet so wicked!—Lye for gain,
And gain so short as age can promise thee!

  Tir. So short a time as I have yet to live
Exceeds thy pointed hour. Remember Laius——

No more—if e'er we meet again, 'twill be
In mutual darkness; we shall feel before us,
To reach each other's hand—Remember Laius.

            [*Exit* Tiresias; *Priests follow.*

OEdip. Remember Laius! that's the burden still.
Murder and incest! But to hear them nam'd
My soul starts in me: " the good centinel
" Stands to his weapons, takes the first alarm,
" To guard me from such crimes." Did I kill Laius?
Then I walk'd sleeping, in some frightful dream;
My soul then stole my body out by night,
And brought me back to bed erē morning-wake.
It cannot be, ev'n this remotest way;
But some dark hint would justle forward now,
And goad my memory——Oh, my Jocasta!

Enter JOCASTA.

  Joc. Why are you thus disturb'd?
  OEdip. Why, wouldst thou think it?
No less than murder.
  Joc. Murder! what of murder?
  OEdip. Is murder then no more? Add parricide
And incest—bear not these a frightful sound?
  Joc. Alas!
  OEdip. How poor a pity is alas,
For two such crimes!—Was Laius us'd to lye?
  Joc. Oh, no! the most sincere, plain, honest man;
One who abhorr'd a lye.
  OEdip. Then he has got that quality in hell.
He charges me——but why accuse I him?

G ij

I did not hear him speak it.   They accuse me,
The priest, Adrastus, and Eurydice,
Of murdering Laius——Tell me, while I think on't,
Has old Tiresias practis'd long this trade?

    Joc. What trade?

    OEdip. Why, this foretelling trade.

    Joc. For many years.

    OEdip. Has he before this day accus'd me?

    Joc. Never.

    OEdip. Have you, ere this, enquir'd who did this
       murder?

    Joc. Often; but still in vain.

    OEdip. I am satisfy'd.

Then 'tis an infant-lye; but one day old.
The oracle takes place before the priest;
The blood of Laius was to murder Laius:
I'm not of Laius' blood.

    Joc. Ev'n oracles
Are always doubtful, and are often forg'd:
Laius had one, which never was fulfill'd,
Nor ever can be now.

    OEdip. And what foretold it?

    Joc. That he should have a son by me, fore-doom'd
The murderer of his father.   True, indeed,
A son was born; but, to prevent that crime,
The wretched infant of a guilty fate,
Bor'd through his untry'd feet, and bound with cords,
On a bleak mountain naked was expos'd.
The king himself liv'd many, many years,
And found a different fate; by robbers murder'd,

Where three ways meet.   Yet these are oracles;
And this the faith we owe them.

   OEdip. Say'st thou, woman?
By Heav'n, thou hast awaken'd somewhat in me
That shakes my very soul!

   Joc. What new disturbance?————

   OEdip. Methought thou said'st, or do I dream thou
      said'st it?
This murder was on Laius' person done
Where three ways meet.

   Joc. So common fame reports.

   OEdip. Would it had ly'd!

   Joc. Why, good my lord?

   OEdip. No questions.
'Tis busy time with me; dispatch mine first.
Say, where, where was it done?

   Joc. Mean you the murder?

   OEdip. Couldst thou not answer without naming
      murder?

   Joc. They say in Phocide; on the verge that
      parts it
From Dalia, and from Delphos.

   OEdip. So——How long? When happen'd this?

   Joc. Some little time before you came to Thebes.

   OEdip. What will the gods do with me?

   Joc. What means that thought?

   OEdip. Something—But 'tis not yet your turn to ask,
How old was Laius, what his shape, his stature,
His action, and his mien? Quick, quick, your answer.

   Joc. Big made he was, and tall; his port was fierce,

Erect his countenance; manly majesty
Sat in his front, and darted from his eyes,
Commanding all he viewed; his hair iust grisled,
As in a green old age.   Bate but his years,
You are his picture.

    OEdip. [*Aside.*] Pray Heav'n he drew me not! Am
        I his picture?

    Joc. So I have often told you.

    OEdip. True, you have:
Add that unto the rest.   How was the king
Attended when he travell'd?

    Joc. By four servants.
He went out privately.

    OEdip. Well counted still!
One 'scap'd, I hear.   What since became of him?

    Joc. When he beheld you first, as king in Thebes,
He kneel'd, and, trembling, begg'd I would dismiss
        him.
He had my leave; and now he lives retir'd.

    OEdip. This man must be produc'd; he must, Jo-
        casta.

    Joc. He shall—Yet have I leave to ask you why?

    OEdip. Yes, you shall know; for where should I
        repose
The anguish of my soul, but in your breast?
I need not tell you Corinth claims my birth;
My parents, Polybus and Merope,
Two royal names; their only child am I.
It happen'd once, 'twas at a bridal feast,
One, warm with wine, told me I was a foundling.

Not the king's son: I, stung with this reproach,
Struck him; my father heard of it; the man
Was made ask pardon, and the business hush'd.

Joc. 'Twas somewhat odd.

OEdip. And strangely it perplex'd me.
I stole away to Delphos, and implor'd
The god to tell my certain parentage.
He bade me seek no farther; 'twas my fate
To kill my father, and pollute his bed,
By marrying her who bore me.

Joc. Vain, vain oracles!

OEdip. But yet they frighted me.
I look'd on Corinth as a place accurs'd;
Resolv'd my destiny should wait in vain,
And never catch me there.

Joc. Too nice a fear.

OEdip Suspend your thoughts, and flatter not too
    soon.
Just in the place you nam'd, where three ways meet,
And near that time, five persons I encounter'd;
One was too like (Heav'n grant it prove not him!)
The person you describe for Laius: insolent
And fierce they were, as men who liv'd on spoil;
I judg'd them robbers, and by force repell'd
The force they us'd. In short, four men I slew;
The fifth, upon his knees, demanding life,
My mercy gave it——Bring me comfort now.
If I slew Laius, what can be more wretched?
From Thebes and you my curse has banish'd me;
From Corinth, fate.

Joc. Perplex not thus your mind.
My husband fell by multitudes oppress'd ;
So Phorbas said.   This band you chanc'd to meet;
And murder'd not my Laius, but reveng'd him.

   OEdip. There's all my hope : let Phorbas tell me
      ·this,
And I shall live again.
To you, good gods, I make my last appeal ;
Or clear my virtue, or my crime reveal.
If wandering in the maze of fate I run,
And backward trod the paths I sought to shun,
Impute my errors to your own decree ;
My hands are guilty, but my heart is free.   [*Exeunt.*

ACT IV.   SCENE I.

Enter PYRACMON *and* CREON.

Pyracmon.

SOME business of import, that triumph wears,
You seem to go with; nor is it hard to guess
When you are pleas'd, " by a malicious joy,
" Whose red and fiery beams cast through your vi-
      sage
" A glowing pleasure.   Sure" you smile revenge,
And I could gladly hear.
   Cre. Wouldst thou believe,
This giddy, hair-brain'd king, whom old Tiresias
Has thunderstruck with heavy accusation,

Tho' conscious of no inward guilt, yet fears?
He fears Jocasta, fears himself, his shadow;
He fears the multitude; and, which is worth
An age of laughter, out of all mankind,
He chooses me to be his orator:
Swears that Adrastus and the lean-look'd prophet
Are joint conspirators; and wish'd me to
Appease the raving Thebans; which I swore
To do.

   Pyr. A dangerous undertaking;
Directly opposite to your own interest.

   Cre. No, dull Pyracmon; when I left his presence,
With all the wings with which revenge could imp
My flight, I gain'd the midst o' the city;
There, standing on a pile of dead and dying,
I to the mad and sickly multitude,
With interrupting sobs, cry'd out, Oh, Thebes!
Oh, wretched Thebes, thy king, thy OEdipus,
This barbarous stranger, this usurper, monster,
Is by the oracle, the wise Tiresias,
Proclaim'd the murderer of thy royal Laius!
Jocasta, too, no longer now my sister,
Is found complotter in the horrid deed.
Here I renounce all tie of blood and nature,
For thee, oh, Thebes, dear Thebes, poor bleeding
       - Thebes!
And there I wept; and then the rabble howl'd,
And roar'd, and with a thousand antic mouths,
Gabbled revenge; revenge was all the cry.

Pyr. This cannot fail; I see you on the throne,
And OEdipus cast out.

   Cre. Then straight came on
Alcander, with a wide and bellowing crowd,
Whom he had wrought; I whisper'd him to join,
And head the forces while the heat was in them.
So, to the palace I return'd, to meet
The king, and greet him with another story.
But see, he enters.

     Enter OEDIPUS *and* JOCASTA, *attended.*

   OEdip. Said you that Phorbas is arriv'd, and yet
Entreats he may return, without being ask'd
Of aught concerning what we have discover'd?

   Joc. He started when I told him your intent;
Replying, what he knew of that affair
Would give no satisfaction to the king;
Then, falling on his knees, begg'd as for life,
To be dismiss'd from court: he trembled too,
As if convulsive death had seiz'd upon him,
And stammer'd in his abrupt pray'r so wildly,
That had he been the murderer of Laius,
Guilt and distraction could not have shook him more.

   OEdip. By your description, sure as plagues and
       death
Lay waste our Thebes, some deed that shuns the light
Begot those fears; if thou respect'st my peace,
Secure him, dear Jocasta; for my genius
Shrinks at his name.

Joc. Rather let him go ;
So my poor boding heart would have it be,
Without a reason.

   OEdip. Hark, the Thebans come !
Therefore retire : and once more, if thou lov'st me,
Let Phorbas be retain'd.

   Joc. You shall, while **I**
Have life, be still obey'd :
In vain you sooth me with your soft endearments,
And set the fairest countenance to view ;
Your gloomy eyes, my lord, betray a deadness
And inward languishing : that oracle
Eats like a subtle worm its venom'd way,
Preys on your heart, and rots the noble core,
Howe'er the beauteous outside shews so lovely.

   OEdip. Oh, thou wilt kill me with thy love's excess !
All, all is well ; retire, the Thebans come. [*Ex.* Joc.

   Ghost. OEdipus !

   OEdip. Ha ! again that scream of woe !
Thrice have I heard, thrice since the morning dawn'd
It hallow'd loud, as if my guardian spirit
Call'd from some vaulted mansion, OEdipus !
Or is it but the work of melancholy ?
When the sun sets, shadows, that shew'd at noon
But small, appear most long and terrible ;
So when we think fate hovers o'er our heads,
Our apprehensions shoot beyond all bounds,
Owls, ravens, crickets, seem the watch of death,
Nature's worst vermin scare her god-like sons ;
Echoes, the very leavings of a voice,

Grow babbling ghosts, and call us to our graves:
Each mole-hill thought swells to a huge Olympus,
While we fantastic dreamers heave and puff,
And sweat with an imagination's weight;
As if, like Atlas, with these mortal shoulders
We could sustain the burden of the world.

　　　　　　　　　　[Creon *comes forward.*

Cre. Oh, sacred sir, my royal lord——

OEdip. What now ?

Thou seem'st affrighted at some dreadful action,
Thy breath comes short, thy darted eyes are fix'd
On me for aid, as if thou wert pursu'd.
I sent thee to the Thebans : speak thy wonder;
Fear not, this palace is a sanctuary,
The king himself's thy guard.

　　　　Cre. For me, alas!

My life's not worth a thought, when weigh'd with
　　　　yours !
But fly, my lord: fly, as your life is sacred.
Your fate is precious to your faithful Creon,
Who therefore, on his knees, thus prostrate, begs
You would remove from Thebes, that vows your ruin.
When I but offer'd at your innocence,
They gather'd stones, and menac'd me with death,
And drove me through the streets, with imprecations
Against your sacred person, and those traitors
Which justify'd your guilt : which curs'd Tiresias
Told, as from Heav'n, was cause of their destruction.

　　OEdip. Rise, worthy Creon, haste and take our
　　　　guard,

Rank them in equal part upon the squâre,
Then open every gate of this our palace,
And let the torrent in.   Hark, it comes.   [*Shout.*
I hear them roar: begone, and break down all
The dams that would oppose their furious passage.

                [*Exit* Creon *with Guards.*

       Enter ADRASTUS, *his Sword drawn.*

     Adr. Your city
Is all in arms, all bent to your destruction.
I heard but now, where I was close confin'd,
A thund'ring shout, which made my gaolers vanish,
Cry, Fire the palace; where's the cruel king?
Yet, by th' infernal gods, those awful pow'rs
That have accus'd you, which these ears have heard,
And these eyes seen, I must believe you guiltless;
For, since I knew the royal OEdipus,
I have observ'd in all his acts such truth,
And god-like clearness; that to the last gush
Of blood and spirits I'll defend his life,
And here have sworn to perish by his side.

     OEdip. Be witness, gods, how near this touches me.

                [*Embracing him.*

Oh, what, what recompence can glory make?

     Adr. Defend your innocence, speak like yourself,
And awe the rebels with your dauntless virtue.
But hark! the storm comes nearer.

     OEdip. Let it come.
The force of majesty is never known

                     H

But in a general wreck : then, then is seen
The difference 'twixt a threshold and a throne.

Enter CREON, PYRACMON, ALCANDER, TIRESIAS,
and Thebans.

   Alc. Where, where's this cruel king? Thebans,
      behold
There stands your plague, the ruin, desolation
Of this unhappy—— Speak; shall I kill him?
Or shall he be cast out to banishment?
   All Theb. To banishment, away with him.
   OEdip. Hence, you barbarians, to your slavish
      distance!
Fix to the earth your sordid looks; for he
Who stirs, dares more than madmen, fiends, or furies.
" Who dares to face me, by the gods, as well
" May brave the majesty of thundering Jove."
Did I for this relieve you when besieg'd
By this fierce prince, when coop'd within your walls,
And to the very brink of fate reduc'd?
When lean-jaw'd famine made more havoc of you
Than does the plague? But I rejoice I know you,
Know the base stuff that temper'd your vile souls.
The gods be prais'd, I needed not your empire,
Born to a greater, nobler, of my own;
Nor shall the sceptre of the earth now win me
To rule such brutes, so barbarous a people.
   Adr. Methinks, my lord, I see a sad repentance,
A general consternation spread among them.
   OEdip. My reign is at an end; yet, ere I finish——

I'll do a justice that becomes a monarch,
A monarch who, i' th' midst of swords and javelins,
Dares act as on his throne encompass'd round
With nations for his guard.   Alcander, you
Are nobly born, therefore shall lose your head :
                                 [*Seizes him.*
Here, Hæmon, take him; but for this, and this,
Let cords dispatch them.   Hence, away with them.
                 [*Exit* Hæmon, *with* Alcander, *&c.*
    Tir. Oh, sacred prince, pardon distracted Thebes,
Pardon her, if she acts by Heav'n's award ;
" If that th' infernal spirits have declar'd
" The depth of fate, and if our oracles
" May speak, oh, do not too severely deal,
" But let thy wretched Thebes at least complain :"
If thou art guilty, Heav'n will make it known :
If innocent, then let Tiresias die.
    Œdip. I take thee at thy word; run, haste and save
        Alcander :
I swear the prophet or the king shall die.
Be witness, all you Thebans, of my oath ;
And Phorbas be the umpire.
    Tir. I submit.   [*Trumpets sound.*
    Œdip. What mean those trumpets?

     Enter HÆMON, *with* ALCANDER, *&c.*

    Hæm. From your native country,
Great sir, the fam'd Ægeon is arriv'd,
That renown'd favourite of the king your father:
              H ij

He comes as an ambassador from Corinth,
And sues for audience.

OEdip. Haste, Hæmon, fly, and tell him that I burn
T' embrace him.

Hæm. The queen, my lord, at present holds him
In private conference ; but behold her here.

Enter JOCASTA, EURYDICE, &c.

Joc. Hail, happy OEdipus, happiest of kings!
Henceforth be blest, blest as thou canst desire,
Sleep without fears the blackest nights away ;
Let furies haunt thy palace, thou shalt sleep
Secure, thy slumbers shall be soft and gentle
As infant dreams.

OEdip. What does the soul of all my joys intend ?
And whither would this rapture ?

Joc. Oh, I could rave,
Pull down those lying fanes, and burn that vault,
From whence resounded those false oracles,
That robb'd my love of rest : if we must pray,
Rear in the streets bright altars to the gods,
Let virgins' heads adorn the sacrifice ;
And not a grey-beard forging priest come near,
To pry into the bowels of the victim,
And with his dotage mad the gaping world.
But see, the oracle that I will trust,
True as the gods, and affable as men.

Enter ÆGEON.   *Kneels.*

OEdip. Oh, to my arms, welcome, my dear Ægeon ;

Ten thousand welcomes, oh, my foster father,
Welcome as mercy to a man condemn'd!
Welcome to me,
As, to a sinking mariner,
The lucky plank that bears him to the shore!
But speak; oh, tell me what so mighty joy
Is this thou bring'st, which so transports Jocasta?

    Joc. Peace, peace, Ægeon, let Jocasta tell him!
Oh, that I could for ever charm, as now,
My dearest OEdipus; thy royal father,
Polybus, king of Corinth, is no more.

    OEdip. Ha! can it be? Ægeon, answer me.
And speak in short what my Jocasta's transport
May over-do.

    Æge. Since in few words, my royal lord, you ask
To know the truth; king Polybus is dead.

    OEdip. Oh, all you powers, is't possible? What,
       dead!
But that the tempest of my joy may rise
By just degrees, and hit at last the stars,
Say, how, how dy'd he? Ha! by sword, by fire,
Or water? By assassinates, or poison? Speak:
Or did he languish under some disease?

    Æge. Of no distemper, of no blast he died,
But fell like autumn fruit that mellow'd long:
Ev'n wonder'd at, because he dropp'd no sooner.
Fate seem'd to wind him up for fourscore years;
Yet freshly ran he on ten winters more;
Till, like a clock worn out with eating time,
The wheels of weary life at last stood still.

" *OEdip.* Oh, let me press thee in my youthful
  arms,
" And smother thy old age in my embraces.
" Yes, Thebans, yes, Jocasta, yes, Adrastus,
" Old Polybus, the king, my father's dead. '
" Fires shall be kindled in the midst of Thebes;
" I' th' midst of tumult, wars, and pestilence,
" I will rejoice for Polybus's death.
" Know, be it known to the limits of the world;
" Yet farther, let it pass yon dazzling roof,
" The mansion of the gods, and strike them deaf
" With everlasting peals of thund'ring joy.
 " *Tir.* Fate! Nature! Fortune! what is all this
  world ?"
 OEdip. Now, dotard; now, thou blind old wizard
  prophet,
Where are your boding ghosts, your altars now;
Your birds of knowledge, that in dusky air
Chatter futurity? and where are now
Your oracles, that call'd me parricide?
Is he not dead? deep laid in his monument?
And was not I in Thebes when fate attack'd him?
Avaunt, begone, you visors of the gods!
Were I as other sons, now I should weep;
But, as I am, I've reason to rejoice;
And will, though his cold shade should rise and
  blast me.
Oh, for this death, let waters break their bounds,
Rocks, valleys, hills, with splitting Io's ring:
Io, Jocasta, Io Pæan sing

Tir. Who would not now conclude a happy end!
But all fate's turns are swift and unexpected.

Æge. Your royal mother, Merope, as if
She had no soul since you forsook the land,
Waves all the neighb'ring princes that adore her.

OEdip. Waves all the princes! Poor heart! for
     what? Oh, speak.

Æge. She, tho' in full-blown flow'r of glorious
     beauty,
Grows cold, ev'n in the summer of her age;
And, for your sake, has sworn to die unmarried.

OEdip. How! for my sake, die, and not marry! Oh,
My fit returns.

Æge. This diamond, with a thousand kisses bless'd,
With thousand sighs and wishes for your safety,
She charg'd me give you, with the general homage
Of our Corinthian lords.

OEdip. There's magic in it, take it from my sight;
There's not a beam it darts but carries hell,
Hot flashing lust, and necromantic incest:
Take it from these sick eyes; oh, hide it from me.
No, my Jocasta, though Thebes cast me out,
While Merope's alive, I'll ne'er return!
Oh, rather let me walk round the wide world
A beggar, than accept a diadem
On such abhorr'd conditions.

Joc. You make, my lord, your own unhappiness,
By these extravagant and needless fears.

OEdip. Needless! Oh, all you gods! By Heav'n
     I'd rather

Embrue my hands up to my very shoulders
In the dear entrails of the best of fathers,
Than offer at the execrable act
Of damn'd incest: therefore no more of her.

Æge. And why, oh, sacred sir, if subjects may
Presume to look into their monarch's breast,
Why should the chaste and spotless Merope
Infuse such thoughts as I must blush to name?

OEdip. Because the god of Delphos did forewarn me
With thundering oracles.

Æge. May I entreat to know them?

OEdip. Yes, my Ægeon; but the sad remembrance
Quite blasts my soul: see then the swelling priest!
Methinks I have his image now in view:
He mounts the Tripos in a minute's space,
His clouded head knocks at the temple-roof,
While from his mouth
These dismal words are heard:
" Fly, wretch, whom fate has doom'd thy father's
blood to spill,
And with prepost'rous births thy mother's womb to
fill."

Æge. Is this the cause
Why you refuse the diadem of Corinth?

OEdip. The cause? Why, is it not a monstrous one?

Æge. Great sir, you may return: and tho' you
should
Enjoy the queen (which all the gods forbid),
The act would prove no incest.

OEdip. How, Ægeon?

Though I enjoy'd my mother, not incestuous!
" Thou rav'st, and so do I ; and these all catch
" My madness; look they're dead with deep distrac-
　　tion."
Not incest ! What, not incest with my mother ?

Æge. My lord, queen Merope is not your mother.

OEdip. Ha ! did I hear thee right ? Not Merope
My mother !

Æge. Nor was Polybus your father.

OEdip. Then all my days and nights must now be
　　spent
In curious search to find out those dark parents
Who gave me to the world; speak then, Ægeon,
By all the gods celestial and infernal,
By all the ties of nature, blood, and friendship,
Conceal not from this rack'd despairing king
A point or smallest grain of what thou know'st :
Speak then, oh, answer to my doubts directly.
If royal Polybus was not my father,
Why was I call'd his son ?

Æge. He, from my arms,
Receiv'd you as the fairest gift of nature.
Not but you were adorn'd with all the riches
That empire could bestow in costly mantles
Upon its infant heir.

OEdip. But was I made the heir of Corinth's crown,
Because Ægeon's hands presented me ?

Æge. By my advice,
Being past all hope of children,
He took, embrac'd, and own'd you for his son.

OEdip. Perhaps I then am yours; instruct me, sir
If it be so, I'll kneel and weep before you,
With all th' obedience of a penitent child,
Imploring pardon.
Kill me, if you please,
I will not writhe my body at the wound ·
But sink upon your feet with a last sigh,
And ask forgiveness with my dying hands.

Æge. Oh, rise, and call not to this aged cheek
The little blood which should keep warm my heart;
You are not mine, nor ought I to be blest
With such a god-like offspring. Sir, I found you
Upon the mount Cithæron.

OEdip. Oh, speak, go on, the air grows sensible
Of the great things you utter, and is calm:
The hurry'd orbs, with storms so rack'd of late,
Seem to stand still, as if that Jove were talking.
Cithæron! Speak, the valley of Cithæron! .

Æge. Oft-times before I thither did resort,
Charm'd with the conversation of a man
Who led a rural life, and had command
O'er all the shepherds, who about those vales
Tended their numerous flocks: in this man's arms
I saw you smiling at a fatal dagger,
Whose point he often offer'd at your throat;
But then you smil'd, and then he drew it back,
Then lifted it again, you smil'd again;
'Till he at last in fury threw it from him,
And cry'd aloud, The gods forbid thy death.
Then I rush'd in, and, after some discourse,

To me he did bequeath your innocent life;
And I the welcome care to Polybus.

   OEdip. To whom belongs the master of the shep-
      herds ?

   Æge. His name I knew not, or I have forgot:
That he was of the family of Laius
I well remember.

   OEdip. And is your friend alive ? for if he be,
I'll buy his presence, though it cost my crown.

   Æge. Your menial attendants best can tell
Whether he lives or not ; and who has now
His place.

   Joc. Winds, bear me to some barren island,
Where print of human feet was never seen,
O'er-grown with weeds of such a monstrous height,
Their baleful tops are wash'd with bellying clouds;
Beneath whose venomous shade I may have vent
For horrors that would blast the barbarous world.

   OEdip. If there be any here that knows the person
Whom he describ'd, I charge him on his life
To speak ; concealment shall be sudden death:
But he who brings him forth, shall have reward
Beyond ambition's lust.

   Tir. His name is Phorbas;
Jocasta knows him well; but if I may
Advise, rest where you are, and seek no farther.

   OEdip. Then all goes well, since Phorbas is secur'd
By my Jocasta. Haste, and bring him forth :
My love, my queen, give orders. Ha ! what mean

These tears, and groans, and strugglings? Speak, my
    fair,
Why are thy troubles?
   Jac. Yours; and yours are mine:
Let me conjure you take the prophet's counsel,
And let this Phorbas go.
   OEdip. Not for the world.
By all the gods, I'll know my birth, though death
Attends the search: I have already past
The middle of the stream; and to return
Seems greater labour than to venture o'er.
Therefore produce him.
   Jac. Once more, by the gods,
I beg, my OEdipus, my lord, my life,
My love, my all, my only utmost hope,
I beg you, banish Phorbas: oh, the gods,
I kneel, that thou may grant this first request.
Deny me all things else; but for my sake,
And as you prize your own eternal quiet,
Never let Phorbas come into your presence.
   OEdip. You must be rais'd, and Phorbas shall ap-
    pear,
Though his dread eyes were basilisks. Guards, haste,
Search the queen's lodgings: find, and force him hi-
    ther.   *[Exeunt Guards.*
   Jac. Oh, OEdipus, yet send,
And stop their entrance, ere it be too late:
Unless you wish to see Jocasta rent
With furies, slain out-right with mere distraction,

Keep from your eyes and mine the dreadful Phorbas.
Forbear this search, I'll think you more than mortal.
Will you yet hear me ?

OEdip. Tempests will be heard,
And waves will dash, though rocks their basis keep.—
But see, they enter. If thou truly lov'st me,
Either forbear this subject, or retire.

Enter HÆMON, *Guards, with* PHORBAS.

Joc. Prepare then, wretched prince, prepare to
  hear
A story, that shall turn thee into stone.
Could there be hewn a monstrous gap in nature,
A flaw made through the center, by some god,
Through which the groans of ghosts may strike thy
  ears,
They will not wound thee as this story will.
Hark, hark ! a hollow voice calls out aloud,
Jocasta ! Yes, I'll to the royal bed,
Where first the mysteries of our loves were acted,
And double-dye it with imperial crimson ;
Tear off this curling hair,
Be gorg'd with fire, stab every vital part,
And when at last I'm slain, to crown the horror,
My poor tormented ghost shall cleave the ground,
To try if hell can yet more deeply wound. [*Exit.*
 OEdip. She's gone ; and as she went, methought
  her eyes
Grew larger, while a thousand frantic spirits
Seething, like rising bubbles, on the brim,

Peep'd from the watery brink, and glow'd upon me.
I'll seek no more; but hush my genius up
That throws me on my fate.——Impossible!
Oh, wretched man, whose too, too busy thoughts
Ride swifter than the galloping heav'ns round,
With an eternal hurry of the soul;
Nay, there's a time when ev'n the rolling year
Seems to stand still, dead calms are in the ocean,
When not a breath disturbs the drowsy waves:
But man, the very monster of the world,
Is ne'er at rest, the soul for ever wakes.
Come then, since Destiny thus drives us on,
Let's know the bottom.   Hæmon, you I sent:
Where is that Phorbas?

   Hæm. Here, my royal lord.

   OEdip. Speak first, Ægeon, say, is this the man?

   Æge. My lord, it is: though time has plough'd
         that face
With many furrows since I saw it first;
Yet I'm too well acquainted with the ground, quite
         to forget it.

   OEdip. Peace! stand back a while.
Come hither, friend; I hear thy name is Phórbas.
Why dost thou turn thy face? I charge thee answer
To what I shall enquire: wert thou not once
The servant to King Laius here in Thebes?

   Phor. I was, great Sir, his true and faithful servant,
Born and bred up in court, no foreign slave.

   OEdip. What office hadst thou? What was thy em-
         ployment?

Phor. He made me lord of all his rural pleasures ;
For much he lov'd them: oft I entertain'd
With sporting swains, o'er whom I had command.

OEdip. Where was thy residence? To what part o'
    th' country
Didst thou most frequently resort?

Phor. To mount Cithæron, and the pleasant vallies
Which all about lie shadowing its large feet.

OEdip. Come forth, Ægeon. Ha! why start'st thou,
    Phorbas?
Forward, I say, and face to face confront him;
Look wistly on him, through him, if thou canst,
And tell me on thy life, say, dost thou know him?
Didst thou e'er see him? e'er converse with him
Near mount Cithæron?

Phor. Who, my lord, this man?

OEdip. This man, this old, this venerable man:
Speak, didst thou ever meet him there?

Phor. Where, sacred sir?

OEdip. Near mount Cithæron; answer to the pur-
    pose,
'Tis a king speaks; and royal minutes are
Of much more worth than thousand vulgar years:
Didst thou e'er see this man near mount Cithæron?

Phor. Most sure, my lord, I have seen lines like
    those
His visage bears; but know not where nor when.

Æge. Is't possible you should forget your ancient
    friend?
There are perhaps

I ij

Particulars, which may excite your dead remem-
brance.
Have you forgot I took an infant from you,
Doom'd to be murder'd in that gloomy vale?
The swaddling-bands were purple, wrought with gold.
Have you forgot too how you wept, and begg'd
That I should breed him up, and ask no more?

Phor. Whate'er I begg'd, thou, like a dotard
speak'st
More than is requisite. And what of this?
Why is it mention'd now? And why, oh, why
Dost thou betray the secrets of thy friend?

Æge. Be not too rash. That infant grew at last
A king; and here the happy monarch stands.

Phor. Ha! whither wouldst thou? Oh, what hast
thou utter'd!
For what thou hast said, death strike thee dumb for
ever!

OEdip. Forbear to curse the innocent; and be
Accurst thyself, thou shifting traitor, villain,
Damn'd hypocrite, equivocating slave.

Phor. Oh, heav'ns! wherein, my lord, have I of-
fended?

OEdip. Why speak you not according to my charge?
Bring forth the rack: since mildness cannot win you,
Torments shall force.

Phor. Hold, hold, oh, dreadful sir;
You will not rack an innocent old man.

OEdip. Speak then.

Phor. Alas, what would you have me say?

OEdip. Did this old man take from your arms an
infant?

Phor. He did: and, oh, I wish to all the gods,
Phorbas had perish'd in that very moment.

OEdip. Moment! Thou shalt be hours, days, years,
a-dying.
Here, bind his hands; he dallies with my fury:
But I shall find a way——

Phor. My lord, I said
I gave the infant to him.

OEdip. Was he thy own, or given thee by another?

Phor. He was not mine; but given me by another.

OEdip. Whence? and from whom? What city? Of
what house?

Phor. Oh, royal sir, I bow me to the ground,
Would I could sink beneath it: by the gods,
I do conjure you to enquire no more.

OEdip. Furies and hell! Hæmon, bring forth the
rack,
Fetch hither cords, and knives, and sulphurous flames:
He shall be bound, and gash'd, his skin flead off,
And burnt alive.

Phor. Oh, spare my age.

OEdip. Rise then, and speak.

Phor. Dread sir, I will.

OEdip. Who gave that infant to thee?

Phor. One of King Laius' family.

OEdip. Oh, you immortal gods! But say, who
was't?

Which of the family of Laius gave it?
A servant, or one of the royal-blood?

Phor. Oh, wretched state! I die, unless I speak;
And, if I speak, most certain death attends me!

OEdip. Thou shalt not die. Speak then, who was it?
　　Speak,
While I have sense to understand the horror;
For I grow cold.

Phor. The Queen Jocasta told me
It was her son by Laius.

OEdip. Oh, you gods!—But did she give it thee?

Phor. My lord, she did.

OEdip. Wherefore? For what?——Oh, break not
　　yet my heart;
Though my eyes burst, no matter. Wilt thou tell me,
Or, must I ask for ever; for what end,
Why gave she thee her child?

Phor. To murder it

OEdip. Oh, more than savage! murder her own
　　bowels!
Without a cause!

Phor. There was a dreadful one,
Which had fortold, that most unhappy son
Should kill his father, and enjoy his mother.

OEdip. But one thing more.
Jocasta told me thou wert by the chariot
When the old king was slain. Speak, I conjure thee,
For I shall never ask thee aught again,
What was the number of th' assasinates?

Phor. The dreadful deed was acted but by one;
And sure that one had much of your resemblance.

   OEdip. 'Tis well! I thank you, gods! 'tis wond_
rous.

Daggers, and poisons! Oh, there is no need
For my dispatch : and you, you merciless pow'rs,
Hoard up your thunder-stones; keep, keep, your
bolts
For crimes of little note.   `   [*Falls.*

   Adr. Help, Hæmon, help, and bow him gently
forward;

" Chafe, chafe his temples: how the mighty spirits,
" Half-strangled with the damp his sorrows rais'd,
" Struggle for vent! But see, he breathes again,
" And vigorous nature breaks through opposition."
How fares my royal friend ?

   OEdip. The worse for you.

Oh, barbarous men, and, oh, the hated light,
Why did you force me back to curse the day;
To curse my friends; to blast with this dark breath
The yet untainted earth and circling air ?
To raise new plagues, and call new vengeance down,
Why did you tempt the gods, and dare to touch me ?
" Methinks there's not a hand that grasps this hell,
" But should run up like flax all blazing fire."
Stand from this spot, I wish you as my friends,
And come not near me, lest the gaping earth
Swallow you too——Lo, I am gone already.

         [*Draws, and claps his sword to his breast, which*
            Adrastus *strikes away with his foot.*

Adr. You shall no more be trusted with your life:
Creon, Alcander, Hæmon, help to hold him.

OEdip. Cruel Adrastus! Wilt thou, Hæmon too?
Are these the obligations of my friends?
Oh, worse than worst of my most barbarous foes!
Dear, dear Adrastus, look with half an eye
On my unheard of woes, and judge thyself,
If it be fit that such a wretch should live!
Or, by these melting eyes, unus'd to weep,
With all the low submissions of a slave,
I do conjure thee give my horrors way;
Talk not of life, for that will make me rave:
As well thou mayst advise a tortur'd wretch,
All mangled o'er from head to foot with wounds,
And his bones broke, to wait a better day.

Adr. My lord, you ask me things impossible;
And I with justice should be thought your foe,
To leave you in this tempest of your soul.

Tir. Tho' banish'd Thebes, in Corinth you may
          reign;
Th' infernal pow'rs themselves exact no more:
Calm then your rage, and once more seek the gods.

OEdip. I'll have no more to do with gods, nor
          men!
" Hence, from my arms, avaunt! Enjoy thy mother!
" What violate, with bestial appetite,
" The sacred veils that wrapt thee yet unborn!
" This is not to be borne! Hence: off, I say;
" For they who let my vengeance, make themselves
" Accomplices in my most horrid guilt.

" *Adr.* Let it be so: we'll fence Heav'n's fury from
        you,
" And suffer all together: this, perhaps,
" When ruin comes, may help to break your fall."
  OEdip. Oh, that, as oft I have at Athens seen
The stage arise, and the big clouds descend;
So now, in very deed I might behold
The pond'rous earth, and all yon' marble roof
Meet, like the hand of Jove, and crush mankind!
For all the elements, and all the pow'rs
Celestial, nay, terrestrial, and infernal,
Conspire the rack of out-cast OEdipus.
Fall darkness then, and everlasting night
Shadow the globe; may the sun never dawn,
The silver moon be blotted from her orb;
And for an universal rout of nature,
Through all the inmost chambers of the sky,
May there not be a glimpse, one starry spark,
But gods meet gods, and justle in the dark;
That jars may rise, and wrath divine be hurl'd,
Which may to atoms shake the solid world. [*Exeunt.*

ACT V. SCENE I.

Enter CREON, ALCANDER, *and* PYRACMON.

Creon.

THEBES is at length my own; and all my wishes,
Which sure were great as royalty e'er form'd,

Fortune and my auspicious stars have crown'd.
O diadem, thou center of ambition,
Where all its different lines are reconcil'd,
As if thou wert the burning-glass of glory!

   Pyr. Might I be counsellor, I would entreat you
To cool a little, sir;
Find out Eurydice;
And with the resolution of a man
Mark'd out for greatness, give the fatal choice
Of death or marriage.

   Alc. Survey curs'd OEdipus,
As one, who, tho' unfortunate, belov'd,
Though innocent, and therefore much lamented
By all the Thebans; you must mark him dead:
Since nothing but his death, not banishment,
Can give assurance to your doubtful reign.

   Cre. Well have you done, to snatch me from the
      storm
Of racking transport, where the little streams
Of love, revenge, and all the under passions,
As waters are by sucking whirlpools drawn,
Were quite devour'd in the vast gulph of empire;
Therefore, Pyracmon, as you boldly urg'd,
Eurydice shall die, or be my bride.
Alcander, summon to their master's aid
My menial servants, and all those whom change
Of state, and hope of the new monarch's favour,
Can wish to take our part. Away! What now?
                       [*Exit* Alcander.

Enter HÆMON.

When Hæmon weeps, " without the help of ghosts,"
I may foretell there is a fatal cause.

Hæm. Is't possible you should be ignorant
Of what has happen'd to the desperate king?

Cre. I know no more but that he was conducted
Into his closet, where I saw him fling
His trembling body on the royal bed.
All left him there, at his desire, alone :
But sure no ill, unless he dy'd with grief,
Could happen, for you bore his sword away.

Hæm. I did; and having lock'd the door, I stood;
And through a chink I found, not only heard,
But saw him, when he thought no eye beheld him :
At first, deep sighs heav'd from his woeful heart
Murmurs, and groans that shook the outward rooms.
And art thou still alive, O wretch! he cry'd :
Then groan'd again, as if his sorrowful soul
Had crack'd the strings of life, and burst away.

Cre. I weep to hear; how then should I have
      griev'd,
Had I beheld this wondrous heap of sorrow!
But to the fatal period.

Hæm. Thrice he struck,
With all his force, his hollow groaning breast,
And thus, with out-cries, to himself complain'd.
But thou canst weep then, and thou think'st 'tis well,
These bubbles of the shallowest, emptiest sorrow,
Which children vent for toys, and women rain

For any trifle their fond hearts are set on;
Yet these thou think'st are ample satisfaction
For bloodiest murder, and for burning lust:
No, parricide; if thou must weep, weep blood;
Weep eyes instead of tears: O, by the gods,
'Tis greatly thought, he cry'd, and fits my woes.
Which said, he smil'd revengefully, and leapt
Upon the floor; thence gazing at the skies,
" His eye-balls fiery red, and glowing vengeance;
" Gods, I accuse you not, tho' I no more
" Will view your heav'n, 'till with more durable glasses,
" The mighty soul's immortal perspectives,
" I find your dazzling beings:" take, he cry'd,
Take, eyes, your last, your fatal farewell-view;
Then with a groan, that seem'd the call of death,
With horrid force lifting his impious hands,
He snatch'd, he tore, from forth their bloody orbs,
The balls of sight, and dash'd them on the ground.

   Cre. A master-piece of horror; new and dreadful!
   Hæm. I ran to succour him; but, oh, too late;
For he had pluck'd the remnant strings away.
What then remains, but that I find Tiresias,
Who, with his wisdom, may allay those furies
That haunt his gloomy soul?   [*Exit.*
   Cre. Heav'n will reward
Thy care, most honest, faithful, foolish Hæmon!
But see, Alcander enters, well attended.

    Enter ALCANDER, *attended.*

I see thou hast been diligent.

Alc. Nothing these,
For number, to the crowds that soon will follow :
Be resolute,
And call your utmost fury to revenge.

Cre. Ha! thou hast given
Th' alarm to cruelty; and never may
These eyes be clos'd, till they behold Adrastus
Stretch'd at the feet of false Eurydice.
But see, they're here? retire awhile, and mark.

Enter ADRASTUS *and* EURYDICE, *attended.*

Adr. Alas, Eurydice, what fond rash man,
What inconsiderate and ambitious foul,
That shall hereafter read the fate of OEdipus,
Will dare, with his frail hand, to grasp a sceptre?

Eur. 'Tis true, a crown seems dreadful, and I wish
That you and I, more lowly plac'd, might pass
Our softer hours in humble cells away :
Not but I love you to that infinite height,
I could (O wondrous proof of fiercest love!)
Be greatly wretched in a court with you.

Adr. Take then this most lov'd innocence away :
Fly from tumultuous Thebes, from blood and murder
Fly from the author of all villanies,
Rapes, death, and treason; from that fury Creon.
Vouchsafe that I, o'er-joy'd, may bear you hence,
And at your feet present the crown of Argos.
                    [Creon *and Attendants come up to him.*

Cre. I have o'erheard thy black design, Adrastus,
And therefore, as a traitor to this state,

K

Death ought to be thy lot : let it suffice
That Thebes surveys thee as a prince ; abuse not
Her proffer'd mercy, but retire betimes,
Lest she repent, and hasten on thy doom.

 Adr. Think not, most abject,
Most abhorr'd of men,
Adrastus will vouchsafe to answer thee.
Thebans, to you I justify my love :
I have address'd my prayer to this fair princess ;
But, if I ever meant a violence,
Or thought to ravish, as that traitor did,
What humblest adorations could not win ;
Brand me, you gods, blot me with foul dishonour,
And let men curse me by the name of Creon !

 Eur. Hear me, O Thebans, if you dread the wrath
Of her whom fate ordain'd to be your queen,
Hear me, and dare not, as you prize your lives,
To take the part of that rebellious traitor.
By the decree of royal OEdipus,
By Queen Jocasta's order, by what's more,
My own dear vows of everlasting love,
I here resign to prince Adrastus' arms
All that the world can make me mistress of.

 Cre. O, perjur'd woman !
Draw all ! and when I give the word fall on.
Traitor, resign the princess, or this moment
Expect, with all those most unfortunate wretches,
Upon this spot straight to be hewn in pieces.

 Adr. No, villain, no ;
With twice those odds of men,

I doubt not in this cause to vanquish thee.
Captain, remember to your care I give
My love; ten thousand thousand times more dear
Than life or liberty.

    Cre. Fall on, Alcander.
Pyracmon, you and I must wheel about
For nobler game, the princess.

    Adr. Ah, traitor, dost thou shun me?
Follow, follow,
My brave companions, see the cowards fly.

    [*Exeunt fighting :* Creon's *Party beaten off by* Adr.

Enter OEDIPUS.

    OEdip. O, 'tis too little this, thy loss of sight,
What has it done? I shall be gaz'd at now
The more; be pointed at, there goes the monster!
Nor have I hid my horrors from myself;
For tho' corporeal light be lost for ever,
The bright reflecting soul, through glaring optics,
Presents in larger size her black ideas,
Doubling the bloody prospects of my crimes:
Holds fancy down, and makes her act again,
With wife and mother. " Tortures, hell and furies!
" Ha! now the baleful offspring's brought to light!
" In horrid form they rank themselves before me;
" What shall I call this medley of creation?
" Here's one, with all th' obedience of a son,
" Borrowing Jocasta's look, kneels at my feet,
" And calls me father; there a sturdy boy,
" Resembling Laius just as when I kill'd him,

K ij

" Bears up, and with his cold hand grasping mine,
" Cries out, how fares my brother OEdipus?
" What, sons and brothers! Sisters and daughters
    too!
" Fly all, begone, fly from my whirling brain;"
Hence, incest, murder; hence, you ghastly figures!
O gods! gods, answer; is there any means?
Let me go mad, or die.

Enter JOCASTA.

Joc. Where, where is this most wretched of man-
    kind,
This stately image of imperial sorrow,
" Whose story told, whose very name but mention'd,
" Would cool the rage of fevers, and unlock
" The hand of lust from the pale virgin's hair,
" And throw the ravisher before her feet?"
OEdip. By all my fears, I think Jocasta's voice!
Hence; fly; begone! " O thou far worse than worst
" Of damning charmers! O abhorr'd, loath'd crea-
    ture!
" Fly, by the gods, or by the fiends, I charge thee,"
Far as the east, west, north, or south of heav'n;
But think not thou shalt ever enter there:
The golden gates are barr'd with adamant,
'Gainst thee, and me; and the celestial guards,
Still as we rise, will dash our spirits down.
" *Joc.* O wretched pair! O greatly wretched we!
" Two worlds of woe!
" *OEdip.* Art thou not gone then? ha!

" How dar'st thou stand the fury of the gods?
" Or com'st thou in the grave to reap new pleasures?
   " *Joc.* Talk on; till thou mak'st mad my rolling
     brain;
" Groan still more death; -and may those dismal
     sources
" Still bubble on, and pour forth blood and tears.
" Methinks, at such a meeting, Heav'n stands still;
" The sea nor ebbs nor flows: this mole-hill earth
" Is heav'd no more: the busy emmets cease:
" Yet hear me on——
   " *OEdip.* Speak then, and blast my soul.
   " *Joc.* O, my lov'd lord, tho' I resolve a ruin
" To match my crimes; by all my miseries,
" 'Tis horror, worse than thousand thousand deaths,
" To send me hence without a kind farewell.
   " *OEdip.* Gods, how she shakes me! Stay thee, O
     Jocasta.
" Speak something ere thou goest for ever from me.
   " *Joc.* 'Tis woman's weakness, that I should be
     pity'd;
" Pardon me then, O greatest, tho' most wretched
" Of all thy kind: my soul is on the brink,
" And sees the boiling furnace just beneath:
" Do not thou push me off, and I will go,
" With such a willingness, as if that Heav'n
" With all its glory glow'd for my reception.
   " *OEdip.* O, in my heart, I feel the pangs of nature;
" It works with kindness o'er: give, give me way;
" I feel a melting here, a tenderness,

" Too mighty for the anger of the gods!

" Direct me to thy knees : yet oh forbear,

" Lest the dead embers should revive.

" Stand off——and at just distance

" Let me groan my horrors—here

" On the earth, here blow my utmost gale ;

" Here sob my sorrows, till I burst with sighing ;

" Here gasp and languish out my wounded soul."

Joc. In spite of all those crimes the cruel gods

Can charge me with, I know my innocence ;

Know yours : 'tis fate alone that makes us wretched,

For you are still my husband.

    OEdip. Swear I am,

And I'll believe thee ; steal into thy arms,

Renew endearments, think them no pollutions,

But chaste as spirits' joys : gently I'll come,

Thus weeping blind, like dewy night, upon thee,

And fold thee softly in my arms to slumber.

        [*The Ghost of* Laius *ascends by degrees, pointing at*

           Jocasta.

    Joc. Begone, my lord ! Alas, what are we doing ?

Fly from my arms ! Whirlwinds, seas, continents,

And worlds, divide us ! Oh, thrice happy thou,

Who hast no use of eyes ; for here's a sight

Would turn the melting face of Mercy's self

To a wild fury.

    OEdip. Ha ! what seest thou there ?

    Joc. The spirit of my husband ! Oh, the gods !

How wan he looks !

    OEdip. Thou rav'st ; thy husband's here.

Joc. There, there he mounts
In circling fire among the blushing clouds!
And see, he waves Jocasta from the world!

Ghost. Jocasta, OEdipus.   [*Vanish with thunder.*

OEdip. What wouldst thou have?
Thou know'st I cannot come to thee, detain'd
In darkness here, and kept from means of death.
I've heard a spirit's force is wonderful;
At whose approach, when starting from his dungeon,
The earth does shake, and the old ocean groans,
Rocks are remov'd, and tow'rs are thunder'd down:
And walls of brass, and gates of adamant
Are passable as air, and fleet like winds.

Joc. Was that a raven's croak, or my son's voice?
No matter which; I'll to the grave and hide me:
Earth, open, or I'll tear thy bowels up.
Hark! he goes on, and blabs the deed of incest.

OEdip. Strike then, imperial ghost; dash all at once
This house of clay into a thousand pieces;
That my poor ling'ring soul may take her flight
To your immortal dwellings.

Joc. Haste thee then,
Or I shall be before thee: see; thou canst not see;
Then I will tell thee that my wings are on:
I'll mount, I'll fly, and with a port divine
Glide all along the gaudy milky soil,
To find my Laius out: ask every god
In his bright palace, if he knows my Laius,
My murder'd Laius!

OEdip. Ha! how's this, Jocasta?
Nay, if thy brain be sick, then thou art happy.

Joc. Ha! will you not? Shall I not find him out?
Will you not shew him? Are my tears despis'd?
Why, then I'll thunder; yes, I will be mad,
And fright you with my cries: yes, cruel gods,
Though vultures, eagles, dragons tear my heart,
I'll snatch celestial flames, fire all your dwellings,
Melt down your golden roofs, and make your doors
Of crystal fly from off their diamond hinges;
Drive you all out from your ambrosial hives,
To swarm like bees about the field of heav'n:
This will I do, unless you shew me Laius,
My dear, my murder'd lord. Oh, Laius! Laius!
      Laius!   [*Exit.*

OEdip. Excellent grief! why, this is as it should be!
No mourning can be suitable to crimes
Like ours, but what death makes or madness forms.
" I could have wish'd, methought, for sight again,
" To mark the gallantry of her distraction:
" Her blazing eyes darting the wand'ring stars,
" T' have seen her mouth the heav'ns, and mate the
      gods.
" While with her thund'ring voice she menac'd high,
" And every accent twang'd with smarting sorrow;"
But what's all this to thee? Thou, coward, yet
Art living, canst not, wilt not find the road
To the great palace of magnificent death;
Though thousand ways lead to his thousand doors,

Which day and night are still unbarr'd for all.

[*Clashing of swords: drums and trumpets without.*

Hark! 'tis the noise of clashing swords! the sound
Comes near: oh, that a battle would come o'er me!

If I but grasp a sword, or wrest a dagger,
I'll make a ruin with the first that falls.

Enter HÆMON, *with Guards.*

Hæm. Seize him, and bear him to the western tow'r.
Pardon me, sacred sir; I am inform'd
That Creon has designs upon your life ·
Forgive me then, if, to preserve you from him,
I order your confinement.

OEdip. Slaves, unhand me!
I think thou hast a sword: 'twas the wrong side.
Yet, cruel Hæmon, think not I will live;
He that could tear his eyes out, sure can find
Some desperate way to stifle this curs'd breath.
" Or if I starve! but that's a ling'ring fate;
" Or if I leave my brains upon the wall!
" The airy soul can easily o'er-shoot
" Those bounds with which thou striv'st to pale her
        in ;
" Yes, I will perish in despite of thee;
" And, by the rage that stirs me, if I meet thee
" In th'other world, I'll curse thee for this usage."

[*Exit.*

Hæm. Tiresias, after him ; and with your counsel
Advise him humbly ; charm, if possible,
These feuds within : while I without extinguish,

Or perish in th' attempt, the furious Creon;
That brand which sets our city in a flame.

    Tir. Heaven prosper your intent, and give a period
To all our plagues: what old Tiresias can,
Shall straight be done. Lead, Manto, to the tow'r.

                [*Exeunt* Tir. *and* Man.

    Hæm. Follow me all, and help to part this fray,

                [*Trumpets again.*

Or fall together in the bloody broil.   [*Exeunt.*

Enter CREON, *with* EURYDICE, PYRACMON, *and his Party, giving ground to* ADRASTUS.

    Cre. Hold, hold your arms, Adrastus, prince of
        Argos,
Hear, and behold; Eurydice is my prisoner.

    Adr. What wouldst thou, hell-hound?

    Cre. See this brandish'd dagger ·
Forego th' advantage which thy arms have won,
Or, by the blood which trembles through the heart
Of her whom more than life I know thou lov'st,
I'll bury to the haft, in her fair breast,
This instrument of my revenge.

    Adr. Stay thee, damn'd wretch: hold, stop thy
        bloody hand.

    Cre. Give order then, that on this instant, now,
This moment, all thy soldiers straight disband.

    Adr. Away, my friends, since fate has so allotted;
Begone, and leave me to the villain's mercy.

    Eur. Ah, my Adrastus! call 'em, call 'em back!
Stand there; come back, O, cruel, barbarous men!

Could you then leave your lord, your prince, your
    king,
After so bravely having fought his cause,
To perish by the hand of this base villain ?
Why rather rush you not at once together
All to his ruin ? drag him through the streets,
Hang his contagious quarters on the gates;
Nor let my death affright you.
   Cre. Die first thyself then.
   Adr. O, I charge thee hold.
Hence from my presence all : he's not my friend
That disobeys : see, art thou now appeas'd ?
                           [*Exeunt Attendants.*
Or is there ought else yet remains to do,
That can atone thee ? slack thy thirst of blood
With mine : but save, O save that innocent wretch.
   Cre. Forego thy sword, and yield thyself my pri-
    soner.
   Eur. Yet, while there's any dawn of hope to save
Thy precious life, my dear Adrastus,
Whate'er thou dost, deliver not thy sword;
With that thou may'st get off, tho' odds oppose
    thee ·
For me, O fear not; no, he dare not touch me ;
His horrid love will spare me. Keep thy sword;
Lest I be ravish'd after thou art slain.
   Adr. Instruct me, gods, what shall Adrastus do ?
   Cre. Do what thou wilt, when she is dead : my sol-
    diers

With numbers will o'erpow'r thee.   Is't thy wish
Eurydice should fall before thee ?

   Adr. Traitor, no :
Better that thou, and I, and all mankind,
Should be no more.

   Cre. Then cast thy sword away,
And yield thee to my mercy, or I strike.

   Adr. Hold thy rais'd arm ; give me a moment's
        pause.
My father, when he blest me, gave me this ;
My son, said he, let this be thy last refuge ;
If thou forego'st it, misery attends thee :
Yet love now charms it from me ; which in all
The hazards of my life I never lost.
'Tis thine, my faithful sword ; my only trust ;
Though my heart tells me, that the gift is fatal.

   Cre. Fatal ! yes, foolish, love-sick prince, it shall ;
Thy arrogance, thy scorn,
My wound's remembrance,
Turn, all at once, the fatal point upon thee.
Pyracmon, to the palace ; dispatch
The king : hang Hæmon up ; for he is loyal,
And will oppose me. Come, sir, are you ready ?

   Adr. Yes, villain, for whatever thou canst dare.

   Eur. Hold, Creon ! or thro' me, thro' me you
        wound.

   Adr. Off, madam, or we perish both.   Behold,
I'm not unarm'd ; my poignard's in my hand :
Therefore, away——

2

Eur. I'll guard your life with mine.

Cre. Die both, then; there is now no time for dally-
ing. [*Kills* Eurydice.

Eur. Ah, Prince, farewell! farewell, my dear Ad-
rastus. [*Dies.*

Adr. Unheard-of monster! eldest-born of hell!
Down to thy primitive flame. [*Stabs* Creon.

Cre. Help, soldiers, help!
Revenge me!

Adr. More, yet more; a thousand wounds!
I'll stab thee still, thus, to the gaping furies.
[Adrastus *falls, killed by the soldiers.*

Enter HÆMON, *Guards, with* ALCANDER *and* PY-
RACMON *bound; the Assassins are driven off.*

Oh, Hæmon, I am slain! nor need I name
Th' inhuman author of all villanies;
There he lies, gasping.

Cre. If I must plunge in flames,
Burn first my arm; base instrument, unfit
To act the dictates of my daring mind.
Burn, burn for ever, oh, weak substitute
Of that, the god, Ambition! [*Dies.*

Adr. She's gone—Oh, deadly marksman! in the
heart!
Yet in the pangs of death, she grasps my hand:
Her lips, too, tremble, as if she would speak
Her last farewell. Oh, OEdipus, thy fall
Is great! and nobly now thou go'st attended.

L

They talk of heroes and celestial beauties,
And wondrous pleasures in the other world :
Let me but find her there; I ask no more. .   [*Dies.*

Enter a Captain to HÆMON, *with* TIRESÍAS *and*
MANTO.

Cap. Oh, sir, the queen, Jocasta, swift and wild,
As a robb'd tygress bounding o'er the woods,
Has acted murders that amaze mankind.
In twisted gold I saw her daughters hang
On the bed royal, and her little sons
Stabb'd through the breasts upon the bloody pillows.
  Hæm. Relentless Heav'ns ! Is then the fate of Laius
Never to be aton'd.   How sacred ought
Kings lives be held, when but the death of one
Demands an empire's blood for expiation !
But see, the furious, mad Jocasta's here.

SCENE II.

Draws, and discovers JOCASTA *held by her Women,*
  " *and stabbed in many places of her bosom, her hair*
  " *dishevelled, her Children slain upon the bed.*"

Was ever yet a sight of so much horror
And pity brought to view !
  Joc. Ah, cruel women !
Will you not let me take my last farewell
Of those dear babes ? Oh, let me run and seal

My melting soul upon their bubbling wounds!
I'll print upon their coral mouths such kisses,
As shall recall their wand'ring spirits home.
Let me go, let me go, or I will tear you piece-meal.
Help, Hæmon, help!
Help, OEdipus! help, gods! Jocasta dies!

Enter OEDIPUS *above.*

OEdip. I've found a window, and, I thank the gods,
'Tis quite unbarr'd.　Sure, by the distant noise,
The height will fit my fatal purpose well.
　Joc. What, hoa, my OEdipus! See where he stands!
His groping ghost is lodg'd upon a tow'r,
Nor can it find the road.　Mount, mount, my soul!
I'll wrap thy shiv'ring spirit in lambent flames; and
　　　so we'll sail.
But see, we're landed on the happy coast;
And all the golden strands are cover'd o'er
With glorious gods, that come to try our cause.
Jove, Jove, whose majesty now sinks me down,
He who himself burns in unlawful fires,
Shall judge, and shall acquit us.　Oh, 'tis done!
'Tis fix'd by fate upon record divine;
And OEdipus shall now be ever mine.　　　[*Dies.*
　OEdip. Speak, Hæmon, what has Fate been doing
　　　there?
What dreadful deed has mad Jocasta done?
　Hæm. The queen herself, and all your wretched
　　　offspring,
Are by her fury slain.

OEdip. By all my woes,
She has out-done me in revenge and murder;
And I should envy her the sad applause:
But, oh, my children! Oh, what have they done?
This was not like the mercy of the Heav'ns,
To set her madness on such cruelty.
This stirs me more than all my sufferings,
And with my last breath I must call you tyrants.

    Hæm. What mean you, sir?

    OEdip. Jocasta, lo, I come!
Oh, Laius, Labdacus, and all you spirits
Of the Cadmean race, prepare to meet me!
All weeping, rang'd along the gloomy shore,
Extend your arms t' embrace me; for I come.
May all the gods, too, from their battlements,
Behold, and wonder at a mortal's daring:
And when I knock the goal of dreadful death,
Shout, and applaud me with a clap of thunder.
Once more, thus wing'd by horrid Fate, I come
Swift as a falling meteor; lo, I fly,
And thus go downwards to the darker sky.

    [*Thunder. He flings himself from the window. The
        Thebans gather about his body..*

    Hæm. Oh, prophet! OEdipus is now no more!
Oh, curs'd effect of the most deep despair!

    Tir. Cease your complaints, and bear his body
        hence;
The dreadful sight will daunt the drooping The-
        bans,
Whom Heav'n decrees to raise with peace and glory.

Yet, by these terrible examples warn'd,
The sacred fury thus alarms the world.
Let none, though ne'er so virtuous, great, and high,
Be judg'd entirely bless'd before they die.

[*Exeunt omnes.*

EPILOGUE.

WHAT Sophocles could undertake alone,
Out poets found a work for more than one;
And therefore two lay tugging at the piece,
With all their force, to draw the pond'rous mass from
      Greece.
A weight that bent ev'n Seneca's strong muse,
And which Corneille's shoulders did refuse.
So hard it is th' Athenian harp to string;
So much two consuls yield to one just king.
Terror and pity this whole poem sway;
The mightiest machines that can mount a play.
How heavy will those vulgar souls be found,
Whom two such engines cannot move from ground!
When Greece and Rome have smil'd upon this birth,
You can but damn for one poor spot of earth;
And when your children find your judgment such,
They'll scorn their sires, and wish themselves born Dutch:
Each haughty poet will infer with ease,
How much his wit must underwrite to please.
As some strange churl would brandishing advance
The monumental sword that conquer'd France;
So you, by judging this, your judgment teach,
Thus far you like, that is, thus far you reach.

Since, then, the vote of full two thousand years
Has crown'd this plot, and all the dead are theirs,
Think it a debt you pay, not alms you give,
And, in your own defence, let this play live.
Think them not vain, when Sophocles is shown;
To praise his worth, they humbly doubt their own.
Yet, as weak states each other's pow'r assure,
Weak poets by conjunction are secure:
Their treat is what your palates relish most,
Charm, song, a shew, a murder, and a ghost!
We know not what you can desire or hope,
To please you more, but burning of a Pope.

THE END.

XIMENA;

OR,

THE HEROIC DAUGHTER.

A

TRAGEDY,

By COLLEY CIBBER.

ADAPTED FOR

THEATRICAL REPRESENTATION,

AS PERFORMED AT THE

THEATRE-ROYAL, COVENT.GARDEN.

REGULATED FROM THE PROMPT-BOOK,

By Permission of the Manager.

LONDON:

Printed for the Proprietors, under the Direction of
JOHN BELL, British Library, STRAND,
Bookseller to His Royal Highness the Prince of Wales.
MDCCXCII.

XIMENA.

I⊤ will be scarcely necessary to add more to the above title, than that this Play is a translation from the CID of Corneille.—A Drama, which has so frequently been the subject of critical investigation, leaves to the observer, upon its transfusion into another tongue, little beyond remark upon the diction, and the sufficiency of its adaptation to British audiences.

CIBBER, in the two last Acts, has added something to the intrigue of the business—for the scenes he admitted to be finely *natural* in the original, he yet conceived in contrivance defective.—His alterations disturb the rude dignity of the original. So it was that, with a hand more daring still, TATE, from the *Herculaneum* of dramatic structures, seized the magnificent monument of LEAR, and patched it with an AMOUR—*à la François.*

In a strange Dedication, which we shall not suffer now to sully the fame of our *comic* COLLEY, he was weak enough to treat STEELE as an *Eagle*, and ADDISON as a *Wren.*—Such prophanation he was afterward wise enough to retrench.—We spare his memory the opprobrium of seeing it here.

PROLOGUE.

As oft in form'd assemblies of the fair,
The strait-lac'd prude will no loose passion bear,
Beyond set bounds no lover must address,
But secret flame in distant sighs express;
Yet if by chance some gay coquette sails in,
A joyous murmur breaks the silent scene,
Each heart reliev'd by her enliv'ning fire,
Feels easy hope, and unconfin'd desire;
Then shuddering prudes with secret envy burn,
And treat the fops, they could not catch, with scorn.
So plays are valued; not confin'd to rules,
Those prudes, the critics, call them feasts for fools;
And if an audience 'gainst those rules is warm'd,
Or by the lawless force of genius charm'd,
Their whole confederate body is alarm'd:
Then every feature's false, though ne'er so taking,
The heart's deceiv'd, though 'tis with pleasure aching,
They'll prove your charmer's not agreeable
Thus far'd it with the Cid of fam'd Corneille.
In France 'twas charg'd with faults were past enduring,
But still had beauties that were so alluring,
It rais'd the envy of the grave Richlieu,
And, spite of his remarks, cramm'd houses drew:

Of this assertion, if the truth you'll know,
Two lines will prove it from the great Boileau :
En vain contre le *Cid* un ministre se ligue,
Tout *Paris* pour *Chimene* a les yeux de *Rodrigue.*
In vain against the Cid the statesman arms,
Paris with Rodrick feels Ximena's charms.
This proves, when passion truly wrought appears,
In plays imperfect, 'twill command your tears :
Yet think not from what's said, we rules despise,
To raise your wonder from absurdities :
As France improv'd it from the Spanish pen,
We hope, now British, 'tis improv'd again.
And though lost tragedy has long seem'd dead,
Yet having lately rais'd her awful head,
To-night with pains and cost we humbly strive
To keep the spirit of that taste alive :
But if, like Phaeton, in Corneille's car,
Th' unequal muse unhappily should err,
At least you'll own from glorious heights she fell,
And there's some merit in attempting well.

Dramatis Perſonae.

COVENT-GARDEN.

Men.

Don Ferdinand, *King of* Castille, - Mr. Hull.

Don Alvarez, *his late general, and fa-* } Mr. Bensley.
ther of Don Carlos, - - -

Don Gormaz, *Count of* Gormaz, *the present* } Mr. Clarke.
general, and father of Ximena, -

Don Carlos, *in love with* Ximena, - - Mr. Smith.

Don Sanchez, *his secret rival, though* } Mr. Savigny.
lately betrothed to Belzara,

Don Alonzo, *an officer,* - - - - Mr. Wroughton.

Don Garcia, *ditto.*

A Page.

Women.

Ximena, *daughter to* Gormaz, - Mrs. Yates.

Belzara, *her friend, forsaken by Don* } Mrs. Mattocks.
Sanchez, - - - -

Scene, *the Royal Palace in* Sevillé.

XIMENA;

OR,

THE HEROIC DAUGHTER.

ACT I. SCENE I.

Enter ALVAREZ *and* CARLOS.

Alvarez.

ALLIANCE! ha! and with the race of Gormaz!
My mortal foe! The king enjoins it, saidst thou?
Let me not think thou couldst descend to ask it.
Take heed, my son, nor let the daughter's eyes
Succeed in what the father's sword has fail'd;
Since I to age have stood his hate unmov'd,
Be not thou vanquish'd by her female wiles,
Nor stain thy honour with insulted love.

Car. O, taint not with so hard a thought her virtues,
Which she has prov'd sincere, from obligations:
'Tis to her suit I owe my late advancement.
You know, my lord, the fortune of this sword
Redeem'd her from the Moors, when late their captive;
For which, at her return to court, she swell'd
The action with such praises to the king,

He bade her name the honours could reward it:
She, conscious of our houses' hate, surpris'd,
And yet disdaining that her heart should fall
In thanks below the benefit receiv'd,
Warm'd with th' occasion, begg'd his royal favour
Would rank me in the field, the next her father.
The king comply'd, and with a smile insisted,
That from her own fair hand I should receive
The grace.   This forc'd me then to visit her ·
To say what follow'd from our interview,
Might tire, at least, if not offend your ear.

   Alv. Not so, my Carlos, but proceed.

   Car. In brief;
The queen, who now in highest favour holds
The fair Ximena, soon perceiv'd our passion,
Approv'd and cherish'd it; our houses' discord,
She knew of old, had often shook the state;
Whereon she kindly to the king propos'd
This happy union, as the sole expedient
To cure those wounds, and fortify his throne ·
Nay, she, Ximena, if I knew her thoughts,
Chiefly to that regard resigns her heart.
O! she disclaims, contemns her beauty's power,'
And builds no merit but on stable virtue.

   Alv. If so, I should indeed applaud her spirit.

   Car. Oh! had you search'd her soul like me, you
       would
Repose your life, your fame, upon her truth.

   Alv. On thee at least I'm sure I may; I know
Thou lov'st thy honour equal to Ximena,

And to that guard I dare commit thy love,
Keep but that union sacred——

   Car. When I break it,
May your displeasure, and Ximena's scorn,
Unite their force to torture me with shame :——
But see, she comes! her eye, my Lord, has reach'd
   you.

o

Enter XIMENA.

Mark her concern, tle softness of her fear,
O'ercast with doubt and diffidence to meet you ;
One gentle word from you would chase the cloud,
And let forth all the lustre of her soul.

   Alv. Hail, fair Ximena! beauteous brightness, hail!
Propitious be this meeting to us all.
With equal joy and wonder I survey thee.
How lovely's virtue in so bright a form!
Thy father's fierceness all is lost in thee ;
Well have thy eyes reproach'd our houses' jars,
And calm'd the tempests that have wreck'd our peace;
What we with false resentments but inflam'd,
Thy nobler virtues have appeas'd with honour.

   Xim. These praises from another mouth, my Lord,
Might dye these glowing cheeks with crimson shame ;
But as they flow thus kindly from Alvarez,
From the heroic sire of my deliverer,
As you bestow 'em, my exulting heart,
Tho' undeserv'd, receives with joy the sound ;
But for those virtues you ascribe to me,
Alas! they are but copy'd all from thence ;

Carlos, I saw, was brave, victorious, great,
Compassionate——I am at best but grateful——
Could I be less reduc'd with obligations?
Could I retain our houses' ancient hate,
When Carlos' deeds so greatly had forgot it?
If Heaven had will'd our feuds should never end,
It would have chose some other arm to save me ·
But if its kinder providence decrees,
Ximena's yielded heart should cure those ills,
And bind our passions in the chains of peace;
Be witness that, all gracious Heaven, I've gain'd
The end, the haven of my hopes on earth,
And fill'd the proudest sails of my ambition.

   Alv. O, Carlos, Carlos, we are both subdu'd!
Where can such heavenly sweetness find a foe?
What Gormaz may resolve, his heart can tell,
But mine no longer can resist such virtue;
His pride perhaps may triumph o'er my weakness,
And wrong Ximena to insult Alvarez:
Be mine that shame, but then be mine this glory,
                        [*He joins their hands.*
That I surrender to his daughter's merit
All that her heart demands, or mine can give:
If he's obdurate, let her wrongs reproach him.

   Enter SANCHEZ *and* ALONZO *observing them.*
No thanks, my fair; for both or neither are
Oblig'd: whatever may be due to me,
Let love and mutual gratitude repay.

   D. San. Death to my eyes! Alvarez joins their
     hands!   [*Aside.*

Alon. Forbear! is this a time for jealousy? [*Aside.*

D. San. Thou, that hast patience, then, relieve my
  torture.   [*Aside.*

Car. Oh, Ximena! how my heart's oppress'd with
  shame——

Thou giv'st me a confusion equal to

My joy; I yet am laggard in my duty;

I must despair to reach with equal virtues

Dread Gormaz' heart, as thou hast touch'd Alvarez'

Xim. That hope we must to Providence resign.

The king intends this day to sound his temper,

Which, tho' severe, I know is generous,

In honour great, as in resentments warm,

Fierce to the proud, but to the gentle yielding;

The goodness of Alvarez must subdue him.

Alon. My lord, I heard the king enquiring for you.

Alv. Sir, I attend his Majesty—I thank you.

Xim. Saw you the count, my father, in the presence?

Alon. Madam, I left him with the king this instant,

Withdrawn to th' window, and in conference.

Xim. 'Twas his command I should attend him there.

Alv. Come, fair Ximena, if thy father's ear

Inclines like mine, unprejudic'd to hear;

His hate subdu'd will public good regard,

And crown thy virgin virtues with reward.

       [*Exeunt* Alv. Car. Xim.

D. San. Help me, Alonzo, help me, or I sink;

Th' oppression is too great for Nature's frame,

And all my manhood reels beneath the load.

O, rage! O, torment of successless love!

       B ij

Alon. Alas! I warn'd you of this storm before,
Yet you, incredulous and deaf, despis'd it;
But since your hopes are blasted in their bloom,
Since vow'd Ximena never can be yours,
Forget the folly, and resume your reason;
Recover to your vows your love betroth'd,
Return to honour, and the wrong'd Belzara.

D. San. Why dost thou still obstruct my happiness,
And thwart the passion that has seiz'd my soul?
A friend should help a friend in his extremes,
And not create, but dissipate his fears.
'Tis true, I see Ximena's heart is given,
But then her person's in a father's power:
He, I've no cause to fear, will slight my offers.
Thou know'st th' aversion that he bears Alvarez
Bars like a rock her wishes from their harbour:
While Carlos has a fear, shall I despair?
Has not the count his passions too to please,
And will he starve his hate to feed her love?
May I not hope he rather may embrace
The fair occasion of my timely vows,
To torture Carlos with a sure despair,
And force Ximena to assist his triumph.
Nay, she, perhaps, when his commands are fix'd,
In pride of virtue may resist her love,
Suppress the passion, and resign to duty.

dis-

quiet,
When honour courts you in a calm to joy?
Belzara's charms are yielded to your hopes,

Contracted to your vows, and warm'd to love,:
Ximena scarce has knowledge of your flame,
Without reproach she racks you with despair,
And must be perjur'd could her heart relieve you.

D. San. Let her relieve me, I'll forgive the guilt,
Forget it, smother in her arms the thought,
And drown the charming falsehood in the joy.

Alon. What wild extravagance of youthful heat
Obscures your honour, and destroys your reason?

D. San. I am not of that lifeless mould of men,
That plod the beaten road of virtuous love;
With me 'tis joyous, beauty gives desire,
Desire by nature gives instinctive hope;
The phœnix, woman, sets herself on fire,
Hope gives us love, our love makes them desire,
And in the flames they raise, themselves expire.

Alon. Nor love, nor hope, can give you here success.

D. San. Let those despair whose passions have their
        bounds,
Whose hopes in hazards, or in dangers die:
Shew me the object worthy of my flame,
Let her be barr'd by obligations, friends,
By vows engag'd, by pride, aversion, all
The common letts that give the virtuous awe,
My love would mount the tow'ring falcon's height,
Cut thro' them all, like yielding air, my way,
And downward dart me rapid on my quarry.

Alon. Farewell, my lord, some other time perhaps
This rapture may subside, and want a friend;
I shall be glad to advise when you can hear.

B iij

But see, Belzara comes, with eyes confus'd,
That speak some new disorder in her heart.
Would you be happy, friend, be just; preserve
Inviolate the honest vows you've made her.
Farewell, I leave you to embrace th' occasion. [*Exit.*

Enter BELZARA.

Bel. I come, Don Sanchez, to inform you of
A wrong that near concerns our mutual honour;
'Tis whisper'd thro' the court, that you retract
Your solemn vows by contract made to me,
And with a perjur'd heart pursue Ximena:
Such false reports should perish in their birth:
I've done my honest part, and disbeliev'd 'em,
Do yours, and by your vows perform'd destroy them.

D. San. Madam, this tender care of me deserves
Acknowledgments beyond my power to pay;
But virtue always is the mark of malice,
Contempt the best return that we can make it.

Bel. Virtue should have so strict a guard, as not
To suffer ev'n suspicion to approach it.
For tho', Don Sanchez, I dare think you just,
Yet while the envious world believes you false,
I feel their insults, and endure the shame.

D. San. Malice succeeds when its report's believ'd;
Seem you to slight it, and the monster's mute.

Bel. I could have hop'd some cause to make me
      slight it:
This cold concern to satisfy my fears,
Proclaims the danger, and confirms them true.

D. San. Then you believe me false?

Bel. Believe it! Heaven!
Am I to doubt what, ev'n your looks, your words,
Your faint evasions, faithlessly confess?
Ungrateful man! when you betray'd my heart,
You should have taught me too to bear the wrong.

D. San. When tears with menaces relieve their grief,
They flow from pride, not tenderness distress'd.

Bel. Insulting, horrid thought! am I accus'd
Of pride, complaining from a breaking heart?

D. San. Behold th' unthrifty proof of woman's love!
Pursue you with the sighs of faithful passion,
You starve our pining hopes with painted coyness;
But if our honest hearts disdain the yoke,
Or seek from sweet variety relief,
Alarm'd to lose what you despis'd secure,
Your trembling pride retracts its haughty air,
And yields to love, pursuing when we fly.
These lavish tears when I deserv'd your heart,
Had held me sighing to be more your slave;
But to bestow them when that heart's broke loose,
When more I merit your contempt than love,
Arraigns your justice, and acquits my falsehood.

Bel. Injurious, false, and barbarous reproach!
Have I with-held my pity from your sighs,
Or us'd with rigour my once boundless power?
Am I not sworn by testify'd consent,
By solemn vows contracted, yielded yours?
But what avails the force of truth's appeal,
Where th' offender is himself the judge?

But yet, remember, tyrant, while you triumph,
I am Don Henrick's daughter, whom you dare betray;
Henrick, whose fam'd revenge of injur'd honour,
Dares step as deep in blood, as you in provocations.

    D. San. Since then your seeming grief's with rage
      reliev'd,
Hear me with temper, madam, once for all.
You urge our solemn contract sworn ; I own
The fact, but must deny the obligation :
'Twas not to me, but to a father's will,
To Henrick's dread commands, your pride submitted.
Since then your merit's to obedience due,
Seek your reward from duty, not from Sanchez :
Your slights to me live yet recorded here,
Nor can your forc'd submissions now remove them.
Ximena's softer heart has rais'd me to
A flame, that gives at once revenge and rapture.
How far Don Henrick may resent the change,
I neither know, nor with concern shall hear :
Nay, trust your injur'd patience to inflame him.

    Bel. Inhuman, vain provoker of my heart,
I need not urge the ills that must o'ertake thee ;
Thy giddy passions will, without my aid,
Punish their guilt, and to themselves be fatal.
Ximena's heart is fix'd as far above
Thy hopes, as truth and virtue from thy soul.
To her avenging scorn I yield thy love ;
There, faithless wretch, indulge thy vain desires,
And starve, like tortur'd Tantalus, in plenty ;
Gaze on her charms forbidden to thy taste,

Famish'd and pining at the tempting feast,
Still rack'd, and reaching at the flying fair,
Pursue thy falsehood, and embrace despair. [*Exit.*

D. San. So raging winds in furious storms arise,
Whirl o'er our heads, and are when past forgotten.

Enter ALONZO.

Alon. Why, Sanchez, are you still resolv'd on ruin?
I met Belzara in disorder'd haste :
At sight of me she stopt, and would have spoke
But grief, alas, was grown too strong for words :
When turning from my view her mournful eyes,
She burst into a show'r of gushing tears,
And in the conflict of her shame retir'd.
Oh, yet collect your temper into thought,
And shun the precipice that gapes before you :
A moment hence, convinc'd, your eyes will see
Ximena parted from your hopes for ever

    D. San. Why dost thou double thus my new dis-
        quiets?
For pains foreseen are felt before they come.

Enter King, GORMAZ, ALVAREZ, CARLOS, XI-MENA, *&c.*

Alon. Behold the king, Alvarez, and her father,
Be wise, tho' late, and profit from the issue.

    King. Count Gormaz, you, and you Alvarez, hear,
Tho' in the camp your swords, in court your counsel,
Have justly rais'd your fame to envy'd heights,
Yet let me still deplore your race and you,

That from a long descent of lineal heat,
Your private feuds as oft have shook the state ;
And what's the source of this upheld defiance ?
Alas ! the stubborn claim of ancient rank,
Held from a two day's antedated honour,   •
Which gave the younger house pre-eminence.
How many valiant lives have eas'd our foes
Of fear, destroy'd by this contested title ;
And what's decided by this endless valour ?
Whose honour yet confesses the superior ?
While both dare die, the quarrel is immortal
Or say that force on one part has prevail'd,
Is there such merit in unequal strength ?
If violence is virtue, brutes may boast it :
Lions with lions grapple, and dispute ;
But men are only great, truly victorious,
When with superior reason they subdue.
Can you then think you are in honour bound
To heir the follies of your ancestors ?
Since they have left you virtues and renown,
Transmit not to posterity their blame.
   Alv. and Gor. My gracious lord——
   King. Yet hold ; I'll hear you both.
Of your compliance, Gormaz, I've no doubt ;
This quarrel in your nobler breast was dying,
Had not, Alvarez, you reviv'd it.
   Alv. I !
Wherein, my gracious lord, stand I suspected ?
   King. What else could mean that sullen gloom you
     wore,

That conscious discontent, so ill conceal'd
In your abrupt retirement from our court,
When late the valiant count was made our general?
Was't not your own request you might resign it?
Which tho', 'tis true, you long had fill'd with honour,
Was it for you to circumscribe our choice?
T' oppose from private hate the public good,
And in his case whose merit had preferr'd him?
When his fierce temper, from reflection calm,
Inclin'd to let the embers of his heat expire,
Was it well done thus to revive the flame,
To wake his jealous honour to resentment,
And shake that union we had laid to heart?
If thou hast ought to urge, that may defend
Thy late behaviour, or accuse his conduct,
Unfold it free, we are prepar'd to hear.

   Alv. Alas, my lord! the world misjudges me,
My hate suppos'd is not so deeply rooted;
Age has allay'd those fevers of my honour,
And weary nature now would rest from passions.
The noble count, whose warmer blood may boil,
Perhaps is still my foe: I am not his,
Nor envy him those honours of his merit.
Where virtue is, I dare be just, and see it.
Your majesty has spoke your wisdom in
Your choice, for I have seen his arm deserve it.
In all the sieges, battles I have won,
I knew not better to command, than he
To execute: those wreaths of victory
That flourish still upon this hoary brow,

Impartial I confess, his active sword
Has lopt from heads of Moors, and planted there.

   King. How has report, my Gormaz, wrong'd this
      man ?

   Alv. Nor was the cause of my retirement more,
Than that I found it time to ease my age,
Unfit for farther action, and bequeath
My son the needless pomp of my possessions.

   King. Is't possible ? Could'st thou conceal this
      goodness ?
Could secret virtue take so firm a root,
While slander like a canker kill'd its beauties ?
Gormaz, if yet thou art not passion's slave,
Take to thyself the glory to reward him.

   Gor. My lord, the passions that have warm'd this
      breast,
Yet never stirr'd but in the cause of honour.
Honour's the spring that moves my active life,
And life's a torment while that right's invaded.
Shew me the man whose merit claims my love,
Whose milder virtues modestly assail me,
And honour throws me at his feet submissive.
I proof of this, there needs but now to own,
The generous advances of Alvarez,
Have turn'd my fierce resentments into shame.
What can I more ? My words but faintly speak me.
But since my king seems pleas'd with my conversion,
My heart and arms are open to embrace him.

   King. Receive him, soldier, to thy heart, and give
Your king this glory of your mutual conquest.
                    [*They embrace.*

Xim Auspicious omen!

Car. O transporting hope!

D. San. Adders and serpents mix in their embraces.

                                      [*Apart.*

King. O, Gormaz! O, Alvarez! stop not here,
Confine not to yourselves your stinted virtue,
But in this noble ardour of your hearts,
Secure to your posterity your peace :

                         [Carlos *and* Ximena *kneel.*
Behold the lifted hands, that beg the blessing,
The hearts that burn to ratify the joy,
And to your heirs unborn transmit the glory.

Gor. Receive her, Carlos, from a father's hand,
Whose heart by obligations was subdu'd.

Alv. Accept, Ximena, all my age holds dear,
Not to my bounty, but thy merit due.

King. O, manly conquest! O, exalted worth!
What honours can we offer to applaud it?
To grace this triumph of Ximena's eyes,·
Let public jubilee conclude the day.
Sound all our sprightly instruments of war,
Fifes, clarions, trumpets, speak the general joy.

Alv. Raise high the clangor of your lofty notes,
Sound peace at home————

Gor. And terror to our foes.

King. Let the loud cannon from the ramparts roar.

Gor. And make the frighted shores of Afric ring.

Car. Long live, and ever glorious live, the king!
            [*Trumpets and vollies at a distance.*

Alv. O, may this glorious day for ever stand
Fam'd in the rolls of late recorded time.

King. This happy union fix'd, my lords, we now
Must crave your counsel in our state's defence——
Letters this morn alarm us with designs
The Moors are forming to invade our realms:
But let them be, we're now prepared to meet them.

The prince that would sit free from foreign fears,
Should first with peace compose intestine jars;
Of hearts united while secure at home,
His rash invaders to their graves must come.   [Exeunt.

ACT II.   SCENE I.

Enter Don SANCHEZ.

Sanchez.

RELENTLESS fortune! thou hast done thy part,
Neglected nothing to oppose my love.
But thou shalt find, in thy despite, I'll on.
Wert thou not blind indeed, thou hadst foreseen
The honour done this hour to old Alvarez,
His being nam'd the prince's governor,
(Which I well knew th' ambitious Gormaz aim'd at)
Must like a wildfire's rage embroil their union,
Rekindle jealousies in Gormaz' heart,
Whose fatal flame must bury all in ashes:
But see, he comes, and seems to ruminate
With pensive grudge the king's too partial favour.

Enter GORMAZ *on the other Side.*

Gor. The king, methinks, is sudden in his choice——
'Tis true, I never sought (but therefore is
Not less the merit) nor obliquely hinted,
That I desir'd the office——He has heard
Me say, the prince, his son, I thought was now
Of age to change his prattling female court,
And claim'd a governor's instructive guidance——
Th' advice, it seems, was fit—but not th' adviser——
Be't so—why is Alvarez then the man?
He may be qualify'd—I'll not dispute——
But was not Gormaz too of equal merit?
Let me not think Alvarez plays me foul——
That cannot be——he knew I would not bear it——
And yet why he's so suddenly preferr'd——
I'll think no more on't—Time will soon resolve me.

D. San. Not to disturb, my lord, your graver
  thoughts,
May I presume——
 Gor. Don Sanchez may command me.
This youthful lord is sworn our house's friend;
If there's a cause for jealous thought, he'll find it.
          [*Aside.*
 D. San. I hear, my lord, the king has fresh advice
  receiv'd
Of a design'd invasion from the Moors,
Holds it confirm'd, or is it only rumour?
 Gor. Such new alarms indeed his letters bring,
But yet their grounds seem'd doubtful at the council.
     C ij

D. San. May it not prove some policy of state?
Some bugbear danger of our own creating?
The king, I have observ'd, is skill'd in rule,
Perfect in all the arts of tempering minds,
And—for the public good—can give alarms
Where fears are not, and hush them where they are.
    Gor. 'Tis so! he hints already at my wrongs.
    D. San. Not! but such prudence well becomes a
        prince;
For peace at home is worth his dearest purchase.
Yet he that gives his just resentments up,
Tho' honour'd by the royal mediation,
And sees his enemy enjoy the fruits,
Must have more virtues than his king to bear it——
Perhaps, my lord, I am not understood,
Nay, hope my jealous fears have no foundation;
But when the ties of friendship shall demand it,
Don Sanchez wears a sword that will revenge you.
                       [*Going.*
    Gor. Don Sanchez, stay—I think thou art my friend:
Thy noble father oft has serv'd me in
The cause of honour, and his cause was mine.
What thou hast said, speaks thee Balthazar's son,
I need not praise thee more——If I deserve
Thy love, refuse not what my heart's concern'd
To ask; speak freely of the king, of me,
Of old Alvarez, of our late alliance,
And what has follow'd since: then sum the whole,
And tell me truly, where the account's unequal.
    D. San. My lord, you honour with too great a trust

The judgment of my inexperienc'd years;
Yet for the time I have observ'd on men,
I've always found the generous open heart
Betray'd, and made the prey of minds below it.
Oh! 'tis the curse of manly virtue, that
Cowards, with cunning, are too strong for heroes:
And since you press me to unfold my thoughts,
I grieve to see your spirit so defeated,
Your just resentments by vile arts of court
Beguil'd, and melted to resign their terror.
Your honest hate, that had for ages stood
Unmov'd, and firmer from your foes' defiance,
Now sapp'd, and undermin'd by his submission.
Alvarez knew you were impregnable
To force, and chang'd the soldier for the statesman;
While you were yet his foe profess'd,
He durst not take these honours o'er your head;
Had you still held him at his distance due,
He would have trembled to have sought this office:
When once the king inclin'd to make his peace,
I saw too well the secret on the anvil,
And soon foretold the favour that succeeded:
Alas! this project has been long concerted,
Resolv'd in private 'twixt the king and him,
Laid out and manag'd here by secret agents,
While he, good man, knew nothing of the honour,
But from his sweet repose was dragg'd t' accept it.
Oh, it inflames my blood to think this fear
Should get the start of your unguarded spirit,

C iij

And proudly vaunt it in the plumes he stole
From you l
   Gor. Oh, Sanchez, thou hast fir'd a thought,
That was before but dawning in my mind l
Oh, now afresh it strikes my memory,
With what dissembled warmth the artful king
First charg'd his temper with the gloom he wore,
When I supply'd his late command of general I
Then with what fawning flattery **to me**
Alvarez l 'fear disguis'd his trembling hàte,
And sooth'd my yielding temper to believe him.
   D. San. Not flattery, my lord; tho' I must grant
'Twas praise well-tim'd, and therefore skilful.
   Gor. Now, on my soul, from him 'twas loathsome
       daubing l
I take thy friendship, Sanchez, to my heart;
And were not my Ximena rashly promis'd——
   D. San. Ximena's charms might grace a monarch's
       bed,
Nor dares my humble heart admit the hope,
Or, if it durst, some fitter time should shew it :
Results more pressing **now** demand your thought ;
First ease the pain of your depending doubt,
Divide this fawning courtier from the friend.
   Gor. Which way shall I receive, or thank thy love ?
   D. San. My lord, you over-rate me now—But see,
Alvarez comes—now probe his hollow heart,
Now while your thoughts are warm with his deceit,
And mark how calmly he'll evade the charge.
My lord, I'm gone.   [*Exit.*

Gor. I am thy friend for ever.

Enter ALVAREZ.

Alv. My lord, the king is walking forth to see
The prince, his son, begin his horsemanship :
If you're inclin'd to see him, I'll attend you.

Gor. Since duty calls me not, I've no delight
To be an idle gaper on another's business.
You may indeed find pleasure in the office,
Which you've so artfully contriv'd to fit.

Alv. Contriv'd, my lord! I'm sorry such a thought
Can reach the man whom I so late embrac'd.

Gor. Men are not always what they seem—This honour,
Which, in another's wrong, you've barter'd for,
Was at the price of those embraces bought.

Alv. Ha! bought! For shame, suppress this poor suspicion!
For if you think, you cann't but be convinc'd
The naked honour of Alvarez scorns
Such base disguise—Yet pause a moment——
Since our great master, with such kind concern,
Himself has interpos'd to heal our feuds,
Let us not, thankless, rob him of the glory,
And undeserve the grace by new false fears.

Gor. Kings are, alas! but men, and form'd like us,
Subject alike to be by men deceiv'd :
The blushing court from this rash choice will see
How blindly he o'erlooks superior merit.
Could no man fill the place but worn Alvarez ?

 Alv. Worn more with wounds and victories than
  age.
Who stands before him in great actions past?
But I'm to blame to urge that merit now,
Which will but shock what reasoning may convince.
 Gor. The fawning slave! Oh, Sanchez, how I
  thank thee!   [*Aside.*
 Alv. You have a virtuous daughter, I a son,
Whose softer hearts our mutual hands have rais'd
Ev'n to the summit of expected joy;
If no regard to me, yet let, at least,
Your pity of their passions rein your temper.
 Gor. Oh, needless care! to nobler objects now,
That son, be sure, in vanity, pretends;
While his high father's wisdom is preferr'd
To guide and govern our great monarch's son,
His proud aspiring heart forgets Ximena.
Think not of him, but your superior care;
Instruct the royal youth to rule with awe
His future subjects, trembling at his frown;
Teach him to bind the loyal heart in love,
The bold and factious in the chains of fear;
Join to these virtues too your warlike deeds,
Inflame him with the vast fatigues you've borne,
But now are past, to shew him by example,
And give him in the closet safe renown;
Read him what scorching suns he must endure,
What bitter nights must wake, or sleep in arms,
To countermarch the foe, to give th' alarm,
And to his own great conduct owe the day;

Mark him on charts the order of the battle,
And make him from your manuscripts a hero.

Alv. Ill-temper'd man ! thus to provoke the heart,
Whose tortur'd patience is thy only friend !

Gor. Thou only to thyself canst be a friend :
I tell thee, false Alvarez, thou hast wrong'd me,
Hast basely robb'd me of my merit's right,
And intercepted our young prince's fame.
His youth with me had found the active proof,
The living practice of experienc'd war ;
This sword had taught him glory in the field,
At once his great example and his guard ;
His unfledg'd wings from me had learnt to soar,
And strike at nations trembling at my name :
This I had done ; but thou, with servile arts,
Hast, fawning, crept into our master's breast,
Elbow'd superior merit from his ear,
And, like a courtier, stole his son from glory.

Alv. Hear me, proud man ! for now I burn to speak,
Since neither truth can sway, nor temper touch thee ;
Thus I retort with scorn thy sland'rous rage :
Thou, thou the tutor of a kingdom's heir !
Thou guide the passions of o'er-boiling youth,
That canst not in thy age yet rule thy own !
For shame ! retire, and purge th' imperious heart,
Reduce thy arrogant, self-judging pride,
Correct the meanness of thy groveling soul,
Chase damn'd suspicion from thy manly thoughts,
And learn to treat with honour thy superior.

Gor. Superior, ha ! dar'st thou provoke me, traitor ?

Alv. Unhand me, ruffian, lest thy hold prove fatal.

Gor. Take that, audacious dotard !   [*Strikes him.*

Alv. Oh, my blood,

Flow forward to my arm, to chain this tyger !

If thou art brave, now bear thee like a man,

And quit my honour of this vile disgrace.

     [*They fight*, Alvarez *is disarm'd.*

Oh, feeble life, I have too long endur'd thee !

 Gor. Thy sword is mine ; take back th' inglorious

   trophy,

Which would disgrace thy victor's thigh to wear.

Now forward to thy charge, read to the prince

This martial lecture of thy fam'd exploits ;

And from this wholesome chastisement, learn thou

To tempt the patience of offended honour.   [*Exit.*

 Alv. Oh, rage ! Oh, wild despair ! Oh, helpless age !

Wert thou but lent me to survive my honour ?

Am I with martial toils worn grey, and see

At last one hour's blight lay waste my laurels ?

Is this fam'd arm to me alone defenceless ?

Has it so often prop'd this empire's glory,

Fenc'd, like a rampart, the Castilian throne,

To me alone disgraceful, to its master useless ?

Oh, sharp remembrance of departed glory !

Oh, fatal dignity, too dearly purchas'd !

Now, haughty Gormaz, now guide thou my prince ;

Insulted honour is unfit t' approach him.

And thou, once glorious weapon, fare thee well,

Old servant, worthy of an abler master,

Leave now for ever his abandon'd side,

And, to revenge him, grace some nobler arm.
My son!

Enter CARLOS.

Oh, Carlos! canst thou bear dishonour?

 Car. What villain dares occasion, sir, the question?
Give me his name; the proof shall answer him.

 Alv. Oh, just reproach! Oh, prompt resentful fire!
My blood rekindles at thy manly flame,
And glads my labouring heart with youth's return.
Up, up, my son—I cannot speak my shame——
Revenge, revenge me!

 Car. Oh, my rage!—Of what?

 Alv. Of an indignity so vile, my heart
Redoubles all its torture to repeat it.
A blow, a blow, my boy!

 Car. Distraction! fury!

 Alv. In vain, alas! this feeble arm assail'd,
With mortal vengeance, the aggressor's heart:
He dally'd with my age, o'erborn, insulted,
Therefore to thy young arm, for sure revenge,
My soul's distress commits my sword and cause:
Pursue him, Carlos, to the world's last bounds,
And from his heart tear back our bleeding honour.
Nay, to inflame thee more, thou'lt find his brow
Cover'd with laurels, and far-fam'd his prowess:
Oh, I have seen him, dreadful in the field,
Cut thro' whole squadrons his destructive way,
And snatch the gore-dy'd standard from the foe!

Car. Oh, rack not with his fame my tortur'd heart,
That burns to know him, and eclipse his glory!

Alv. Tho' I foresee 'twill strike thy soul to hear it;
Yet since our gasping honour calls for thy
Relief——Oh, Carlos!—'tis Ximena's father——

Car. Ha!

Alv. Pause not for a reply——I know thy love,
I know the tender obligations of thy heart,
And even lend a sigh to thy distress.
I grant Ximena dearer than thy life;
But wounded honour must surmount them both.
I need not urge thee more; thou know'st my wrong;
'Tis in thy heart, and in thy hand the vengeance;
Blood only is the balm for grief like mine,
Which, 'till obtain'd, I will in darkness mourn,
Nor lift my eyes to light, till thy return.
But haste, o'ertake this blaster of my name,
Fly swift to vengeance, and bring back my fame.

                         [*Exit.*

Car. Relentless Heav'n! is all thy thunder gone?
Not one bolt left to finish my despair!
Lie still, my heart, and close this deadly wound;
Stir not to thought, for motion is thy ruin.
But see, the frighted poor Ximena comes,
And with her tremblings strikes thee cold as death.
My helpless father too, o'erwhelm'd with shame,
Begs his dismission to his grave with honour.
Ximena weeps; heart-pierc'd Alvarez groans;
Rage lifts my sword, and love arrests my arm:

Oh, double torture of distracting wo!
Is there no mean betwixt these sharp extremes?
Must honour perish, if I spare my love?
Oh, ignominious pity! shameful softness!
Must I, to right Alvarez, kill Ximena?
Oh, cruel vengeance! Oh, heart-wounding honour!
Shall I forsake her in her soul's extremes,
Depress the virtue of her filial tears,
And bury in a tomb our nuptial joy?
Shall that just honour that subdu'd her heart,
Now build its fame relentless on her sorrows.
Instruct me, Heav'n, that gav'st me this distress,
To choose, and bear me worthy of my being!
Oh, Love, forgive me, if my hurry'd soul
Should act with error in this storm of fortune;
For Heav'n can tell what pangs I feel to save thee!
But hark! the shrieks of drowning honour call!
'Tis sinking, gasping, while I stand in pause;
Plunge in, my heart, and save it from the billows.
It will be so——the blow's too sharp a pain,
And vengeance has at least this just excuse,
That ev'n Ximena blushes while I bear it:
Her generous heart, that was by honour won,
Must, when that honour's stain'd, abjure my love.

Oh, peace of mind, farewell! Revenge, I come,
And raise thy altar on a mournful tomb! [Exit.

D

ACT III. SCENE I.

Enter GARCIA *and* GORMAZ.

Gormaz.

THE king is master of his will and me :
But be it as it may—what's done's irrevocable.

Gar. My lord, you ill receive this mark of favour,
And while thus obstinate, inflame your fault.
When sovereign power descends to ask of subjects
The due submission which its will may force,
Your danger's greater from such slighted mildness,
Than should you disobey its full commands.

Gor. The consequence, perhaps, may prove it so.

Gar. Have you no fear of what his frown may do ?

Gor. Has he no fear of what my wrongs may do ?
Men of my rank are not in hours undone ;
When I am crush'd, I fall with vengeance round me.

Gar. The rash indignity you've done Alvarez,
Without some proof of wrong, bears no excuse.

Gor. I am myself the judge of what I feel ;
I feel him false, and, feeling, must resent.

Gar. Shall it be deem'd a falsehood to accept
A dignity by royal hands conferr'd ?

Gor. He should have wav'd it ; first consulted me.
He might have held me still his friend sincere,
Have shar'd my fortunes, as a friend entreating ;
But basely thus to out me of my right,

By treacherous aĉts to do me private wrong,
Is what I never can forgive, and have resented.

Gar. But in this violence you offend the king,
The sanĉtion of whose choice claim'd more regard.

Gor. Why am I fretted with these chains of honour,
Less free than others in my just resentments;
Who, unprovok'd myself, do no man wrong,
But injur'd, am as storms implacable?

Gar. My lord, this stubborn temper will undo you.

Gor. Then, sir, Alvarez will be satisfy'd.

Gar. Be yet persuaded, and compose this broil.

Gor. My resolution's fix'd; let's wave the subjeĉt.

Gar. Will you refuse all terms of reparation?

Gor. All, all, that are not from my honour due!

Gar. Dare you not trust that honour with the king?

Gor. My life's my king's, my honour is my own.

Gar. What's then, in short, your answer? For the
        king
Expeĉts it on my first return.

Gor. 'Tis this,
That I dare die, but cannot bow to shame.

Gar. My lord, I take my leave.

Gor. Don Garcia's servant.   [*Exit* Garcia.
Who fears not death, smiles at the frowns of power.

Enter CARLOS.

Car. My lord, your leave to talk with you.

Gor. Be free.
I did expeĉt you on this late occasion.

Car. I'm glad to find you do my honour right ;
And hope you'll not refuse it wrong'd Alvarez.

Gor. He had a sword to right himself.

Car. That sword is here

Gor. 'Tis well ; the place—and let our time be short.

Car. One moment's respite, for Ximena's sake :
She has not wrong'd me, and my heart would spare her:
We both, without a stain to either's honour,
May pity her distress, and pause to save her :
Nor need I blush that I suspend my cause,
Since with its vengeance her sure woes are blended.
Not for myself, but for her tender sake,
I bend me to the earth, and beg for mercy.
Let not her virtues suffer for her love ;
Oh, lay not on her innocence the grief
Of a mourn'd father's, or a lover's blood !
Oh, spare her sighs, prevent her streaming tears ;
Stop this effusion of my bleeding honour,
And heal, if possible, its wounds with peace !

Gor. What you have offer'd for Ximena's sake,
Will, in her gratitude, be full repaid ;
And for the peace you ask, that's yours to give.
Submission 'tis in vain to hope ; for know,
I have this hour refus'd it to the king.
Thy father's arts betray'd my friendship's faith ;
I felt the wrong, and, as I ought, reveng'd it.
We're now on equal terms : but if his cause
So deep is in thy heart, that thou resolv'st,
With fruitless vengeance, to provoke my rage,
Then thou, not I, art author of thy ruin.

Car. Support me now, Ximena, guard my heart,
And bar this pressing provocation's entrance. [*Aside.*
Have I, my lord, in person wrong'd you?
   Gor. No.
   Car. Why then these fatal cruelties to me,
That I must lose, or wrong Ximena's love?
For she must scorn me, should I bear my shame;
Or fly me, tho' my honour should revenge it.
   Gor. Place that to thy misfortune, not to me.
   Car. Not to you!
Am I not forc'd by wrongs I blush to name,
To prosecute this fatal reparation,
Which, had you temper or a feeling here,
Had you the spirit to confess your error,
Your heart's confusion had subdu'd Alvarez,
And thrown you at his injur'd feet for pardon?
   Gor. If thou com'st here to talk me from my sense,
Or think'st with words t' extenuate his guilt,
Thou offer'st to the winds thy forceless plea.
I will not bear the mention of his truth;
His falsehood's here, 'tis rooted in my heart,
And justifies a worse revenge than I have taken.
   Car. Oh, patience, Heav'n! Oh, tortur'd rage!
      Not speak
The pious pangs of my torn soul insulted!
Have I for this how'd down my humble knee,
To swell thy triumph o'er my father's wrongs,
And hear him tainted with a traitor's practice?
Oh, give me back that vile submissive shame,
That I may meet thee with retorted scorn,

D iij

And right my honour with untainted vengeance!.
Yet no——withhold it, take it to acquit my love;
That sacrifice was to Ximena due;
Her helpless sufferings claim'd that pang; and since
I cannot bring dishonour to her arms,
Thus my rack'd heart pours forth its last adieus,
And makes libation of its bleeding peace.
Farewell, dear injur'd softness—follow me.

    Gor. Lead on——yet hold—should we together
        forth,
It may create suspicion, and prevent us.
Propose the place; I'll take some different circle.

    Car. Behind the ramparts near the Western Gate.

    Gor. Expect me on the instant.

    Car. Poor Ximena!   [*Exit.*

    Gor. Deep as resentment lodges in my heart,
It feels some pity there for Carlos' passion——
It shall be so——his brave resentment's just;

                    [*Writes in tablets.*

And hard his fate both ways——This legacy
Shall right my honour and my enemy.   [*Exit.*

       Enter BELZARA *and* XIMENA.

    Bel. Look up, Ximena, and suppress thy fears;
What tho' a transient cloud o'ercast thy joy,
Shall we conclude from thence a wreck must follow?

    Xim. Can I resist the fears that reason forms?
Have I not cause to tremble in the storm,
While horror, ruin, and despair's in view?
Can I support the good Alvarez' shame,

Whose generous heart took pity on our love,
And not let fall a grateful tear to mourn it?
Can I behold fierce Carlos, stung with his disgrace,
Breaking like fire from these weak-holding arms,
And not sink down with terror at his rage?
Must I not tremble for the blood may follow?
If by his arm my hapless father falls,
Am I not forc'd with rigour to revenge him?
If Carlos by my father's sword should bleed,
Am I not bound with double grief to mourn him?
One gave me life, shall I not revere him?
The other is my life, can I survive him?

   Bel. Her griefs have something of such mournful
      force,
That, tho' not equal to my own, I feel them. [*Aside.*
   Xim. Carlos, you see too, shuns my sight; no news,
No tidings yet arrive, tho' I have sent
My swiftest fears a thousand ways to find him.
Who can support these terrors of suspense?
   Bel. Be not thus torn with wild uncertain fears;
Carlos may yet arrive, and save your peace:
He is too much a lover to resist
The tender pleadings of Ximena's sorrow;
One word, one sigh from you arrests his arm,
And makes the tempest of his rage subside.
   Xim. And say that I could conquer him with tears,
And terrors could subdue his piteous heart,
To yield his honour and its cause to love,
What will the world not say of his compliance?
Can I be happy in his fame's disgrace?

Can love subsist on shame, that sprung from honour?
Shall I reduce him to such hard contempt,
And raise on infamy our nuptial joy?
Ah, no! no means are left for my relief:
Let him resist, or yield to my distress,
Or shame or sorrow's sure to meet me.

Bel. Ximena has, I see, a soul refin'd,
Too great, too just, too noble to be happy:
True virtue must despair from this vile world
To crown its days with unallay'd reward.
But see, your servant is return'd—Good news,
Kind Heav'n!

Enter a Page.

Xim. Speak quickly, hast thou seen Don Carlos?

Page. Madam, where your commands directed me,
I've made the strictest search in vain to find him.

Xim. Now, now, Belzara, where's that hope thou
　　　　gav'st me?

Bel. Nor hast thou gain'd no knowledge of his steps?
Has no one seen him pass, or heard of him?

Page. As I return'd, the centinel that guards
The gate inform'd me, that he saw him scarce
Ten minutes hence pass in disorder'd haste
From out this very house alone.

Bel. Alone!

Page. Alone! and after soon my lord, wrapp'd in
His cloak, without a servant, follow'd him.

Xim. Oh, Heav'n!

Bel. No servant, saidst thou?

Page None; and as
My lord came forth, the soldier standing to
His arms, he sign'd forbiddance, and reply'd,
Be sure you saw me not.

 Xim. Then ruin's sure;
They are engag'd, and fatal blood must follow.
Excuse, my dear, this hurry of my fate;
One moment lost may prove an age too late.   [*Exit.*

 Bel. Howe'er my own afflictions press my heart,
I bear a part in poor Ximena's grief;
Tho' e'en the worst that can befall her hopes,
May better be endur'd than what I feel.
Oh, nothing can destroy her lover's truth!
Carlos may prove unhappy, not inconstant;
Whate'er disasters may obstruct her joy,
The comfort of his truth is sure to find her;
That thought ev'n pains of parting may remove,
Or fill up all the space of absence with delight.
But I, alas! am left to my despair alone,
Confin'd to sigh in solitude my woes,
Or hide with anguish what I blush to bear.
In vain the woman's pride resents my wrongs,
Unconquer'd Love maintains his empire still,
And with new force insults my heart's resistance.

Enter ALONZO *hastily.*

 Alon. Your pardon, madam—Have you seen Lord
  Gormaz?
I come to warn him that he stir not hence;
The guards are order'd to attend his door.

Bel. Alas, they are too late! Carlos and he
Are both gone forth, 'tis fear'd, with fatal purpose;
And poor Ximena, drown'd in tears, has follow'd
        them.

Alon. Then 'tis, indeed, too late—I wish my friend,
The rash Don Sanchez, had not blown this fire.
Be not concern'd, madam ; I know your griefs,
And, as a friend, have labour'd to prevent them.
You have not told Ximena of his falsehood ?

Bel. Alas, I durst not! knowing that her friendship
Would for my sake so coldly treat his vows,
That 'twould but more provoke him to insult me.

Alon. You judge him right ; patience will yet recall
        him ;
'Tis not his love, but pride, pursues Ximena;
A youthful heat, that with the toil will tire.
Be comforted ; I'll still observe his steps,
And when I find him staggering, catch him back
To love, and warm him with his vows of honour.
But duty calls me to the king——Shall I
Attend you, madam ?

Bel. Sir, I thank your care.
My near concern for poor Ximena's fate
Keeps me impatient here, till her return.   [*Exeunt.*

Enter KING, GARCIA, SANCHEZ, *Attendants.*

King. Since mild entreaties fail, our power shall
        force him.
Could he suppose his insult to our person offer'd,
His outrage done within our palace walls,

Deserv'd the lenity we've deign'd to shew him?
Is yet Alonzo with our orders gone?

   Gar. He is, my lord, but not return'd.

   D. San. Dread sir,

For what the count has offer'd to Alvarez
I dare not plead excuse; but as his friend,
Would beg your royal leave to mitigate
His seeming disobedience to your pleasure.
Restraint, however just, oppos'd against
The tide of passion, makes the current fiercer,
Which of itself in time had ebb'd to reason;
Your will surpris'd him in his heart's emotion,
Ere thought had leisure to compose his mind;
Great souls are jealous of their honour's shame,
And bend reluctant to enjoin'd submission:
Had your commands oblig'd him to repair
Alvarez' wrongs with hazards in your service,
Were it to face the double-number'd foe,
To pass the rapid stream thro' showers of fire,
To force the trenchment, or to storm the breach,
I'll answer he'd embrace with joy the charge,
And march intrepid in commands of honour.

   King. We doubt not of his daring in the field;
But he mistakes, if he concludes from thence,
That to persist in wrong is height of spirit,
Or to have acted wrong is always base:
Perfection's not the attribute of man,
Nor therefore can a fault confess'd degrade him;
The lowest minds have spirits to offend,
But few can reach the courage to confess it.

Submitting to our will, the count had lost
No fame, nor can we pardon his refusal
What you have said, Don Sanchez, speaks the friend ;
What we resolve, 'tis fit should speak the king :
We both have said enough—The public now
Requires our thought.   We are inform'd ten sail
Of warlike vessels, mann'd with our old foes,
The Moors, were late discover'd off our coast,
And steering to the river's mouth their course.

    Gar. The lives, sir, they have lost in like attempts
Must make them cautious to repeat the danger ;
This is no time to fear them.

    King. Nor contemn ;
Too full security has oft been fatal.
Consider with what ease the flood, at night,
May bring them down t' insult our capital.
Let at the port, and on the walls, our guards
Be doubled ; till the morn that force may serve.
Gormaz has tim'd it ill to be in fault,
When his immediate presence is requir'd.

    Gar. My liege, Alonzo is return'd.

Enter ALONZO.

    King, 'Tis well——
Have you obey'd us ? Is the count confin'd ?

    Alon. Your orders, sir, arriv'd unhappily
Too late ; the count, with Carlos, was before
Gone forth, to end their fatal difference :
As I came back, I met the gathering crowd
In fright, and hurrying to the western gate,

To see, as they reported, in the field,
The body of some murder'd nobleman
Struck with my fears, I hasted to the place,
Where to my sense's horror, when arriv'd,
1 found them true, and Gormaz just expir'd ;
While fair Ximena, to adorn the wo,
Bath'd his pale breathless body with her tears,
Calling with cries for justice on his head,
Whose rueful hand had done the barbarous deed.
The pitying crowd took part in her distress,
And join'd her moving plaints for due revenge ;
While some, in kinder feeling of her griefs,
Remov'd the mournful object from her eyes,
And to the neighbouring convent bore the body,
Which, when committed to the abbot's care,
I left the pressing throng to tell the news.

 King. Ximena's griefs are follow'd with our own ;
For tho' in some degree the haughty count
Drew on himself the son's too just revenge,
We cannot lose, without a deep concern,
So true a subject, and so brave a soldier :
However pity may for Carlos plead,
Death ends his failings, and demands our grief.

 Alon. Sir, here, in the tablets of th' unhappy count,
In his own hand these written lines were found.

 King. [*Reading.*] " Alvarez wrong'd me in my
   master's favour ;
Carlos is brave, and has deserv'd Ximena."
Strange, generous spirit ! now we pity thee.

E

Alon. Behold, sir, where the lost Ximena comes,
O'erwhelm'd with sorrow, to demand your justice.

Enter XIMENA.

Xim. Oh, sacred sir, forgive my grief's intrusion !
Behold a helpless orphan at your feet,
Who for a father's blood implores your justice.

Enter ALVAREZ, *hastily.*

Alv. Oh, turn, dread, royal master, turn your eyes,
See on the earth your faithful soldier prostrate,
Whose honour's just revenge entreats your mercy !
　　Xim. Oh, godlike monarch, hear my louder cries !
Alv. Oh, be not to the old and helpless deaf !
Xim. Revenge yourself, your violated laws.
Alv. Support not violence in rude aggressors.
Xim. Be greatly good, and do the injur'd justice.
Alv. Be greater still, and shew the valiant mercy.
　　Xim. Oh, sir, your crown's support and guard is
　　　　gone !
The impious Carlos' sword has kill'd my father—
　　Alv. And, like a pious son, aveng'd his own.
　　King. Rise, fair Ximena, and Alvarez rise !
With equal sorrow we receive your plaints ;
Both shall be heard apart——Proceed, Ximena ;
Alvarez, in your place you speak ; be patient
　　Xim. What can I say ? But miseries like mine
May plead with plainest truths their piteous cause.
Is he not dead ? Is not my father kill'd ?
Have not these eyes beheld his ghastly wound,

And mix'd with fruitless tears his streaming blood?
That blood, which in his royal master's cause
So oft has sprung him through your foes victorious;
That blood, which all the raging swords of war
Could never reach, a young presumptuous arm
Has dar'd within your view to sacrifice!
These eyes beheld it stream—Excuse my grief;
My tears will better than my words explain me.

    King. Take heart, Ximena; we're inclin'd to hear
       thee.

    Xim. Oh, shall a life so faithful to the king
Fall unreveng'd, and stain his glory?
Shall merit so important to the state
Be left expos'd to sacrilegious rage,
And fall the sacrifice of private passion?
Alvarez says his honour was insulted;
Yet, be it so, was there no king to right it?
Who better could protect it than the donor?
Shall Carlos wrest the sceptre from your hand,
And point the sword of justice whom to punish?
Oh, if such outrage may escape with pardon,
Whose life's secure from his self-judging rage?
Oh, where's protection, if Ximena's tears,
And tender passion could not save her father?

    King. Alvarez, answer her.

    Alv. My heart's too full:
Divided, torn, distracted with its griefs,
How can I plead poor Carlos' cause, when I
Am touch'd with pity of Ximena's wo?
Her suffering piety has caught my soul,

E ij

And only leaves me sorrow to defend me :
Ximena has a grief I cannot disallow,
Nor dare I hope for pardon, but your pity ;
Carlos, ev'n yet, may merit some compassion ;
Perhaps I'm partial to his piety,
And see his deeds with a fond father's eye ;
But that I still must leave to royal mercy.
Oh, sir, imagine what the brave endure,
When the chaste front of honour is insulted,
Her fame abus'd, and ravish'd by a blow I
Oh, piercing, piercing must the torture be,
If soft Ximena wanted pow'r t' appease it I
Pardon this weakness of o'erflowing nature ;
I cannot see such filial virtue perish,
And not let fall a tear to mourn its hardship.
 Xim. Oh, my divided heart I Oh, poor Alvarez I
            [*Aside.*
 King. Compose thy griefs, my good old friend ; we
  feel them.
 Alv. If Gormaz' blood must be with blood re-
  veng'd,
Oh, do not, sacred sir, misplace your justice !
Mine was the guilt, and be on me the vengeance :
Carlos but acted what my sufferings prompted ;
The fatal sword was not his own, but mine ;
I gave it, with my wrongs, into his hand,
Which had been innocent had' mine been able.
On me your vengeance will be just and mild ;
My days, alas I are drawing to their end,
But Carlos spar'd may yet live long to serve you.

Preserve my son, and I embrace my fate;
Since he has sav'd my honour from the grave,
Oh, lay me gently there to rest for ever!
 King. Your mutual plaints require our tend'rest
   thought:
Our council shall be summon'd to assist us——
Look up, my fair, and calm thy sorrows;
Thy king is now thy father, and will right thee.
Alvarez, on his word, has liberty;
Be Carlos found to answer to his charge.
Sanchez, wait you Ximena to her rest,
Whom, on the morrow's noon, we full will answer.

 Hard is the task of justice, where distress
 Excites our mercy, yet demands redress. [Exeunt.

ACT IV. SCENE I.

XIMENA's *Apartment.*

BELZARA *alone.*

SURE some ill-boding planet must preside,
Malignant to the peace of tender lovers!
Undone Ximena! Oh, relentless honour,
That first subdu'd thy generous heart, then rais'd
Thy lover's fatal arm to pierce it through
Thy father's life, and make thy virtue wretched!
The hapless Carlos too is lost for ever!
Condemn'd to fly an exile from her sight,

In whom he only lives !——Oh, Heav'n ! he's here !
His miseries have made him desperate.

Enter CARLOS.

Carlos, what wild distraction has possess'd thee,
That thus thou seek'st thy safety in thy ruin ?
Is this a place to hide thy wretched head,
Where justice and Ximena's sure to find thee ?
   Car. I would not hide me from Ximena's sight;
Banish'd from her, I every moment die.
Since I must perish, let her frowns destroy me ;
Her anger's sharper than the sword of justice.
   Bel. Alas, I pity thee ! but would not have
Thee tempt the first emotions of her heart,
While duty and resentment yet transport her :
I wait each moment her return from court,
Which now, be sure, will be with friends attended.
O fly, for pity's sake, regard her fame,
Should you be seen, what must the world conclude ?
Would you increase her miseries, to have
Malicious tongues report her love conceal'd
Beneath the roof her father's murderer.
But see, she comes ! O, hide thee but a moment !
Kill not her honour too, let that persuade.thee.
                         [*Exit* Carlos.
Don Sanchez here ! O, Heavens ! how I tremble.
                              [*Retires.*

Enter Don SANCHEZ *and* XIMENA.

   D. San. This noble conquest, madam, of your love,

To after-ages must record your fame.
Just is your grief, and your resentment great,
And great the victim that should fall before it;
But words are empty succours to distress:
Therefore command my actions to relieve you.
Would you have sure revenge, employ this sword,
My fortune, and my life is yours to right you;
Accept my service, and you'll overpay it.

Bel. O faithless, barbarous man! but I'll divert
Thy cruel aim, and use my power for Carlos. [*Aside.*

Xim. O, miserable me!

Bel. Take comfort, madam.

D. San. Belzara here! then I have lost th' occasion;
Yet I may urge enough to give her pain: [*Aside.*
Commanding me, you make your vengeance sure.

Xim. That were t' offend the king, to whom I have
Appeal'd, and whence I now must only wait it.

D. San. Revenge from justice, madam, moves so
          slow,
That oft the watchful criminal escapes it.
Appeal to your resentment, you secure it.
Carlos, you found, would trust no other-power,
And 'tis but just you quit him as he wrong'd you.

Bel. Alas! Don Sanchez, madam, feels not love,
He little thinks how Carlos fills your heart;
What shining glory in his crime appears;
What pangs it cost him to take part with honour;
That you must hate the hand that could destroy him.
Sanchez, to shew the real friend, would use
His secret int'rest with the king to spare him,

For tho' you're bound in duty to pursue him,
Yet love, alas! would with a conscious joy,
Applaud the power that could unbid preserve him.

   Xim. O, kind Belzara! how thou feel'st my suf_
      ferings;
Yet I must think Don Sanchez means me well.

   D. San. Confusion! how her subtle tongue has
      foil'd me——————   [*Aside.*
Madam, some other time I'll beg your leave
To wait your service, and approve my friendship.

   Xim. Oh, every friend but Carlos is at hand
To help me! Grief, sir, is unfit to thank you.

   D. San. Oh! if such beauties 'midst her sorrows
      shine,
What darting charms must point her smiling eyes.
                      [*Exit.*

   Xim. At length I'm free, at liberty to think,
And give my miseries a loose of sórrow.
O, Belzara! Carlos has kill'd my father!
Weep, weep, my eyes, pour down your baleful show'rs,
He that in grief should be my heart's support,
Has wrought my sorrows, and must fall their victim.
When Carlos is destroy'd, what comfort's left me?
Spite of my wrongs, he still inhabits here:
O, still his fatal virtues plead his cause;
His filial honour charms my woman's heart,
And there, ev'n yet, he combats with my father.

   Bel. Restrain these headstrong sallies of your heart,
And try with slumbers to compose your spirits.

   Xim. O! where's repose for misery like mine?

How grievous, Heaven! how bitter is my portion!
O, shall a parent's blood cry unreveng'd?
Shall impious love suborn my heart to pay
His ashes but unprofitable tears,
And bury in my shame the great regards of duty?

Bel. Alas! that duty is discharg'd; you have
Appeal'd to justice, and should wait its course.
Nor are you bound with rigour to enforce it;
His hard misfortunes may deserve compassion.

Xim. O! that they do deserve, it is my grief;
Could I withdraw my pity from his cause,
Were falsehood, pride, or insolence his crime,
My just revenge, without a pang, should reach him.
But as he is supported with excuse,
Defended by the cries of bleeding honour,
Whose cruel laws none but the great obey;
My hopeless heart is tortur'd with extremes,
It mourns in vengeance, and at mercy shudders.

Bel. O, what will be at last the dire resolve
Of your afflicted soul?

Xim. There is but one
Can end my sorrows, and preserve my fame;
The sole resource my miseries can have
Is to pursue, destroy; then meet him in the grave.

[*Going.*

CARLOS *meets her.*

Amazement! horror! have my eyes their sense?
Or do my raving griefs create this phantom?

Support me! help me! hide me from the vision!
For 'tis not Carlos come to brave my sorrows.

         [*Carlos kneels.*

 Bel. O turn your eye in pity of his griefs,
Resign'd, and prostrate at your feet for mercy.

 Xim. What will my woes do with me?

 Bel. Now!
Now, conquering love, shoot all thy darts to save him;
Now snatch the palm from cruel honour's brow;
Maintain thy empire, and relieve the wretched:
O, hang upon his tongue thy thrilling charms,
To hold her heart, and kill the hopes of Sanchez.

           [*Exit.*

 Car. O, pierce not thus with thy offended eyes,
The wretched heart that of itself is breaking.

 Xim. Can I be wounded, and not shrink with pain?
Can I support with temper, him that shed
My father's blood, triumphant in my ruin?
O, Carlos! Carlos! was thy heart of stone?
Was nothing due to poor Ximena's peace?
O! 'twas not thus I felt new pains for thee,
When, at my feet, thy sighs of love were pity'd,
And all hereditary hate forgotten!
Tho' bound in filial honour to insult
Thy flame, I broke through all to crown thy vows,
And bore the censure of my race to save thee:
And am I thus requited? Left forlorn!
The tender passion of my heart despis'd!
Could not my terrors move one spark of mercy?

No mild abatement of thy stern revenge?
T' excuse thy crime, or justify my love?

 Car. O, hear me but a moment.

 Xim. O, my heart!

 Car. One mournful word!

 Xim. Ah! leave me to despair!

 Car. One dying last adieu, then wreak thy venge-
  ance:

Behold the sword that has undone thee.

 Xim. Ah! stain'd with my father's blood! O, rue-
  ful object!

 Car. O, Ximena!

 Xim. Take hence that horrid steel,

That, while I bear thy sight, arraigns my virtue.

 Car. Endure it rather to support resentment,

T' inflame thy vengeance, and to pierce thy victim ·

I am more wretched than thy rage can wish me.

 Xim. O, cruel Carlos! in one day' thou hast kill'd

The father with thy sword, the daughter with

Thy sight——O, yet remove that fatal object;

I cannot bear the glare of its reproach;

If thou wouldst have me hear thee, hide the cause,

That wounds reflection to our mutual ruin.

 Car. Thus I obey——but how shall I proceed?

What words can help me to deserve thy hearing?

How can I plead my wounded honour's cause,

Where injur'd love and duty are my judges?

Or how shall I repent me of a crime,

Which, uncommitted, had deserv'd thy scorn?

Yet think not, O, I conjure thee, think not,

But that I bore a thousand racks of love,
While my conflicting honour press'd for vengeance.
O, I endur'd, submitted ev'n to shame,
Begg'd, as for life, for peaceful reparation !
But all in vain ; like water sprinkled on
A fire, those drops but made him burn the more,
And only added to thy father's fierceness.
Reduc'd, at last, to these extremes of torture,
That I must be, or infamous, or wretched,
I sav'd my honour, and resign'd to ruin.
Nor think, Ximena, honour had prevail'd,
But that thy nobler soul oppos'd thy charms,
And told my heart, none but the brave deserv'd thee.
Now having thus discharg'd my honour's debt,
And wash'd my injur'd father's stains away,
What yet remains of life, is due to love.
Behold the wretch whose honour's fatal fame
Is founded on the ruin of thy peace :
Receive the victim, which thy griefs demand,
Prepar'd to bleed, and bending to the blow

    Xim. O, Carlos, I must take thee at thy word,
But must with equal justice too discharge
My ties of love, as fatal bonds of duty.
O, think not, tho' enforc'd to these extremes,
My heart is yet insensible to thee !
O ! I must thank thee for thy painful pause :
The generous shame thy tortur'd honour bore,
When at my father's feet my suff'rings threw thee.
Can I present thee in that dear confusion,
And not with grateful sighs of pity mourn thee?
   1

I can lament thee, but I dare not pardon;
Thy duty done, reminds me of my own;
My filial piety, like thine distress'd,
Compels me to be miserably just,
And asks my love a victim to my fame:
Yet think not duty could o'er love prevail,
But that thy nobler soul assures my heart,
Thou wouldst despise the passion that could save thee.

   Car. Since I must die, let that kind hand destroy me.
Let not the wretch, once honour'd with thy love,
Thy Carlos, once thought worthy of thy arms,
Be dragg'd a public spectacle to justice:
To draw the irksome pity of a crowd,
Who may with vulgar reason call thee cruel.
My death from thee will elevate thy vengeance,
And shew, like mine, thy duty scorn'd assistance.

   Xim. Shall I then take assistance? and from thee?
Accept that vengeance from thy heart's despair?
No, Carlos, no!
I will not judge, like thee, my private wrongs,
But to the course of justice trust my duty,
Which shall, in ev'ry part, untainted flow;
Unmix'd with gain'd advantage o'er thy love,
And from its own pure fountain raise my glory.

   Car. O, can my death with shame advance that glory?
Can I do more than perish to appease thee?
Can my misfortunes too have reach'd thy hate?

   Xim. Can hate have part in interviews like this?
Nay, can I give thee greater proof of love,
Than that I trust my vengeance with thy honour?

F

Art not thou now within my power to seize ?
Yet I'll release thee, Carlos, on thy word.
Give me thy word, that on the morrow noon,
Before the king in person thou wilt answer,
And take the shelter of the night to leave me.

   Car. O, thou hast found the way to fix my ruin!
It must be so, thou shalt have ample vengeance,
Pursu'd by thee, my life's not worth the saving;
But then that fatal honour, my engagement,
That at the hour propos'd I'll meet my fate——
But must we part, Ximena, like sworn foes ?
Has love no sense of all its perish'd hopes?
Dismiss my miseries at least with pity :
May I not breathe upon this injur'd bosom
One parting sigh to ease my wounded soul,
And loose the anguish of a broken heart ?

   Xim. Support me, Heaven—we meet again to-mor-
      row.

   Car. To-morrow we must meet like enemies,
Thy piercing eyes, relentless in revenge,
And all the softness of thy heart forgotten;
This only moment is our life of love.
O, take not from this little interval,
The poor expiring comfort that is left me.

                    [Xim. *weeps.*

My heart's confounded with thy soft compassion,
And dotes upon the virtue that destroys me.

   Xim. O! I shall have the start of thee in wo;
Thou canst but fall for her thou lov'st; but what
Must she endure that loves thee—and destroys thee ?

Yet, Carlos, take this comfort in thy fate,
That if the hand of justice should o'ertake thee,
Thy mournful urn shall hold Ximena's ashes.

Car. O, miracle of love!

Xim. O, mortal sorrow!
But haste, O leave me while my heart's resolv'd;
Fly, fly me, Carlos, lest thou taint my fame;
Lest in this ebbing rigour of my soul,
I tell thee, tho' I prosecute thy fate,
My secret wish is, that my cause may fail me.

Car. O, spirit of compassion! O, Ximena!
What pangs and ruin have our parents cost us?
Farewell, thou treasure of my soul, O stay!
Take not at once my short-liv'd joys away.
While thus I fix me on thy mournful eyes,
Let my distresses to extremes arise:
Thy victim's now secure; for thus to part,
I sate thy vengeance with a broken heart. [*Exeunt.*

Enter ALVAREZ, *with Noblemen, Officers, and others.*

1 *Nob.* These few, my lord, are on my part engag'd;
In half an hour Don Henrique de Las Torres,
With sixty more, will wait upon your cause,
Resolv'd, and ready, all like us, to right you:
Since the just quarrel of your house must live,
Since the brave blood of Carlos is pursu'd,
The race of Gormaz shall attend his ashes.

Alv. My lord, this mark of your exalted honour
Will bind me ever grateful to your friendship:
Tho' I still hope the mercy of the King

Will spare the criminal, whose guilt is honour.
The service I have done the state has found
A bounteous master always to reward it;
Nor am I yet so wedded to my rest,
But that I still can, on occasion, break it.
The Moors are anchored now within the river,
And, as I'm told, near landing to insult us——
Wherefore, I would entreat you at this time,
To wave my private danger for the public.
Since chance has form'd us to so brave a body,
Let us not part inactive to our honour;
Let's seize this glad occasion of th' alarm,
Let's chase these robbers in our king's defence,
And bravely merit, not demand his mercy.

   1 *Nob.* Alvarez may command us, who is still
Himself, and owns no cause unmix'd with honour.

     Enter a Servant, who whispers ALVAREZ.

   Alv. How, now! the news.
Just enter'd, and alone!
O, Heav'n, my pray'rs are heard! my noble friends,
Something to our present purpose has occurr'd;
Let me entreat you, forward to the garden,
Where you will find a treble number of
Our forces assembl'd on the like occasion;
Myself will in a moment bring you news,
That will confirm and animate our hopes. [*Ex.* Nob.

         Enter CARLOS.

My Carlos! O, do I live once more t' embrace thee,

Prop of my age, and guardian of my fame!
Nor think, my champion, that my joy's thus wild,
For that thou only hast reveng'd my honour,
(Tho' that's a thought might bless me in the grave)
No, no, my son, for thee am I transported;
Alas! I am too sensible what pains
Thy heart must feel from anguish of thy love;
And had I not new hopes that will support thee,
Some present prospect of thy pain's relief,
My sense of thy afflictions would destroy me.

Car. What means this kind compassion of my griefs?
Is there on earth a cure for woes like mine?
O, sir, you are so tenderly a father,
So good, I can't repent me of my duty:
Be not, however, jealous of my fame,
If yet I mix your transports with a sigh,
For ruin'd love and for the lost Ximena:
For since I drag, with my despair, my chain,
Her sated vengeance only can relieve me.

Alv. No more depress thy spirits with despair,
While glory and thy country's cause should wake it;
The Moors, not yet expected, are arriv'd,
The tide and silent darkness of the night
Lands, in an hour, their forces at our gates:
The court's dismay'd, the people in alarm,
And loud confusion fills the frighted town.
But Fortune, ere this public danger reach'd us,
Had rais'd five hundred friends, the foes of Gormaz,
Whose swords resolve to vindicate thy vengeance,
And here without expect thee at their head.

Forward, my son, their number soon will swell,
Sustain the brunt and fury of the foe.
And if thy life's so painful to be borne,
Lay it at least with honour in the dust,
Cast it not fruitless from thee; let thy king
First know its value ere his laws demand it——
But time's too precious to be talk'd away.
Advance, my son, and let thy master see,
What he has lost in Gormaz, is redeem'd in thee.

   Car. Relenting Heaven at last has found **the means**
To end my miseries with guiltless honour.
Why should I live a burthen to myself,
A trouble to my friends, a terror to Ximena?
Not all the force of mercy, or of merit,
Can wash a father's blood from her remembrance,
Or reconcile the horror to her love.
Yet I'll not think her duty so severe,
But that to see me fall my country's victim
Would please her passion, tho' it shock'd her ven-
        geance.
It must be so——Dying with honour, I
Discharge the son, the subject, and the lover.
O! when this mangled body shall be found,
A bare and undistinguish'd carcase, 'midst the slain,
Will she not weep in pity of my wrongs,
And own her wounds have ample expiation?
Her duty then may with a secret tear,
Confess her vengeance great, and glorious my despair.
                        [*Exeunt.*

ACT V. SCENE I.

Enter BELZARA.

Belzara.

VICTORIOUS Carlos, now resume thy hopes,
Demand thy life, and silence thy Ximena.
Hard were thy fate indeed, if she alone
Should be the bar to triumphs nobly purchas'd.
But see, she comes, with mournful pomp of wo,
To prosecute this darling of the people,
And damp with ill-tim'd griefs the public joy.

Enter XIMENA *in mourning, attended.*

Ximena! Oh! I more than ever now
Deplore the hard afflictions that pursue thee;
While thy whole native country is in joy,
Art thou the only object of despair?
Is this a time to prosecute thy cause,
When public gratitude is bound t' oppose thee?
When on the head of Carlos, which thy griefs
Demand, Fortune has pour'd protection down?
The Moors repuls'd, his country sav'd from rapine,
His menac'd king confirm'd upon his throne,
From every heart but thine, will find a voice
To lift his echoed praises to the Heavens.

Xim. Is't possible? Are all these wonders true?
Am I the only mark of his misdoing?
Could then his fatal sword transpierce my father,

Yet save a nation to defeat my vengeance?
Still as I pass, the public voice extols
His glorious deeds, regardless of my wrongs;
The eye of pity, that but yesternight
Let fall a tear in feeling of my cause,
Now turns away, retracting its compassion,
And speaks the general grudge at my complaining.
But there's a king, whose sacred word's his law;
Supported by that hope, I still must on,
Nor, till by him rejected, can be silent.

    Bel. Your duty should recede, when public good
Must suffer in the life your cause pursues.

    Xim. But can it be? Was it to Carlos' sword
The nation thus transported owes its safety?
O, let me taste the pleasure and the pain!
Tell me, Belzara, tell me all his glory;
O, let me surfeit on the guilty joy,
Delight my passion, and torment my virtue.

    Bel. Alonzo, who was present, will inform us.

Enter ALONZO.

Alonzo, if your business will permit.

    Alon. The abbot, at whose house Count Gormaz lies,
Has sent in haste to speak with me; I guess,
To fix the order of his funeral.   [*Aside to* Belzara.

    Bel. Spare us at least a moment from th' occasion,
Ximena has not yet been fully told
The action of our late deliverance;
The fame of Carlos may compose her sorrows.

    Alon. Permit the action then to praise itself.

Late in the night, at Lord Alvarez' house,
Five hundred friends were gather'd in his cause,
T' oppose the vengeance that pursu'd his son;
But in the common danger, brave Alvarez,
With valiant Carlos at their head, preferr'd
The public safety to their private honour,
And march'd with swords determin'd 'gainst the
      Moors.
This brave example, ere they reach'd the harbour,
Increas'd their numbers to three thousand strong.
  Bel. Were the Moors landed ere you reach'd the
      port?
  Alon. Not till some hours after. When we arriv'd,
Our troops were form'd, Ximena was the word,
And Carlos foremost to confront the foe.
The Moors not yet in view, he order'd first
Two thirds of our divided force to lie
Conceal'd i' th' hatches of our ships in harbour;
The rest, whose numbers every moment swell'd,
Halted with Carlos, on the shore, impatient,
And silent on their arms reposing, pass'd,
The still remainder of the wasting night.
At length the brightness of the moon presents
Near twenty sail approaching with the tide;
Our order still observ'd, we let them pass;
Nor at the port, or walls, a man was seen.
This deadness of our silence wings their hopes
To seize th' occasion, and surprise us sleeping,
And now they disembark, and meet their fate.
For at the instant they were half on shore,

Uprose the numbers in our ships conceal'd,
And to the vaulted Heaven thunder'd their huzzas,
Which Carlos echo'd from his force on shore :
At this amaz'd, confusion seiz'd their troops,
And ere their chiefs could form them to resist,
We press'd them on the water, drove them on
The land, then fir'd their ships to stop their flight :
Howe'er, at length, their leaders bravely rallying,
Recover'd them to order, and a while
Sustain'd their courage, and oppos'd our fury :
But, when their burning ships began to flame,
The dreadful blaze presenting to their view
Their slaughter'd heaps that fell where Carlos fought,
(For O, he fought as if to die were victory)
Their fruitless courage then resign'd their hopes ;
And now their wounded king, despairing, call'd
Aloud, and hail'd our general to surrender,
Whom Carlos answering, receiv'd his prisoner.
At this, the rest had on submission quarter,
Our trumpets sound, and shouts proclaim our victory:
While Carlos bore his captive to his father,
Whose heart transported at the royal prize,
Dropp'd tears of joy, and to the king convey'd him ;
Where now he's pleading for his son's distress,
And asks but mercy for his glorious triumph. [*Exit.*

   Xim. Too much! it is too much, relentless Heav'n!
Th' oppression's greater than my soul can bear !
O, wounding virtue! O, my tortur'd heart !
Art only thou forbidden to applaud him ?
Cannot a nation sav'd appease thy vengeance ?

Why, why, just Heaven ! are his deeds so glorious,
And only fatal to the heart that loves him ?

Bel. Compose, Ximena, thy disorder ; see,
The king approaches, smiling on Alvarez,
Whose heart o'erflowing, gushes at his eyes,
And speaks his plea too strong for thy complaint.

Xim. Then sleep, my love, and virtue arm t' oppose
　　him ;
Let me look backward on his fatal honour,
Survey this mournful pomp of his renown,
These woful trophies of his conquer'd love,
That thro' my father's life pursu'd his fame,
And made me in his nuptial hopes an orphan :
O, broken spirit ! wouldst thou spare him now,
Think on thy father's blood ! exert the daughter,
Suppress thy passion, and demand thy victim.

　　Enter KING, ALVAREZ, SANCHEZ, &c.

　King. Dismiss thy fears, my friend, and man thy
　　heart,
For while his actions are above reward,
Mercy's of course included in the debt.
Our ablest bounty's bankrupt to his merit :
Our subjects rescu'd from so fierce a foe,
The Moors defeated, ere the rude alarm
Allow'd us time to order our defence,
Our crown protected, and our sceptre fix'd,
Are actions that secure acknowledgment.

　Alv. My tears, sir, better than my words will thank
　　you.

Enter GARCIA.

Gar. Don Carlos, sir, without attends your pleasure,
And comes surrender'd as his word engag'd,
To answer the appeal of fair Ximena.

King. Attend him to our presence.

Xim. O, my heart!

King. Ximena, with compassion we shall hear thee,
But must not have thy griefs arraign our justice,
If in his judge thou find'st an advocate :
Not less his virtues, than thy wrongs will plead.

Xim. O, fainting cause! but thus my griefs demand
     him.   [*Kneeling.*
     [*While the King raises* Ximena, *enter* Alonzo,
         and whispers Alvarez.

Alv. This instant, say'st thou? Can I leave my son?

Alon. The matter's more important than your stay.
Make haste, my lord.

Alv. What can thy transport mean?
Be plain.

Alon. We have no time to lose in words,
Away, I say.

Alv. Lead on, and ease my wonder.   [*Exeunt.*

Enter CARLOS, *and kneels to the King.*

King. Oh, rise, my warrior, raise thee to my breast,
And in thy master's heart repeat thy triumphs.

Car. These honours, sir, to any sense but mine,
Might lift its transports to ambition's height;
But while Ximena's sorrows press my heart,

Forgive me, if despairing of repose,
I taste no comfort in the life she seeks,
And urge the issue of her grief's appeal.

King. Ximena, 'tis most true, has lost a father,
But thou hast sav'd her country from its fate ;
And the same virtue that demands thy life,
Owes more than pardon to the public weal.

Xim. My royal lord, vouchsafe my griefs a hearing;
Oh, think not, sir, because my spirits faint,
That the firm conscience of my duty staggers.
The criminal I charge has kill'd my father;
And, tho' his valour has preserv'd the state,
Yet every subject is not wrong'd like me,
Therefore, with ease, may pardon what they feel not
As he has sav'd a nation from its foe,
The thanks that nation owes him are but just,
And I must join the general voice t' applaud him:
But all the tribute that my heart can spare him,
Is tears of pity ; while my wrongs pursue him,
What more than pity can those wrongs afford ?
What less than justice can my duty ask ?
If public obligations must be paid him,
Let every single heart give equal share :
(Carlos has prov'd, that mine is not ungrateful)
But must my duty yield such disproportion ?
Must on my heart a father's blood be levy'd,
And my whole ruin pay the public thanks ?
If blood for blood might be before demanded,
Is it less due, because his fame's grown greater ?

G

Shall virtue, that should guard, insult your laws,
And tolerate your passions to infringe 'em?
If to defend the public, may excuse
A private wrong, how is the public safe?
How is the nation from a foe preserv'd,
If ev'ry subject's life is at his mercy?
My duty, sir, has spoken, and kneels for judgment.

   Car. Oh, noble spirit, how thou charm'st my sense,
And giv'st my heart a pleasure in my ruin.   [*Aside.*

   King. Raise thee, Ximena, and compose thy thoughts,
As thou to Carlos' deeds hast spoke impartial,
So to thy virtue, that pursues him, we
Must give an equal plaudit of our wonder ·
But we have now our duty to discharge,
Which, far from blaming, shall exalt thy own:
If thy chaste fame, which we confess sublime,
Compels thy duty to suppress thy love,
To raise yet higher then thy matchless glory,
Prefer thy native country to them both,
And to thy public tears resign thy victim.
Where a whole people owe their preservation,
Shall private justice do a public wrong,
And feed thy vengeance with the general sorrow?

   Xim. Is then my cause the public's victim?

   King. No.
We've yet a hope to conquer thy resentment,
And rather would compose than silence it:
For if our arguments seem yet too weak
To guard thy virtue from the least reproach,
Behold the generous sanction that protects it;

Read there the pardon which thy father gives him,
And with his dying hand assigns thy beauties.

 Xim. My father's pardon!

 King. Read, and raise thy wonder.

 Xim. [*Reads.*] " Alvarez wrong'd me in my mas-
   ter's favour,

Carlos is brave, and has deserv'd Ximena."

 Car. Oh, soul of honour! now lamented victory!

 King. Now, fair Ximena, now resume thy peace,

Reduce thy vengeance to thy father's will,
And join the hand his honour has forgiven.

 Xim. All-gracious Heaven! have my swollen eyes
   their sense?

 D. San. Oh, tottering hope! but I have yet a thought
That will compel her virtue to pursue him.

 Xim. Why did you shew me, sir, this wounding
   goodness?

This legacy, tho' fit for him to leave,
Would in his daughter be reproach to take;
Honour unquestion'd may forgive a foe,
But who'll not doubt it when it spares a lover?
If you propos'd to mitigate my griefs,
You should have hid this cruel obligation.
Why would you set such virtues in my view,
And make the father dearer than the lover?

 King. Since with such rigour thou pursu'st thy
   vengeance,

And what we meant should pacify, provokes it,
Attend submissive to our last resolve:
For since thy honour's so severely strict,

G ij

As not to ratify thy father's mercy,
We'll right at once thy duty and thy lover :
Give thee the glory of his life pursu'd,   '
And seal his pardon to reward thy virtue.

 Xim. Avert it, Heaven, that e'er my guilty heart
Should impiously insult a father's grave,
And yield his daughter to the hand that kill'd him.

 D. San. Unnatural thought I Madam, suppress
   your tears,
Your murder'd father was my dearest friend ;
Permit me, therefore, on your sinking cause,
To offer an expedient may support it

 Xim. Whatever right or justice may, I am bound
In duty to pursue, and thank your friendship.

 D. San. Thus then to royal justice I appeal,
And in Ximena's right her advocate,
Demand from Carlos your reverse of pardon.

 King. What means thy transport ?

 D. San. Sir, I urge your laws ;
And since her duty's forc'd to these extremes,
There's yet a law from whence there's no appeal,
A right, which e'en your crown's oblig'd to grant her,
The right of combat, which I here demand,
And ask her vengeance from a champion's sword.

 Car. Oh, sacred sir, I cast me at your feet,
And beg your mercy would relieve my woes;
Since her firm duty is inflexible,
Consign her victim to the braver sword.

Oh, nothing is so painful as suspense ;
This way our griefs are equally reliev'd,
Her duty's full discharg'd, your justice crown'd,
And conquest must attend superior virtue.

King. This barbarous law, which yet is unrepeal'd,
Has often against right gross wrongs supported,
And robb'd our state of many noble subjects ;
Nor ever was our mercy tempted more
T' oppose its force, than in our care for Carlos :
But since his peace depends upon his love,
And cruel love insists upon its right,
We'll trust his virtues to the chance of combat,
And let his fate reproach, or win Ximena.

Xim. What unforeseen calamities surround me !

King. Ximena ! now no more complain, we grant
Thy suit ; but where's this champion of thy cause ?
Whose appetite of honour is so keen,
As to confront in arms this laurell'd brow,
And dare the shining honours of his sword ?

D. San. Behold th' assailant of this glorious hero ;
Your leave, dread sir, thus to appel him forth.

[*Draws.*

Bel. Hold, heart, and spare me from the public
    shame. [*Aside.*

D. San. Carlos, behold the champion of Ximena,
Behold th' avenger of brave Gormaz' blood,
Who calls thee traitor to thy injur'd love,
Ungrateful to the sighs that pitied thee,
And proudly partial to thy father's falsehood :

G iij

These crimes my sword shall prove upon thy heart,
And to defend them dares thee to the combat.

 Car. Open the lists, and give th' assailant room,
There on his life my injur'd sword shall prove,
This arm ne'er drew it but in right of honour.
First, for thy slander, Sanchez, I defy thee,
And throwing to thy teeth the traitor's name,
Will wash the imputation with thy blood ;
And prove thy virtue false as is thy spirit:
For not Ximena's cause, but charms have fir'd thee,
Vainly thou steal'st thy courage from her eyes,
And basely stain'st the virtue that subdu'd her.

 D. San. Oh, that thy fame in arms——

 King. Sanchez, forbear——
'Tis not your tongues must arbitrate your strife,
Let in your lists, your vauntings be approv'd.
Whose arm, Ximena, shall defend your cause?

 Xim. Oh, force of duty! sir, the arm of Sanchez.

 D. San. My word's my gage.

 King. 'Tis well, the lists are set,——
Let on the morn the combatants be cited,
And, Felix, you be umpire of the field.

 Car. The valiant, sir, are never unprepar'd.
Oh, sir, at once relieve my soul's suspense,
And let this instant hour decide our fate.

 D. San. This moment, sir,—I join in that with
   Carlos.

 King. Since both thus press it, be it now decided.
Carlos, be ready at the trumpet's call ;

You, Felix, when the combat's done, conduct
The victor to our presence—Now, Ximena,
As thou art just or cruel in thy duty,
Expect the issue will reward or grieve thee.
Sanchez, set forward—Carlos, we allow
Thy pitied love a moment with Ximena.

[*Exit* King *and train.*

D. San. A fruitless moment that must prove his last.

[*Exit.*

Car. Ximena! Oh, permit me ere I die,
To tell thy heart, thy hard unkindness kills me.

Xim. Ah, Carlos, can thy plaints reproach my duty,
Nay, art thou more than Sanchez is, in danger?

Car. Or thou more injur'd than thy hapless father,
Whose greater heart forgave my sense of honour?
Thou canst not think I speak regarding life,
Which, hopeless of thy love's not worth my care;
But, oh! it strikes me with the last despair,
To think that lov'd Ximena's heart had less
Compassion than my mortal enemy;
My life had then indeed been worth acceptance,
Had thy relenting throes of pity sav'd it:
But, as it is pursu'd to these extremes,
Thus made the victim of superfluous fame,
And doom'd the sacrifice of filial rigour,
These arms shall open to thy champion's sword,
And glut the vengeance that supports thy glory.

Xim. Hast thou no honour, Carlos, to defend?

[*Trembling.*

Car. How can I lose what Sanchez cannot gain?

For where's his honour where there's no resistance?
Is it for me to guard Ximena's foe,
Or turn outrageous on the friendly breast,
Which her distressful charms have warn'd to right her.
   Xim. Oh, cruel Carlos! thus to rack my heart
With hard reproaches, that thou know'st are ground-
     less;
Why dost thou talk thus cruelly of death,
And give me terrors unconceiv'd before?
What tho' my force of duty has pursu'd thee,
Hast thou not left thy courage to defend thee?
Oh, is thy quarrel to our race reviv'd?
Couldst thou, to right thy honour, kill my father,
And now not guard it, to destroy Ximena?
   Car. Oh, heav'nly sound! Oh, joy unfelt before!
   Xim. Oh, is my duty then not thought compulsive?
Canst thou believe I'm pleas'd while I pursue thee?
Or think'st thou I'm not pleas'd the king preserv'd
     thee?
And that thy courage yet may ward my vengeance?
Oh, if thou knew'st what transports fill'd my heart,
When first I heard the Moors had fled before thee,
Thy love would feel confusion for my shame,
And scarce forgive the passion thou reproachest.
Oh, Carlos, guard thy life, and save Ximena!
   Car. And save Ximena! Oh, thou hast fir'd my
     heart
With animated love, and sav'd thy Carlos!
                       [*Sound trumpets.*
But hark, the trumpet calls me to the list!

Xim. May Heav'n's high care, and all its angels
    guard thee!
Car. Words would but wrong my heart, my sword
    shall speak it.
Sanchez, I come, impatient to chastise
Thy love, which makes thee now the criminal:
I might have spar'd thee had the rival slept,
But boldly thus avow'd, thou'rt worth my sword—
'Tis said the lion, tho' distress'd for food,
Espying on the turf the huntsman sleeping,
Restrains his hunger, and forbears the prey;
But when his rousing foe, alarm'd and ready,
Uplifts his jav'lin brandish'd to assail him,
The generous savage then erects his crest,
Grinds his sharp fangs, and with fierce eyes inflam'd,
Surveys him worthy of his rage defy'd,
Furious uprearing rushes on the game,
And crowns at once his vengeance and his fame. [*Ex.*
    Xim. Oh, glorious spirit! Oh, hard-fated virtue!
With what reluctance has my heart pursu'd thee?
    Bel. Was ever breast like mine with wo divided?
I fear the dangers of the faithless Sanchez,
And tremble more for his dread sword's success:
Should Carlos fall, what stops him from Ximena?
Keep down my sighs, or seem to rise for her. [*Aside.*
    Xim. Tell me, Belzara, was my terror blameful?
Might not his passion make my heart relent,
And feel, at such a time, a pang to save him?
    Bel. So far was your compassion from a crime,
That 'tis th' exalted merit of your duty:

Had Carlos been a stranger to your heart,
Where were the virtue that your griefs pursu'd him?
Were it no pain to lose him, where the glory?
The sacrifice that's great, must first be dear;
The more you love, the nobler is your victim.

   Xim. Thy partial friendship sees not sure my fault;
I doubt my youthful ignorance has err'd,
And the strict matron, rigidly severe,
May blame this weakness of my woman's heart;
But let her feel my trial first, and if
She blames me then, I will repent the crime.
                 [*Sound trumpet at a distance.*
Hark, hark the trumpet! Oh, tremendous sound!
Belzara, oh, the combat is began!
The agonizing terror shakes my soul:
Help me, support me with thy friendly comforts;
Oh, tell me what my duty owes a parent,
And warm my wishes in his champion's favour!—
Oh, Heav'n, it will not, will not be! my heart
Rebels, and spite of me inclines to Carlos,
Who now again, in Sanchez, fights my father;
Now he attacks him, presses, now retreats,
Again recovers, and resumes his fire,
Now grows too strong, and is at last triumphant!

   Bel. Restrain thy thoughts, collect thy constancy,
Give not thy heart imaginary wounds;
Thy virtue must be Providence's care.

   Xim. Oh, guard me, Heav'n! help me to support
      it—Ah!   [*Trumpets and shouts.*
'Tis done! the dreadful shouts proclaim the victor:

If Carlos conquers, still I've lost a father ;
And if he perishes, then—die Ximena.

   Bel. Conquer who may, no hope supports Belzara.

                                    [*Aside.*

Enter GARCIA.

Came you, Don Garcia, from the combat ?

   Gar. Madam,
The king, to shew he disapproves the custom,
Forbade his own domestics to be present. [*Shouts nearer.*
But I presume 'tis done ; these shouts confirm it :
Hence from this window we may guess the victor.

   Xim. Oh, tell me quickly, while I've sense to hear
      thee !

   Gar. Oh, Heav'n ! 'tis Sanchez ! I see him with his
      sword,
In triumph pressing thro' the crowd his way.

   Xim. Sanchez !—thou'rt sure deceiv'd. Oh, bet-
      ter yet
Inform thy dazzled eyes !

   Gar. 'Tis certain he ;
For now he stops, and seems to warn them back :
The crowd retires, I see him plain, and now
He mounts the steps that lead to this apartment.

   Xim. Then, fatal vengeance, thou art dearly sated.
Now love unbounded may o'erflow my heart,
And Carlos' fate without a crime be mourn'd.
Oh, Sanchez, if poor Carlos told me true,
If 'twas thy love, not honour, fought my cause,

Thy guilt has purchas'd with thy sword my scorn,
And made thy passion wretched as Ximena.

   Bel. Oh, Heav'n support her nobler resolution!
But see, he comes to meet the disappointment.

Enter Don SANCHEZ, *and lays his Sword at* XIMENA'S
              Feet.

   D. San. Madam, this sword, that in your cause was
       drawn———
   Xim. Stain'd with the blood of Carlos, kills Ximena.
   D. San. I come to mitigate your griefs.
   Xim. Avaunt, avoid me, wing thee from my sight!
Oh, thou hast giv'n me for revenge despair,
Hast ravish'd with thy murderous arm my peace,
And robb'd my wishes of their dearest object!
   D. San. Hear me but speak———
   Xim. Canst thou suppose 'twill please me
To hear thy pride triumphant, paint my ruin,
Vaunt thy vain prowess, and reproach my sorrows?
   D. San. Those sorrows, would you hear my story—
   Xim. Hence!
To regions distant as thy soul from joy,
Fly, and in gloomy horrors waste thy life:
Remorse, and pale affliction wait thee to
Thy rest, repose forsake thee, frightful dreams
Alarm thy sleeps, and in thy waking hours,
May woes like mine pursue thy steps for ever.
   Bel. Oh, charming rage! how cordially she hates
       him!   *[Aside.*

Enter KING.

King. What, still in tears, Ximena? Still com-
 plaining?
Cannot thy duty's full discharge content thee?
Repin'st thou at the act of Providence,
And think'st thy cause still wrong'd in Heav'n's de-
 cree?
Xim. Oh, far, sir, from my soul be such a thought!
I bow submissive to high Heaven's appointment;
But is affliction impious in its sorrow?
'Tho' vengeance to a father's blood was due,
Is it less glorious that I priz'd the victim?
Has nature lost its privilege to weep,
When all that's valuable in life is gone?
Oh, Carlos, Carlos, I shall soon be with thee!
 King. Are then these tears for Carlos? Oh, Xi-
 mena,
The vanquish'd Sanchez has deceiv'd thy grief,
And made this trial of thy generous heart!
For know, thy Carlos lives, and lives t' adore thee.
 Xim. What means my royal lord?
 King. Inform her, Sanchez.
 D. San. The fortune of the combat I had told be-
 fore,
Had, sir, her fright endur'd to hear my speech;
I would have told you, madam, as oblig'd
In honour to the conquering sword of Carlos,
How nobly, for your sake, he spar'd your champion,
When on the earth, succumbent and disarm'd,

     • H

I lay: Live, Sanchez, said the generous victor,
The life that fights Ximena's cause is sacred;
Take back thy sword, and at her feet present
The glorious trophy which her charms have won,
The last oblation that despair can make her——
Touch'd with the noble fulness of his heart,
I flew to execute the grateful charge;
But, madam, your affright mistook the victor,
And your impatient griefs refus'd me audience.

 King. Now think, Ximena, one moment think for
  Carlos.

 Xim. Oh, love! Oh, persecuted heart!
Instruct me, Heaven, to support my fame,
To right my passion, and revere my father.

 D. San. And now, with just confusion, sir, I own
In me 'twas guilty love that drew my sword.
But since th' event has crown'd a nobler passion,
I plead the merit of that sword's defeat,
Regret the error, and entreat for pardon.

 King. Sanchez, thy crime is punish'd in itself:
We late have heard of thy retracted vows,
Which on thy strict allegiance we enjoin
Thy honour instantly to ratify——
Suppress thy tears, Belzara, he shall right thee.

 Xim. 'Tis fix'd—a beam of heavenly light breaks
  forth,
And shews my ruin'd peace its last resource.

 Gar. Don Carlos, sir, attends your royal pleasure.

 King. Has he your leave, Ximena, to approach?

 Xim. Oh, sir, yet hold! I dare not see him now:

While my depending justice was my guard,
I saw him fearless from assaults of love;
But now my vanquish'd vengeance dreads his merit,
And conscious duty warns me to avoid him.
Since then my heart's impartial to his virtues,
Oh, do not call me cruel to his love,
If I, in reverence to a father's blood,
Should shut my sorrows ever from his sight!
For tho' you raise above mankind his merit,
And I confess it—still he has kill'd my father——
Nay tho' I grant the fact may plead for mercy,
Yet 'twould in me be impious to reward it;
My eyes may mourn, but never must behold him more,
Yet, ere I part, let, sir, my humblest sense
Applaud your mercy, and confess your justice.
Hence to some sacred cloister I'll retire,
And dedicate my future days to Heav'n——
'Tis done——Oh, lead me to my peaceful cell,
One sigh for Carlos——Now, vain world, farewell!"
                    [*As* Xim. *is going off.*

Enter ALVAREZ *and* ALONZO.

Alv. Turn, turn, Ximena, oh, prepare to hear
A story will distract thy sense with joy,
Drive all thy sorrows from thy sinking heart,
And crown thy duty with triumphant love.
Pardon, dread sir, this tumult of my soul,
That carries in my rudeness my excuse;
Oh, press me not to tell particulars,
But let my tidings leap at once the bounds

H ij

Of your belief, and in one burst of joy
Inform my royal master, that his crown's support,
My vanquish'd friend, thy father, Gormaz lives ;
He lives in health confirm'd from mortal danger:
These eyes have seen him, these bless'd arms em-
  brac'd him.
The means, th' occasion of his death suppos'd, _
Would ask more words than I have breath to utter.
Alonzo knows it all——Oh, where's my Carlos ?

 King. Fly, Sanchez, make him with this news thy
  friend.

 Alv. Oh, lead me, lead me to his heart's relief!
        [*Exeunt* Alv. *and* San.

 Xim. Oh, Heav'n! Alvarez would not sure de-
  ceive me.

 King. Proceed, Alonzo, and impart the whole ;
Whence was his death so firmly credited,
And his recovery not before reveal'd ?

 Alon. My liege, the great effusion of his blood
Had such effect on his deserted spirits,
That I, who saw him, judg'd him quite expir'd :
But when the Abbot, at whose house he lay,
With friendly sorrow wash'd his hopeless wound,
His heaving breast discover'd life's return ;
When calling straight for help, on stricter search,
His wound was found without a mortal symptom :
And when his senses had resum'd their function,
His first words spoke his generous heart's concern
For Carlos and Ximena ; when being told
How far her filial vengeance had pursu'd him,

Is't possible, he cry'd? Oh, Heav'n! then wept,
And begg'd his life might be one day conceal'd,
That such exalted merit of her duty
Might raise her virtue worthy of his love.
But, sir, to tell you how Alvarez met him,
What generous reconcilements pass'd between them,
Would ask more time than public joy could spare.
Let it suffice, the moment he had heard
Ximena had appeal'd brave Carlos to the lists,
We flew with terror to proclaim him living——
But sir, so soon the combat follow'd your
Decree, that, breathless, we arriv'd too late,
And had not his physicians, sir, prescrib'd
His wound repose, himself had ventur'd forth
To throw his errors at your feet for pardon.

    King. Not only pardon, but our love shall greet
        him.

Brave Carlos shall himself be envoy of
Our charge, and gratulate his bless'd recovery—
Has he your leave, Ximena, now t' approach you?

    Xim. My senses stagger with tumultuous joy,
My spirits hurry to my heart's surprise,
And sinking nature faints beneath the transport.

    Enter ALVAREZ, SANCHEZ, *and* CARLOS.

    King. Look up, Ximena, and complete thy joy.
    Xim. My Carlos!—Oh!
    Car. Ximena! Oh, my heart!   [*Embracing.*
    Alv. Oh, Carlos! Oh, Ximena! yet suppress

them ;
First pay your duty there, haste to his feet,
And let his sanction consecrate your love.

   King. Lose not a moment from his sight—Oh, fly!
Tell him his king congratulates his health,
And will with loads of honour crown his virtues;
Nor in his orisons let him forget
The hand of Heav'n, whose providential care
Has order'd all, the innocent to save,
To right the injur'd, and reward the brave.

                    [*Exeunt omnes.*

Spoken by XIMENA.

WELL, SIRS!

I'M come to tell you, that my fears are over,
I've seen papa, and have secur'd my lover.
And, troth, I'm wholly on our author's side,
For had (as Corneille made him) Gormaz dy'd,
My part had ended as it first begun,
And left me still unmarry'd, and undone,
Or, what were harder far than both—a nun.
The French, for form indeed, postpones the wedding,
But gives her hopes within a year of bedding.
Time could not tie her marriage-knot with honour,
The father's death still left the guilt upon her:
The Frenchman stopp'd her in that forc'd regard,
The bolder Briton weds her in reward:
He knew your taste would ne'er endure their billing
Should be so long deferr'd, when both were willing.
Your formal Dons of Spain an age might wait,
But English appetites are sharper set.
'Tis true, this difference we indeed discover,
That, though like lions you begin the lover,
To do you right, your fury soon is over.

Beside, this scene thus chang'd, the moral bears,
That virtue never of relief despairs :
But while true love is still in plays ill-fated,
No wonder you gay sparks of pleasure hate it—
Bloodshed discourages what should delight you,
And from a wife, what little rubs will fright you !
And virtue not consider'd in the bride, ,
How soon you yawn, and curse the knot you've ty'd !
How oft the nymph, whose pitying eyes give quarter,
Finds in her captive she has caught a Tartar !
While to her spouse, that once so high did rate her,
She kindly gives ten thousand pounds to hate her.
So, on the other side, some sighing swain,
That languishes in love whole years in vain,
Impatient for the feast, resolves he'll have her,
And in his hunger vows he'll eat for ever ;
He thinks of nothing but the honey-moon,
But little thought he could have din'd so soon.
Is this not true ? Speak, dearies of the pit,
Don't you find too how horribly you're bit ?
For the instruction, therefore, of the free,
Our author turns his just catastrophe.
Before you wed, let love be understood,
Refine your thoughts, and chase it from the blood :
Nor can you then of lasting joys despair,
For when that circle holds the British fair,
Your hearts may find heroic daughters there.

THE END.

Deacidified using the Bookkeeper process
Neutralizing agent Magnesium Oxide
Treatment Date Nov 2005

PreservationTechnologies
A WORLD LEADER IN PAPER PRESERVATION
111 Thomson Park Drive
Cranberry Township PA 16066
(724) 779-2111

Lightning Source UK Ltd.
Milton Keynes UK
UKOW05f0306041216
289122UK00001B/88/P